U-BOAT IN

191_ ____

BY THE SAME AUTHOR

U-Boats Destroyed:
The Effect of Anti-Submarine Warfare 1914-1918

Available from Periscope Publishing Ltd.
www.periscopepublishing.com

U - BOAT

INTELLIGENCE

1914—1918

ROBERT M. GRANT

PERISCOPE PUBLISHING
PENZANCE

First Published in Great Britain in 1969 by Putnam and Company Ltd.

Republished in 2002 by
Periscope Publishing Ltd.
33 Barwis Terrace
Penzance
Cornwall TR18 2AW

www.periscopepublishing.com

A CIP record for this book is available from the British Library

ISBN No 1-904381-01-4

Printed in England by Anthony Rowe Ltd
Eastbourne

CONTENTS

ILLUSTRATIONS

TEXT ILLUSTRATIONS

CHARTS

PREFACE

THE PRESENT VOLUME represents a continuation of the research undertaken for *U-Boats Destroyed* (Periscope Publishing Ltd., 2002) and like it, is based largely on German records captured at Tambach in 1945. For the use of these documents my continuing thanks are due to Admiral E. M. Eller, Director of Naval History, and to his able associates, and to Commander P. K. Kemp of the Naval Historical Branch, Ministry of Defence, London. My warmest appreciation is also due to the help provided by Admiral P. N. Buckley, Mr. H. F. Langley, Dr. Douglas Robinson and Professor Arthur Marder. Perhaps above all, however, I should express my gratitude to Admiral Sir William James, without whose encouragement I could not have finished the book.

After my first volume appeared it was suggested — notably in a review by Admiral Carney in the *United States Naval Institute Proceedings* — that the background of anti-submarine operations deserved further investigation. By great good luck, when I was teaching at Yale in the autumn of 1964 I found in Sterling Library a collection of wartime Intelligence documents circulated by the French Ministère de la Marine. These were concerned with submarine and anti-submarine activities and have provided invaluable aid. In addition, I have now made use of the final volume of Admiral Spindler's *Handelskrieg mit U-Booten* (1966), which in turn makes occasional use of my article published in the *Proceedings* in January 1938. Beyond this, Admiral Eller has provided continued guidance, especially in regard to the National Archives in Washington, and the Naval Historical Branch has been unfailingly helpful. Finally, I should like to thank numerous authors and publishers for permission to quote material from their books.

Perhaps it should be said that my work is quite different from the masterly survey of *Room 39* by Donald McLachlan. It is not based on personal experience and has therefore had to be built up on the basis of innumerable details from various kinds of sources. Since I am a layman and have some competence only in the general field of historical study, it need hardly be said that none of my conclusions, unless described as derived from wartime documents, is to be regarded as reflecting official views, whether American, British, French, or German.

R.M. GRANT
Divinity School, University of Chicago

I

THE WAYS AND MEANS OF NAVAL INTELLIGENCE

THE PURPOSE OF Naval Intelligence, unlike that of naval history, is severely practical. It is to assemble and analyse as much information as possible about the enemy's materials, methods, and morale so that advantage can be taken of possible weaknesses in his materials, inadequacies in his methods, and failures in his morale, and thereby to inflict damage on his forces while protecting one's own. To a certain extent the approaches of Naval Intelligence coincide with those of the historian. Both are concerned with gathering and interpreting as much information as possible, in order to create a relatively complete and coherent picture of the course of incidents, campaigns, and wars. The difference between their studies is due to the fact that Intelligence work has a time limit. Old information usually has little value, for the aim of Intelligence is to produce results in the immediate future. The historian, on the other hand, can work slowly and, ideally, more thoroughly because his goal is to understand and interpret what has already been accomplished. He does not have the same kind of deadline; the war he studies has already been won or lost. For Intelligence the value of the historian's work lies only in the possibility that situations analogous to those he describes may arise in the future.

The practical interest of a study of the work of Naval Intelligence in World War I is rather limited because of the drastic changes in the nature of the submarine and the methods of anti-submarine warfare, and in methods of communication, which have occurred since 1918. Many of the events of 1914-18 were so conditioned by the geographical situation of the British Isles vis-a-vis Germany that nothing closely resembling them recurred in 1939-45 although it is obvious that British waters, or even the Atlantic, do not provide the only area in which submarine operations take place. In this study we shall pay no attention to the possible implications of our research, however, since our primary purpose is historical.

The war of 1914-18 was marked by the introduction of an extremely important new weapon, the submarine, which could attack and retire without being seen and counterattacked. The basic problem faced by the Allies was therefore how to prevent attacks on naval units or on shipping. Defensively, this meant that naval units had to employ such weapons as the depth charge (in addition to using older methods like ramming and gunfire), and that merchant vessels had to be armed and/or sail in convoys escorted by torpedo-boat destroyers and other naval units. The use of submarine minelayers by the Germans meant that harbours and shipping routes constantly had to be cleared by minesweepers. More offensively, naval units had to be employed in searching for U-boats, with the use of hydrophones to listen for them under water and the utilization of aircraft to spot them on the surface and, sometimes, submerged. Mines were sometimes laid in operations areas.

Because the German submarines were based on German ports, Ostend-Bruges-Zeebrugge in Belgium, and Cattaro and Pola in the Adriatic, they had to pass from and to their bases though waters which the Allies could control. For this reason the laying of minefields was highly significant. The most successful of them was the one laid in the narrow passage between Folkestone and Gris Nez in the Straits of Dover; in 1918 it was illuminated by night and patrols forced U-boats to dive into the mines. Less successful, though fairly dangerous, fields were laid in the Otranto Straits and in the northern North Sea between the Orkney Islands and the Norwegian coast. In addition, the British frequently laid mines off the port of Zeebrugge and in the Bight of Heligoland as well as occasional fields in the Kattegat, east of Denmark. In relation to the location of these minefields the work of Intelligence was obviously very important.

The war of 1914-18 was the first in which use was made of a new means of communication: wireless telegraphy or radio. Once at sea, naval units could now communicate with their bases or with other units at considerable distances. The messages sent could obviously be picked up by the enemy as well as by those for whom they were intended, and at the beginning of the war it had to be decided whether to disrupt enemy communications by jamming them or to intercept them in the hope of finding valuable information. The decision was made easier almost at the beginning of the war after the German cruiser *Magdeburg* ran aground in the Gulf of Finland and came under fire from Russian vessels. A German signalman, about to sink the naval signal book, was killed by a bursting shell, and soon afterwards the Russians picked up his corpse with the book. In a striking example of Allied cooperation, they sent the book to London on October 13, 1914.

Secret messages are usually made secret in two ways. First, they are 'coded'. This means that a message is translated into a highly artificial language by means of a code-book used by the sender and the receiver. Second, they are 'enciphered'. The language of the code-book is modified by substitutions and alterations of various kinds. In order to break an enciphered code message one must first decipher and then decode it. The whole process is sometimes called 'decryption'.

The code-book was therefore indispensable but did not explain the enciphered German radio messages. The meaning of these was worked our by Fleet Paymaster Rotter, whom James calls 'the principal German expert in the Intelligence Division'.

With his naval knowledge to help him to guess the possible purport of the signals, Rotter, by a brilliant piece of deduction, produced the key. It was a substitution table (a=r, b=h, etc.), and at that time in force for three months. Later on it was changed every week, and still later [in 1917] every twenty-four hours.

In considerable measure the work of deciphering was based on logical analysis. It was also facilitated, as P. D. Hobson has stated in the *Encyclopaedia Americana*, by the Germans' 'habit of broadcasting standard test messages in each cipher as it was introduced into service'.

Both sides regularly compromised new codes and ciphers by sending messages in the new form to isolated ships or units and then by having to repeat them in the old code or cipher because the addressee had not yet received the new one.

The class 'isolated ships' obviously includes submarines. Indeed, H. C. Hoy tells the story of a U-boat in distress which was unable to read signals in a new cipher, though the Admiralty was finding them perfectly comprehensible.[1]

In his reminiscences Hans Rose, the famous commander of *U-53*, gives an example of the kind of message he would send. In April 1918, he writes, he transmitted the signal '1-2--9--068 α-U53'. This meant that he had sunk one ship of 2,000 tons, still had nine torpedoes, and was in quadrant 068 alpha at the western end of the English Channel. Once his signal had been deciphered and decoded, the meaning of the first three groups could be inferred from comparison with similar signals made by U-boats over a period of time. What remained to be done was to identify the location and the submarine. The location was given in relation to a series of grid charts that remained unchanged from the beginning of the war up to the middle of July 1918. Locations on these charts could be checked in two ways: first and best, by possession of the charts themselves, either taken from wrecks or acquired by agents, and second, by the use of directional radio interception to pinpoint the submarine's position. When the new chart came into use directional interception was important, but so was the occasional use of old grid square locations by U-boats.

As for the identification of the U-boat, this was facilitated by the fact that until the end of September 1918 the U-boats used call signs, which though frequently changed, were systematically arranged in relation to the various flotillas among which they were distributed. This fact was

1 The case in question was probably that of *U-106*.

established by means of documents taken from wrecked U-boats as well as by a continuing process of logical analysis.

Late in the war U-boats often sent messages providing information about convoys they had sighted. If these signals were read, and even if they were not, the convoys could be rerouted. After the war Admiral Sims expressed his confidence that 'history will show, when all the facts are known, that more shipping was saved through thus keeping track of submarines and routing ships clear of them than by any other single measure.'

Naturally radio interception did not provide the only means of keeping track of the U-boats. From Allied and neutral seamen a steady flow of information gave reports of encounters with submarines and even fairly detailed descriptions of the enemy vessels. All this information was continuously correlated and it became possible to estimate what various U-boats had accomplished on each of their cruises. Without deciphered signals, however, and sometimes even with them, the reconstructions were likely to prove rather inaccurate. Some attempt was also made to keep files on the capabilities of various U-boat officers. In the case of minelaying submarines, the discovery of new minefields off the Allied coasts made it possible, to some extent, to predict future patterns.

Secret agents and deserters have always supplied information about an enemy, and World War I was no exception to the rule. The Allies used agents not only in Germany and Austria-Hungary but also, and perhaps especially, in neutral countries like Spain and Switzerland, where information could be bought or exchanged, and - specifically related to the U-boat war - in German-occupied Belgium and in the neutral countries past which U-boats sailed in transit: Holland, Denmark, and Norway. From such agents the Allies derived details of submarine construction and about officers and men, some information about the dates on which submarines sailed and returned (and sometimes about their operations orders), not so much information about the losses the U-boats were experiencing, and occasionally fairly detailed information about the operations of a particular flotilla.

Depending on the circumstances, the sinking of a U-boat could lead to a good deal of Intelligence material. Some prisoners were rather more talkative than others were, and toward the end of the war they became relatively more indiscreet. They could provide information about U-boat construction, about the cruises of their own submarine, and sometimes about other submarines as well. They could also describe operational procedures in considerable, and sometimes surprising, detail. Occasionally they were carrying documents, which could lead to the destruction of other submarines.

DIVERS AND WRECKED U-BOATS

An equally important source of information was provided by the wrecks of U-boats sunk off the British coast. Thus the mysterious appearance of German mines off the East Coast in June 1915, at first ascribed to surface layers, was first explained after July 3. There had been a heavy explosion in Yarmouth Roads the evening before, and a diver was sent down to investigate. What he found was the wreck of the new small minelayer *UC-2*, lying on the bottom with a 45-degree list. About twelve feet ahead of the conning tower was a cut, about three feet deep, in the upper deck. This had apparently been caused by collision with the steamer *Cottingham*. More significant damage, however, was found about twelve feet abaft the conning tower; there the wreck was nearly cut in two. In the after part the diver found bits of accumulators, some mess tins, and two pieces of clothing. The forward section was more important. There the diver found seven mine-chutes. The first three of them contained one mine apiece, but the four after tubes were empty and could be seen through. The empty tubes and the shattered stern indicated that one of the submarine's mines had detonated under her. Further diving operations suggested that the fore part could be raised for examination, and later in the summer this operation was carried out. A consequence of the examination was the development of the British E-class submarine minelayers.

During 1916 two further small minelayers were raised from the bottom. One was *UC-12*, which blew up on her own mines in Taranto Harbour on March 16 and was raised by the Italian Navy. The other was *UC-5*, stranded on Shipwash Sand on April 27 and towed to Harwich practically intact. In addition, the French salved the wreck of the new coastal submarine *UB-26* just nine days after she was netted, close to Le Havre, on April 5. Her construction and her contents were carefully studied. Among her papers were charts of German minefields off the Belgian coast and of British fields in the Straits of Dover. It is practically certain that this discovery pointed the way to the British fields laid off the Belgian coast on April 24 and therefore caused the loss of *UB-13* the next day. Further Belgian coast minelaying produced the sinkings of *UC-3* in May and of *UC-7* in July.

UB-26 also carried a manual of instructions for U-boat operations in the Channel, and it was discovered that U-boats were accustomed to lie on the bottom in locations mentioned in the manual. No sinkings, however, took place in consequence of the discovery.

We shall later discuss the work of divers in relation to at least five submarines sunk during 1917 and the results obtained by raising *UC-44* from the bottom. During 1918 the figure increased sharply. Divers visited at least fifteen wrecks, and the new *UB-110* was brought to the surface.

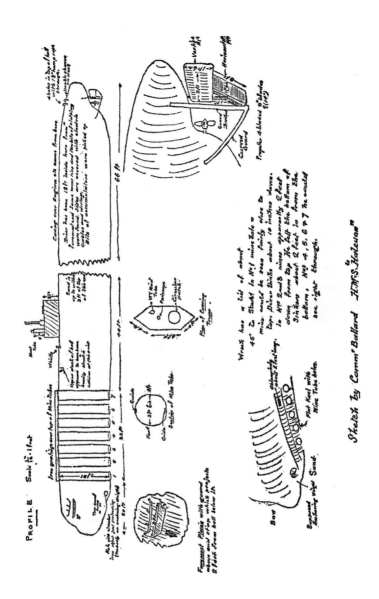

SKETCH OF THE WRECK OF *UC-2*, BASED ON REPORTS OF DIVERS IN
JULY 1915

14

Valuable information was often provided, especially in the cases of UC-44, UB-33, UB-110 and UB-109, from which documents were recovered. The wrecks were significant for analysis of structural details, and therefore the British were eager to acquire examples of minelayers both small (UC-2, UC-5) and large (UC-44), as well as the latest type of UB-boat (UB-110). Intelligence also asked for the central portion of U-48, blown up on the Goodwin Sands late in 1917, but salvage was not practicable. In addition, as we have seen, the French obtained the medium-sized UB-26 and the Italians raised the wreck of UC-12.

Signal books could also be recovered occasionally from Zeppelins - under naval command - downed on Allied territory or nearby waters. Thus in August 1916 the Germans introduced a new signal book, but a copy of it was soon obtained from the Zeppelin L-32, shot down at Great Birstead near Billericay on September 24. It was especially valuable because at the time no U-boats were being sunk in waters where divers could visit the wrecks. Late in February 1917 divers visited the wreck of UC-32 off Sunderland and may have recovered documents from it. The Zeppelin L-48, shot down over England on June 17, was certainly carrying - contrary to orders - a general cipher table for the naval signal book, as well as three lists of code words. On June 22 Admiral Scheer informed the Chief of the Naval Staff that codes and ciphers had to be changed.

Later in the year a few papers were recovered from the stranded and captured UC-61 and a richer haul came from the wreck of UC-44 after she was mined on August 4. The wrecks of other UC-boats seem to have provided little of value, and the capture of code books and a grid chart from the Zeppelin L-49, downed in France, was therefore important. On October 25 Admiral Sir Reginald (W. R.) Hall, Director of Naval Intelligence, wrote a letter to the Chief of the Intelligence Section of the American Army General Staff.

> Commander Babcock, Admiral Sims' aide, has handed to me the important documents which you were good enough to send to Admiral Sims. I hasten to express to you my most grateful thanks for your kindness and promptitude in sending me this most valuable document, which I assure you will be of the greatest value. You may rely that any information contained therein which will be of value to the United States forces will be at once communicated to them.

Whatever the cause may have been, the quality and quantity of U-boat signal deciphering seems to have improved at this point.

During 1918 valuable materials were certainly recovered from the wrecks of UB-33 during May, UB-110 during July, and UB-109 at the end of

August. In addition, the Zeppelin *L-70*, shot down close off the British coast on August 5, yielded a harvest of documents for Intelligence study.

One might wonder to what extent the German command was aware of the activities of British Intelligence. Admiral James has stated that 'when a war lasts long enough it is always possible to detect the efficiency of the enemy's Intelligence service, and the Germans from time to time knew that we were reading their messages and we knew that the German cryptographers were very skilled'. Some U-boat commanders taken prisoner by the British were able to report to Germany the fact that their interrogators seemed to know every move the U-boats made. And when U-boats were pursued by British hunters immediately after making signals they were aware that they had given away their locations.

Perhaps the best testimony on this subject is provided by Admiral Dönitz in his *Memoirs*. He was discussing the second war, but he had been a U-boat commander in 1918 and had written a book based on early experience in 1939. In his opinion 'the best result of D-F [direction-finding] that has come to our knowledge showed an error of 30 miles, and that was in close proximity to the coast of western France'. Our examination of earlier evidence shows that as early as 1918 the accuracy of direction-finding was much superior to this estimate. Dönitz was also sure that there was a widespread network of spies at work in the German bases in occupied France. 'An efficient enemy intelligence service must *in any case* [author's italics] have been able to ascertain the distribution of U-boats among the various bases, the dates of their sailing and return to port, and possibly also the sea areas allocated to boats proceeding on operations.' Certainly the efficient Allied intelligence services of World War I had possessed precisely this information, as the French records make clear.

The question of codes and ciphers was more difficult. During World War II, Dönitz writes, these 'were checked and rechecked, to make sure that they were unbreakable; and on each occasion the head of the Naval Intelligence Service at Naval High Command adhered to his opinion that it would be impossible for the enemy to decipher them'. He admits, however, that (writing in 1958) 'as far as I know, we are not certain whether or not the enemy did succeed in breaking our ciphers during the war'. Later discussions, such as those by Farago and Kahn, clearly show that the ciphers were broken. The same situation obtained during 1914-18, with few exceptions.

Oddly enough, Dönitz makes no mention of the interrogation of prisoners, important during both wars.

From November 1914 to the end of the war the Director of Naval Intelligence was W. R. Hall, first Captain, later Rear-Admiral. Under his guidance British intelligence, especially in regard to the antisubmarine campaign, reached what Admiral James, in charge of 'Room 40' in 1917 and 1918, calls 'its zenith of efficiency and importance'. It might be mentioned that a section of the operation, staffed by Fleet Paymaster Ernest Thring, Commander Alfred Dewar, and others, was responsible for locating and identifying U-boats, plotting their movements, and providing analysis of them. The materials with which Hall had to deal are listed by James as including 'the directional wireless plotting, the decyphering of signals, agents' reports on the activities in German dockyards, reports of sightings by neutral steamers, reports from agents or consular authorities in neutral countries, reports of sightings and attacks from convoys and hunting squadrons, and interrogation of prisoners'. All these materials had to be 'sifted and correlated'.

Because of the importance of intercepting signals, the Admiralty immediately proceeded to construct directional finding stations for this purpose. The furthest north was in Shetland, the furthest west in Ireland. The first of them was erected at Hunstanton, Norfolk, on the Wash, and was thought to be completely secret. 'Sentries were posted,' James writes, 'but one day Leslie Lambert, afterwards well known as a story teller on the BBC, encountered a woman in the station whom he recognized as Queen Alexandra, because he had recently been at Marlborough House doing some conjuring for a children's party. How the Queen evaded the sentries was never learned.' Among the other stations he mentions those at Lowestoft, Lerwick, Aberdeen, York, Flamborough Head, and Birchington (near Margate), as well as five more in Ireland. Ultimately there were many more, and when James was in Room 40 'the pneumatic tube which discharged the signals was always clattering like a machine gun'.[1]

Most of the signals intercepted had to do with transit routes. 'After a mine barrier was laid across the North Sea from Scotland to Norway the submarines reported when they had crossed the barrier, and when returning to base they always reported, when they were passing north of the Shetlands, their time of arrival at the end of one of the swept channels in the Bight and the tonnage they had sunk. We were continually laying minefields at the ends of the swept channels and they *had* to give a position where they could be met by minesweepers, so we always knew whenever a submarine had sailed and when she was returning.'

In addition, there were signals from operations areas. 'When they started concentrated attacks - three or four attacking simultaneously - they interchanged a lot of signals which we picked up and on several occasions the course of convoys was altered and escaped attack. Except when concentrating the submarines did not make many signals when operating on

1 Quotations from Admiral James are either from his book *The Eyes of the Fleet* (London, 1956) or from private correspondence.

17

the trade routes but we always knew how many were operating and could keep the convoys warned.'

The British were of course not alone in the field of interception and analysis. As James points out, 'the French Admiralty had a chain of intercepting stations and a staff of cryptographers who welcomed any help that Room 40 could give them'. For this reason 'the latest information was sent over to Paris by messenger every night'. Kahn, relying on official French sources, gives a less optimistic picture of inter-Allied cooperation. French experts themselves reconstructed a German U-boat code, the four-letter German naval code 'superencipherment and all', and a monalphabetically enciphered flag code for U-boats. They needed further assistance, however.

> Once when Cartier [head of the French cryptologic service] was visiting Hall, he told the director of naval intelligence that his bureau was cryptanalyzing the German naval codes but had only progressed to partial solutions. Hall suggested that Cartier leave the naval traffic to the British, who had an actual copy of the German code, could read the German messages with ease, and would apprise the French of anything of importance to them. Cartier replied by telling Hall how one of the fragmentary French decryptments had enabled them to save one of their auxiliary cruisers from possible torpedoing; the English must have known of the danger from the same intercept, but they had not warned the French. The intelligence chief explained that it was better to lose the ship than to take precautionary measures that risked disclosing the cryptanalysis to the Germans. 'Would you feel the same way if the cruiser had been British?' Cartier asked coldly. Hall dodged that one, and a change of code ended the negotiations.¹

It is fairly clear that quite a few signals were read by the French during 1917 and 1918, although the records to which we have had access are not altogether complete.

When the United States entered the war in April 1917 a great deal of information was shared with the Navy Department by both British and French Intelligence. From January 1918 onwards, indeed, the Admiralty provided Admiral Sims with a daily briefing in regard to operations of the preceding twenty-four hours. Hall supplemented the briefing with letters to Sims whenever new intelligence gave warning of U-boat operations which might do damage to American shipping. In addition, there was an American

---

1 *The Codebreakers* (New York, 1967), p. 277.

Naval Planning Section in London, which was supplied with relevant information.

Because of the necessity for secrecy, it was fairly soon decided not to release information about the sinking of submarines. Early in 1915 announcements about sinkings were made, to be sure, for their effect on enemy morale, and notes in the *Memoirs* of Admiral von Tirpitz show that the announcements took effect.

> March 5 [1915]. We have probably lost *U-8*. We, however, must resign ourselves to losses, especially as, out of regard for the neutrals, drastic restrictions have been laid on submarine warfare concerning compulsory rising to the surface in doubtful cases. March 26. Last night the English Admiralty announced that it had grounds for believing *U-29* (Weddigen) had been sunk in the Irish Sea with all hands. They wouldn't make this public without good reason, and *U-29* is overdue. A most lamentable incident. Weddigen perhaps was too confident, and then there's that perilous cautiousness towards neutrals!

The Admiralty's announcements had actually not given everything away. The sinking of *U-8* had nothing to do with an attack on shipping; she had been caught submerged in the Straits of Dover by a destroyer with an explosive sweep. And while the statement that *U-29* had been sunk in the Irish Sea did suggest that she was attacking shipping, she was actually rammed while attacking British battleships in the North Sea. And especially when decoy vessels were introduced it became important not to let any information out.

As it happened, however, the sinking of *U-27* by the Q-ship *Baralong* was fully described in the American press by crew members of the American steamer *Nicosian*, on the spot when the submarine was sunk on August 4, 1915. In addition, U-boat commanders who were able to escape from decoy vessels soon reported their encounters, and the secret was thus soon lost. (There was nothing especially mysterious about the sinking of *U-12*, but details were brought back to Germany in 1916 when the war pilot Völker escaped from prison in Britain, made his way to Hull, and boarded the Swedish bark *Ionstorp*. Off the Firth of Forth the bark was stopped by the homeward-bound *U-16*, which took Völker off and brought him home. He later perished aboard *U-44*, sunk in August 1917.)

In December 1916 an exchange of prisoners into internment placed Schulthess of *U-23* and Crompton, lieutenant in *U-41*, in Switzerland. Both officers soon transmitted information to Germany. This information had lost most of its value by this time. *U-23* had been torpedoed by a submarine being towed by a trawler; *U-41* had been shelled by a Q-ship. In late 1916, however, the trawler-submarine combination had been abandoned, and the secret of the 'mystery ships' was well known in Germany.

What had more value in Crompton's report was the picture he gave of British interrogation methods.[1] To his surprise, a British captain asked him questions in 'absolutely pure German'. When he refused to give any answers except concerning himself, the captain proceeded to repeat the questions - and to give the answers, in order to show how complete the extent of British information was. They knew many names of U-boat commanders and could often describe U-boat cruises in considerable detail; they knew when and how *U-20* had sunk the *Lusitania*. They were well acquainted with German naval construction and could identify individual shipyards and describe the contracts they held. As for *U-41* herself, they knew the names of almost her entire complement, as well as many details about the officers and the names of the ships she had sunk. 'I was amazed at this espionage,' Crompton wrote. 'England had recognized its importance earlier than we did.'

Accounts provided by U-boat prisoners taken later on in the war clearly show that a main feature of British interrogation was the element of surprise. It was provided by the partial revelation of how much the British already knew. Thus Schmitz, captured from *UC-75* in May 1918, concluded that the British information must have come from agents; a chance remark suggested to him that women were involved. After the interrogators of Fürbringer, captured from *UB-110* that July, used the nicknames of various Flanders commanders, he decided that there were spies in the Casino at Ostend. Actually the nicknames were mostly those of captured captains. Viebeg of *UB-80* was called 'Maxe' because Wenninger, a survivor from *UB-55*, had used this name. Whatever the case may have been in regard to spies, it is a fact that seemingly insignificant details elicited during one interrogation could be used to good effect during another.

SOME SOURCES OF GERMAN INTELLIGENCE

During the autumn of 1917 news about the losses of U-boats occasionally reached Germany. During October Arnold of *UC-33* was able to report that his submarine had been sunk during the previous month and that there was one survivor - obviously himself. American prisoners taken after *U-53* sank the destroyer *Jacob Jones* (and radioed Queenstown to send out rescue for survivors) revealed that their sister ship *Fanning* had depth-charged a U-boat off Milford Haven and rescued survivors. They also said that a U-boat was depth-charged at the end of October and then was visited by divers. The first case was that of *U-58*. The second, actually *UC-42*, could not be identified by the Germans because the submarine was actually lost in September.

---

1 He described the interrogation in a book published in 1940, but the account was undoubtedly sent to Berlin in 1916.

20

By January 6, 1918, the watch officer of *UB-81*, sunk in December, was able to get a letter back to Germany. In it he reported that his own submarine had hit a deep mine off Beachy Head (wrong location) on December 1 (wrong date), that *UC-63* had been torpedoed twenty minutes after leaving the minefield, and that *UC-65* had been torpedoed in mid-Channel off Dartmouth. A little later, a survivor from *U-58* sent back the news that on board a British mining cruiser at Kingstown (Ireland) was the compass of the salved *UC-44*.

None of this information was exceptionally valuable, although U-boats could be warned about the deep mines off Beachy Head. In fact they were so warned by a transmission from Bruges on the night of January 6-7.

During the first fortnight of January 1918 the U-boat officers captured by the British during 1914 and 1915 were released into Dutch custody and internment - the only exceptions being Schulthess and Crompton, to Switzerland in December 1916. There was little that the Germans could learn from these officers, it was believed, because of the rapid development of anti-submarine warfare during the years between. According to Gibson and Prendergast, writing in 1931, 'of the manner in which the U-boat had met Nemesis the German authorities could learn but little' because 'on the British side grim - silence, absolute and ominous, reigned'. After January 1918 the silence was not quite so absolute, for the interned officers brought news from almost every U-boat captain taken prisoner by the British during 1917.

In consequence, a good deal of information was available concerning 1917 losses. Messages came in from Breyer of *UC-32*, from Tebenjohanns of *UC-44*, from Arnold of *UC-33*, from Lafrenz of *UC-65*, and from Amberger of *U-58*. Indeed, only Weisbach of *U-81* did not report, and he had been badly injured when his submarine was sunk. Sauer, a lieutenant on *UC-55*, sent news, for Lilienstern, the captain, had not survived.

The most interesting reports came in from the captains of UC-boats recently sunk. Tebenjohanns stated that his interrogators showed him the list of 'losses of submarines', and on it he read that *UC-42* had been torpedoed by a G-class submarine on March 12 or 13, and that *UC-36* and *UC-66* had been sunk on June 12 or 13. Evidently Tebenjohanns did not have an opportunity to look for long. The list said that *UC-43* was torpedoed on March 10 and that only *UC-66* was sunk on June 12. Arnold suggested that regular mine-laying off British or Irish ports was a mistake. In his view the sinking of *UC-44* had been due to excessive regularity. Sauer reported that *UC-55* had been lost simply because of flooding. He added that according to British officers land stations could detect a U-boat twelve miles away.

Lafrenz provided a good deal of information, some of it doubtless derived from his interrogation. Presumably for the sake of completeness he reported that Weddigen (*U-29*) had been sunk by the *Dreadnought*; this was hardly worth mentioning by 1918. Schwieger (*U-88*) had been depth-charged north of Ireland (this was simply a mistake). Elstester (*U-99*) had been depth-charged between Scotland and Norway - and this was one conclusion the British had reached in 1917. Other British opinions are reflected in the statements that *UB-37* had been sunk by a decoy vessel and *UB-20* had been bombed by planes. On the other hand, the view that *U-106* had been depth-charged in the northern North Sea is quite wrong and may have been offered in order to mislead the Germans.

His reports about UC-boats are not very satisfactory. He correctly stated that his own submarine and *UC-63* were torpedoed, but he wrongly assigned the same cause to the loss of *UC-66*. He rightly reported that *UC-72* had been sunk by a ship - but the British view was that she had been bombed by a plane.

Three other items provided no new information. Lafrenz said that the British were aware of the losses of *U-66* and *U-50*. This was not surprising, for members of his crew had spoken of them. In addition, he reported that Mildenstein of *UC-1* had been lost in a net. British conjectures of the time do not agree with this conclusion, which is what he himself told the interrogators. Under the circumstances, this bit of confusion is not surprising.

Lafrenz's report reflects the developed interrogation technique used by the British in late 1917. According to Bywater, and to one verifiable German account, threats were sometimes also employed, but the evidence is not altogether satisfactory. The commander of the Zeppelin *L-33* alleged that Major Trench, head of the German Department in the Intelligence Division, threatened him with a civil trial for murder. A report from Kölle of *L-45*, published by Robinson, reflects an interrogation in form identical with those undergone by U-boat officers. Major Trench 'showed astonishingly detailed knowledge' about personnel; his information was 'accurate in the most minute detail'.

British interrogators were not only aiming at an 'omniscience effect' but carefully implying that the major source of their information lay within Germany itself. When they asked questions about the use of radio they implied that they were not really well acquainted with the German call letters and procedure and could not read the U-boat signals. Thus Lafrenz was told that *U-106* had been depth-charged in the northern North Sea. The French records clearly indicate, however, that the Allies had read German signals and knew that she had been mined off the Frisian Islands. It is worth noting that in Lafrenz's report there is no mention of U-boats sunk by mines. Presumably his attention was being diverted from this subject.

Early in February German Intelligence conducted further investigations into the information the U-boat officers in Holland had provided. Kapitän-Leutnant W. Lechler was sent to interview them, and on his return he drew the obvious conclusion that the British were extremely well informed about U-boat operations. In his view their knowledge was based first on a highly developed technique of interrogation, second on a remarkably efficient spy system. The latter provided them with technical information, sailing dates, and details about the personal affairs of officers and men. Lechler recommended that officers be urged to maintain silence and that some attempt be made to track down British agents.

The conclusion about agents was corroborated early in March, when Berlin was aware that a British agent had been asking questions about U-boat technology, while a French spy had been making inquiries about the causes of Steinbrinck's success (formerly commander of *UC-65*) and about the U-cruisers.

On April 18 some rather stale news came in from a survivor of *UC-39*, sunk in February 1917. He believed that she had been captured, not sunk. Actually a British destroyer had tried to tow her to port but she could not be kept afloat.

During May and early June the German command was much concerned with the safety of codes and ciphers, for *U-154* had been torpedoed by a British submarine at a rendezvous with *U-153* and *U-62*. After assessing the possibilities it was concluded (wrongly) that the 'gamma ulli' cipher was unbreakable. In any case, it had not been used by submarines of the V Flotilla, from which - it was reported on May 7- important documents had been taken by a deserter to the Allies.

On June 21 word came in from Wenninger of *UB-55*, a British prisoner for the past two months. Since he reported that his submarine had struck deep mines near the Varne shoal, Bruges immediately sent out a radio warning to U-boats at sea. In mid-September another message stated that he had struck a 'double mine' at 11 metres, but by this time Flanders U-boats were no longer heading out through the Straits of Dover.

It was not until October 28 that a letter came in from a prisoner taken off *UB-124*, sunk in July. It brought the news that the interrogators in July were so well informed about U-boat losses that they could even discuss the accidental sinkings of *UB-106*, *UB-84* and *UB-114* at Kiel. This news was significant only for its proof of British efficiency. By now the war was nearly over.

We may add that German Intelligence learned little from the prisoners they interrogated. The survivors from *Jacob Jones* said that American destroyers could make 37 knots. They also stated or admitted that the war was making the rich richer and the poor poorer. One hopes that the interrogators were not led to expect the immediate collapse of American morale. Again, much of the 'information' supplied by two survivors from the British submarine *D-6*, sunk by *UB-73* on June 24, consisted of English complaints about Scottish teenagers and the closing hours of Glasgow pubs.

A volunteer informer taken off the tanker *O. B. Jennings* by *U-140* in the summer of 1918 provided no information of any value.

It would be a mistake to underrate the capabilities of German Intelligence as if there were something innately superior about the skills of the Allies. German radio transmission and reception were developed to a remarkable extent, and the British were amazed by the distances over which U-boats could communicate. By the spring of 1915 directional signals were being sent out from Sylt, Borkum, Nordholz and Bruges, and by the beginning of 1918 Cleve and Tondern had been added to these.[1] Bruges constantly kept check on prospective weather conditions and communicated with U-boats about them. In addition, a close watch over Allied radio signals was kept. This involved the breaking of Allied codes and ciphers. Just because of the nature of the U-boat war, however, these activities were less important than were the intercepted signals picked up by the British and the French.

It should be noted, finally, that while Gladisch refers to the sinkings of two British destroyers in August 1918 as the only successes achieved by German minefields in the Bight,[2] he seems to be unaware of the fact that these fields probably accounted for no fewer than thirteen British submarines.

Adequate recognition has not always been given to the work of Austrian Intelligence, actively engaged not only in producing explosions which sank the Italian battleship *Benedetto Brin* and the cruiser *Leonardo da Vinci* but also in collecting information at the consulate in Zurich for the benefit of U-boats in the Mediterranean and Adriatic seas. In turn, Italian Intelligence was actively involved in a raid on the consulate during the night of February 25-26, 1917. Although the walls of the archives in the consulate were 'filled with poison gas', the raiders cut through them with blow torches and took all the documents to the Italian consulate in Berne. Several executions took place in consequence of what was found in them, especially as regards the sinking of the battleship and the cruiser.[3] Presumably Zurich lost its importance as an information centre. In any event, radio interception was more reliable.

SOME EARLY INTERCEPTS

Among the important signals intercepted early in the war should be mentioned two noted by Ewing in his *Life* of his father, the first head of Room 40. On May 12, 1915, the 'first boat of the III Half-Flotilla' - a submarine which Paymaster Thring identified as *U-20* - reported that on the

---

1 For a discussion of Cleve and Tomdern in relation to Zeppelins see D. H. Robinson, *The Zeppelin in Combat* (London, 1962), p.298.

2 Gladisch, VII, p. 312.

3 N. von Martiny. *Bilddokumente aus Osterreich-Ungarns Seekrieg 1914-1918* (Graz, 1939). II, pp. 334-37.

7th she had sunk the *Lusitania* by firing a single torpedo. And nearly a year later a single code word transmitted by Nauen Radio informed both the German forces and the British that Sir Roger Casement had sailed for Ireland aboard a U-boat.

To be sure, the importance and the nearly absolute reliability of the interceptors' work was not fully recognized within the Admiralty, partly because of organizational difficulties. We need not retell the story of the failure to make use of Room 40 during the battle of Jutland (May 31-June 1, 1916) but can refer to Marder's account.[1] He speaks of 'criminal neglect' while McLachlan uses the expression 'stupid incompetence'.[2] Many of the intercepted signals were 'put on the file unused' in the Operations Division.

What seems to be an analogous case at about the same time is the mining of the cruiser *Hampshire* off Marwick Head (Orkney) on June 5. She was carrying Lord Kitchener to Archangel, but he was not among the twelve survivors. On the morning of June 5 there was a fierce gale from the north-east. Minesweepers tried to clear the route westward from Scapa Flow towards Cape Wrath but had to come back. Under these circumstances Jellicoe decided to send the cruiser neither out to the east nor directly west but up the west coast of Orkney on the route 'ordinarily used by fleet auxiliaries'.

His decision was based on three points: (1) since 1915 no minefield had been laid so far north by the Germans; (2) submarine minelayers had never operated off Scapa Flow; and (3) the midsummer nights were so short that a surface minelayer could not have been at work. This reasoning was obviously unsound, since the first two points were based merely on what had happened hitherto and all of them neglected the possibilities of U-boat minelaying. It might have been noted that 'a very big submarine' - actually the minelayer *U-74* - had been sunk east of Aberdeen on May 27. Furthermore, if the argument was really convincing, why had the minesweepers gone out to the west?

In any event, at 1600 two destroyers sailed, forty-five minutes ahead of *Hampshire*. At 1745 she caught up with them but in the heavy sea they were unable to keep up and at 1830, far behind her, she ordered them to turn back. At 1940 she struck a mine and sank in about fifteen minutes.

A fog of mystery had enshrouded the loss of *Hampshire*, and many strange tales are collected in Donald McCormick's book *The Mystery of Lord Kitchener's Death* (1959). They involve British and Irish plots, radio interception by the Germans, changes in U-boat orders, etc., and it is not necessary to discuss any of them. The facts are as follows.

In May 1916 Admiral Scheer was planning to draw out the British fleet for what turned into the battle of Jutland, and his plans included minelaying

1 *From the Dreadnought to Scapa Flow*, III (London, 1966), pp. 148-54.
2 *Room 39* (London, 1968), p. 39.

operations by three new, large U-boats. *U-74* was the first to sail, on May 13, but apparently she was sunk before she laid mines off the Firth of Forth. *U-72* sailed on May 23 for Moray Firth but, with a bad oil leak, had to return to her base. *U-75* was off Sylt on the evening of May 24 when she made an intercepted signal before heading into the North Sea.

Her orders, issued on May 21, were these. 'Lay mines on warship route from Scapa Flow on west side of the Orkneys to the north, off Marwick Head, distance 2-3 sea miles from the coast. If it is not possible, because of technical reasons, to lay the field exactly on the course the mining is to go from north-east to south-west so that it will also be effective against ships coming from the north-west. Depth seven metres below high water.'

During the night of May 28-29 *U-75* laid her mines off Marwick Head and, indeed, precisely between 5905/0324½ W. and 5909/0328W., or from south-east to north-west. Two intercepts on May 31 and June 1 gave her positions as she headed back to Germany. Since her orders provided for an alternative area to be mined - west of the Shetlands - if she could not lay the field off Marwick Head, it is extremely likely that one of these signals indicated what she had actually done.

It is therefore highly probable that by June 1 Room 40 was cognizant of a new German minefield to the west of Marwick Head, and that this intelligence was passed on to the Operations Division of the Admiralty. There, we must assume, it went on file, lost in the confusion accompanying the battle of Jutland.

Later in the year the situation was quite different, and an intercept from *U-20* led to immediate action. On November 2 the homeward bound *U-20* encountered *U-30* off Bergen, Norway, and that evening received a message asking for help because neither of her sister submarine's engines was functioning. The next morning she found *U-30*, now able to make some headway, and both submarines headed for home. In heavy weather and thick fog, however, both ran aground near Bovbjerg, Denmark, on the 5th. Only *U-30* was able to get free. *U-20* radioed for assistance, and the next morning a half-flotilla of torpedo boats arrived on the scene. Since *U-20* could not be towed free, two of her torpedoes were detonated in the tubes and the wreck was abandoned. (It was finally blown up by the Danish Navy on August 25, 1925.)

The signals had been intercepted and read, and therefore the submarine *J-1* had been sent to patrol off Horns Reef in order to intercept not only the torpedo boats but also the battle cruisers and battleships sent out to support them. About noon on November 5, *J-1* fired four torpedoes at a line of four German battleships. Two of them were hits, and produced damage to *Grosser Kurfürst* and to *Kronprinz*. According to Admiral Scheer, the German authorities supposed that news of the stranded U-boats had reached England from Danish sources. Whether or not this was the case, the intercepted signals were decisive.

II

INTERCEPTION, PRISONERS AND WRECKS

A. Interception December 1916-March 1917

FROM A TIME very early in the war, as we have seen, the Admiralty intercepted signals made by U-boats and were usually able to read them. Presumably there were systematic analyses of these signals, partly in order to determine what call signs belonged to various flotillas and individual U-boats. In the French records to which we have had access there are no clear traces of any system, however, before December 1916. In our opinion, this fact does not prove that such systematic analysis did not exist; it merely suggests that its results were not circulated outside highly restricted circles.

Very few of the signals listed in the French records for December 1916 were intercepted from waters outside the North Sea and the Skagerrak. In those waters nine U-boats, one UB-boat, and two UC-boats were heard from, and a check of the identifications shows that only one call sign was wrongly ascribed. The French listed one signal as having been made by *U-68*, but this was clearly wrong because *U-68* had been sunk in March. The signal probably came from *U-83*, a unit of the same flotilla, even though another signal from *U-83* herself is given in the French list.

The chief value of the signals from German waters consisted of the proof they provided that various U-boats were at sea. Further information, as the French Intelligence analysts pointed out, was needed for tracing their cruises or making guesses about their intentions.

Three signals from German submarines off the French coast, on the other hand, permitted some inferences about what they were doing. At 2200 on December 17 a signal was picked up from *U-70*, thirty-five miles west of the Casquets in the Channel. Twenty-four hours later she made another when she was forty miles west-south-west of Ushant. Obviously she was on her way from the Channel to the Bay of Biscay - and ultimately to the waters just north of the Spanish coast.[1] Again, on December 27 a signal from *U-46*, ninety miles north-north-east of Cape Ortegal, suggested that she might have encountered some difficulties. Actually she was about to return home because of a damaged periscope.[2]

1 See Spindler, III, p. 262.
2 Ibid.,p. 261

The signals listed for January 1917 are much more numerous. No fewer than forty of them came from the North Sea - including five wrongly ascribed to *U-56*, sunk two months earlier. (German records suggest that these were made by *U-60*, which had taken the call sign previously assigned to *U-56*.) Twenty more were picked up from operations areas, and these made it possible to delineate the cruises of several U-boats in some detail. The two cruises we have mentioned as beginning in January could be followed as the submarines returned to Germany. *U-70* made a signal on January 1 from a position off Cape Ortegal, another on January 3 west of Biscay as she headed north, a third on January 10 east of the Orkneys, and a fourth on January 13, farther south-east in the North Sea. A signal from *U-46* on January 5 (5430/0230E.) showed that she had just returned through the Straits of Dover.

Six cruises begun during the first fortnight in January could be outlined by means of intercepts. (1) *U-48* was first heard from on January 1, north-west of Ireland; five days later she was north-west of Spain and, on the 7th, in the Bay of Biscay. Ten days of silence were devoted to operations. Then came two signals on the 17th from the waters west of Ushant. She was evidently returning to the north, and this was proved by two more signals: one from the Skerryvore Passage (north of the North Channel) on the 20th, the other from the Bight, north-west of Horns Reef, on the 25th. (2) Another boat, *U-44*, sent only three messages. The first, north-east of Heligoland on January 1, evidently marked her departure. Another, sent on the 17th from 5500/1300W, presumably announced her impending return.[1] She arrived back in the North Sea on January 25. (3) Something is wrong with the record of the signals ascribed to *U-84*. She was supposed to be north-west of Ireland on January 2, but she had sailed only the day before. She was also believed to be north-west of Spain on January 5, but this too is impossible. Two more signals from *U-84*, to the west of Lands End and Coqueville on the 17th, were probably identified correctly. She certainly made the last two signals ascribed to her. One of these came in on the 21st from a location south-west of Tory Island, the other on the 24th from the North Sea. (4) Signals were also picked up from *U-57*. These included three messages sent from a location near Heligoland on January 9-11; she was obtaining new sailing orders permitting her to go north of Scotland rather than through the Straits of Dover.[2] She then proceeded to the waters south of Ireland, where she made two signals on January 21. Ten days later she was in 5500/1300W., on her way home, and east of the Orkneys on February 5. (5-6) Finally, sequences of signals from *U-43* and *U-59* showed that both had sailed on January 12. On the 24th *U-43* was north of Cape Finisterre, *U-59* south-west of Lands End.[3]

1 Ibid.,p. 265
2 Ibid., p. 267.
3 Ibid. *U-59* was running low on fuel oil.

The reconstruction of these six cruises constituted the principal achievement based on interception during January, although it was also known that a U-boat commanded by Jess (actually *U-79*) returned to the Bight on January 17 (more probably, 27),[1] and that a few other boats had sailed on cruises. *U-45*, off Heligoland on the 14th and east of the Dogger Bank two days later, was evidently outward-bound. Signals from *U-85* were rather confusing. On the 22nd she was off the West Frisian Islands, presumably bound for the Straits of Dover, but four days later she was located off the Danish coast. Actually she was out on a training cruise in the North Sea.[2]

Two signals from *UC-32*, north of Heligoland, on January 17-18, showed that she was at sea, and ten days later a German petty officer was captured in the North Sea, apparently from the same submarine. After his U-boat had captured the drifter *Mayfly* he had been put on board, but a decoy vessel drove off the submarine and in turn he was captured. He told his captors he came from *UC-32*, but in fact his boat was *UC-31*.[3]

INTERCEPTION DURING FEBRUARY-MARCH

In February, as the unrestricted campaign got under way, the pattern of intercepts abruptly changed. Whereas two-thirds of the sixty signals picked up during January had come from the North Sea, in February only one-third of forty-two came from that area. Ten signals were evidently made by U-boats returning to port, since they had previously sent messages from operations areas. Signals from eleven U-boats showed that they were beginning and continuing their cruises.

U-81 was off Bishops Rock on the 1st; another signal off Fastnet on the 6th presumably announced her return, since she was in the Bight of Heligoland on the 15th. A signal from *UC-24* in the Channel on the 2nd presumably marked her safe passage through the Straits; she was in fact bound for the Mediterranean. *U-60* was in the Channel approaches on the 3rd and the 17th, and a signal off Guernsey on the 22nd suggested that she might be going eastward through the Straits. On the 26th, however, she was north of the Shetlands and had evidently taken the north about route.[4] On the 3rd *U-83* was off Ushant and reported her transit through the Straits; another signal on the 12th, south of Bishops Rock, was intercepted by the

1 Ibid., pp. 277-78.
2 Ibid., p. 272.
3 Ibid., p. 283.
4 Her signal on the 22nd had indicated that she would not pass through the Straits because of fog (Spindler, IV, p. 70).

30

British but not received at home.[1] U-85 was off Lands End on the 4th, back in the North Sea on the 16th. U-50 was very talkative. From the western approaches she made six signals on the 15th, 16th and 19th.[2] U-67 could be observed moving north in the Bay of Biscay on the 16th, and back in the Bight on the 24th. U-84 was in the Channel approaches on the 17th, in the North Sea on the 26th. U-49 was off Malin Head on the 23rd, off Fastnet on the 28th, and back off the Hebrides on March 8. U-70 made a signal in the Bight on the 24th and in the southern North Sea the next day. Finally, U-66 was heard from, north of the Shetlands, on February 27.

Radio signals did not provide the only information available to the Allies concerning U-boat operations in February. They knew more about the cruise of U-43 (commanded by Korvetten-Kapitän 'Jursth') because the captain of the British steamer *Hollinside* was a prisoner aboard her for two days and because a prize crew she had set on board the steamer *Famiglia* was captured by the British auxiliary cruiser *Moldavia* on February 9. The cruise of U-81 could be reconstructed not only from the radio signals but also from a German press release of February 15 and from the declarations of eight Spanish prisoners which U-81 took from the steamer *Gravina* on February 7. These prisoners were released to Switzerland in April. The cruise of U-60 was given a good deal of light by the crew of the Norwegian *Storskog*, taken back to Germany after the U-boat sank her on February 7. They identified their captor and stated that she was a new U-boat, operating from Heligoland on her second cruise, and commanded by 'Schultze or Schulze' (actually Schuster). She had two guns, probably 88-millimetre, and four torpedo tubes. By February 7 she had fired 150 shells and 6 torpedoes - about half her ammunition. As she was running short of provisions, she planned to return by the Straits of Dover, but after being depth-charged by a destroyer (probably Torpedo-boat 224 on February 20) she lost oil and touched a net, and went back north of Scotland. The prisoners noted that she had made frequent use of her radio. As for U-83, the report states that there was no trace of her after 1000 on February 17, when a British 'patrol' shelled a U-boat at close range.

Reconstructing the cruise of U-85 was a task based largely on German press releases of February 17 and 19. The first of these stated that a U-boat had recently sunk a total of 51,800 tons - an auxiliary cruiser of 20,000 tons, two transports of 13,600 tons each, and a steamer of 4,600 tons. The second added that the total was sunk within twenty-four hours and that the commander's name was Petz. Radio interception had already shown that U-85, back in the North Sea on February 16, had been in the Channel on

1 *U-53* encountered her off the Scillies on February 4 (Scheer, p. 271); she was sunk by *Farnborough* on the 17th, leaving one survivor (Spindler, IV, pp.100-1).

2 The first four signals indicated that she had passed through the Straits; the last two showed that she was leaving the Bay of Biscay for the south-west of Ireland (cf. Spindler, IV, p. 89).

31

February 4, and it was also known that Petz was in command of *U-85*. In addition, the German claims of shipping sunk could be checked against various 24-hour totals. It was clear that between 1100 on the 6th and 0925 on the 7th some U-boat had been able to sink *Cliftonian* (4,302 tons), *Vedamore* (6,329 tons), and *California* (8,666 tons), and to damage *Explorer* (7,608 tons), although she was able to reach port. This activity, then, could be ascribed to *U-85* - even though the only tonnage even approximately correct was that given for *Cliftonian*. Someone's imagination had been responsible for adding more than a hundred per cent to the total.[1]

During the month of March not a great deal was discovered by means of interception. *U-49*, homeward-bound, was off the Hebrides on the 8th. The cruise of *U-44* could be delineated as she moved along the northern route on the 2nd, operated out in the Atlantic from the 3rd to the 14th, and came back north of Scotland again on the 23rd.

The cruise of *U-48* became more interesting when intercepts were combined with information from other sources. She had been heard from in the Channel on the 6th and back in the Bight of Heligoland on the 15th. Later it was learned that she was undergoing extensive repairs; her commander, Kapitän-Leutnant 'Busz' (Buss), was dead. The damage, it was rightly concluded, had occurred when she collided submerged with the sinking steamer *East Point* on March 9. Her conning tower was crushed by the impact.

A single signal from *U-55*, in the southern North Sea on March 9, seemed strange, since it was known that this U-boat had sailed for the Straits about five days earlier. On March 13 three disarmed torpedoes were found on the beach by Fort Mahan near Boulogne, and it was presumed that a disabled U-boat had fired them in order to get refloated. The most likely U-boat to have been stranded, it was concluded, was *U-55*. This conclusion was correct.

A few other signals may be briefly noted, apart from those made by UC-boats. *U-70* made signals before and after passing eastward through the Straits, while *U-53*, *U-61* and *U-81* took the northern route homeward. In addition, three U-boats made signals from their patrol areas: these were *U-62*, *U-24* and *U-66*. Another boat, *U-86*, was north of the Dogger Bank on March 23 - evidently on her way out, as April signals showed.[2]

B. The April Crisis

April 1917, as it turned out, was the crucial month of the U-boat war. The U-boats were at sea in force, and they sank more tonnage than in any

---

1 The total assigned to *U-85* was still too high; see B. Herzog, *Die deutschen U-Boote 1906-1945* (Munich, 1959), p. 88.
2 West of Ireland April 6-7, in the North Sea April 17.

other month before or after. No fewer than eighteen of them made intercepted signals from the waters west of the British Isles.

Some, to be sure, were clearly terminating their cruises. Thus U-46 was heard from in the Channel approaches on April 3, in the North Sea four days later. U-57 was west-south-west of Barra Head on the 4th and in the Northern North Sea on the 7th. Similarly U-66, north-west of Ireland on the 4th, and U-59, west of Slyne Head on the 6th, were known to be homeward-bound. Later in the month signals from U-55, north-west of Slyne Head on the 17th, and U-53, west-south-west of St. Kilda on the 22nd and north of Unst (Shetlands) on the 29th, showed that they too were returning to port.

These boats were more than adequately replaced during the month, as was known from signals made by ten U-boats arriving in operations areas. Three signals made by U-60 on the 5th and 6th presumably reported her encounter with E-32 and the decoy vessel Aubretia on the former day, while another west of Ireland on the 20th must have marked the beginning of her homeward voyage.[1] Another boat to arrive was U-84, out in the North Sea on April 6 and south-west of the Scillies a fortnight later, then homeward. The cruise of U-50 could be followed in more detail. Southwest of Barra Head on the 13th she sent an intercepted and deciphered message about her meeting with the damaged UC-30. Two more signals made south-west of Fastnet on the 20th and the 21st, probably reported an encounter with the decoy vessel Zylpha on the 17th, while another on the 27th probably indicated both that she had encountered the decoy Viola the day before and that she was leaving her station.

The French records show that signals from three U-boats were not positively identified. It was thought, however, that U-69 was north-west of the Butt of Lewes (Hebrides) on April 18, that U-70 was west of Ireland on the 23rd, and that U-61 was south of Ireland on the 24th. As a matter of fact, all three identifications were correct. These submarines had sailed in mid-April and were arriving in their operations areas.

Another submarine presented a special situation. This was U-52, which had made a signal twenty miles south of Barcelona on April 11 and then proceeded towards the Straits of Gibraltar. Ten days later she arrived in approximately 4800/1100W. The day after that, she was in 5040/1250W. and was evidently heading north-west on her way to Germany.

A little later in the month signals were exchanged by U-43, about to return from the waters south-west of Ireland, and U-93, arriving from the North Channel and about to take the place of U-43. Two signals from each boat were picked up by shore stations. Finally, on April 25 a signal was intercepted from U-81, out from Germany and arriving in 5415/ 1130W. on her way to the waters west off Fastnet.

1 See Spindler, IV, p. 71.

More information about both *U-93* and *U-81* was derived from the interrogation of prisoners. *U-93* had arrived at Emden to join the IV Flotilla on April 6; bad weather had delayed her sailing until the 13th. During her cruise she had sunk ten ships to a total of 24,110 tons. On the 25th she had met *U-43*, 250 miles west of Fastnet, and had fruitlessly worked with her for the next two days. She was about to begin her homeward voyage when she sighted the decoy vessel *Prize* on April 30. When the decoy opened fire, the U-boat's commander, von Spiegel, at first prepared to ram her but then recognized his mistake and tried to escape on the surface at high speed. A shell hit the conning tower and blew him and two others overboard. In spite of damage, *U-93* definitely reached port. On May 12 it was learned that British prisoners aboard her arrived at Camp Brandenburg in Germany. Two days later the Duke of Connaught was sent a telegram by the Crown Princess of Sweden. 'Been asked news of Captain Von Spiegel was wounded and fell overboard during fight with schooner near Fastnet Rocks April 30.' She was assured that he was in good health.

As for *U-81*, she was sunk on May 1 when the patrol submarine *E-54* torpedoed her in approximately 5100/1300W. Her signal on April 25 had suggested that she might possibly operate in this area, for in it she stated that she had found nothing but sailing vessels in the North Channel. Three days after the sinking the British submarines' patrol area was shifted to the latitude of 55° North in the hope of catching U-boats in transit, but no results were achieved thereby.

The British submarines had been patrolling west of Fastnet since early March, without success, and according to Hurd the Admiralty knew 'as early as April 20' that the Germans were cognizant of similar patrols off St. Kilda (west of the Hebrides), Muckle Flugga (Shetlands), and Utsire Light (coast of Norway).[1] He does not say how the Admiralty knew this, but we may assume that their knowledge was due to the interception of signals made to, or possibly by, homeward-bound U-boats. The date April 20 suggests that perhaps a warning to the homeward-bound *UC-30* was intercepted.

Around this time the Anti-Submarine Division was much concerned, and with good reason, with U-boat activities south-west of Ireland. A letter from Admiral Duff to Admiral Bethell at Plymouth reflects the concern.[2]

I want especially to recommend to your notice the vicinity of 49°N., and between 9°and 10°W. This is for your personal information, as I have good reasons for believing the enemy submarines are pretty constantly there or thereabouts. Occasional harrying of this area would, I am sure, tend to keep Approach-routes clear, and yet need not lead to any suspicion on the part of the enemy that we are keeping a special watch

1 *The Merchant Navy*, III, p. 201.
2 Duff Papers (Greenwich): Duff to Bethell, April 21, 1917.
on it. The south-west of Ireland has been a veritable shambles for the last few days, and I fully expect a determined attack from the south at any time. If it comes, I hope you may be in a position to apply drastic treatment for 48 hours, or so.

The 'shambles' had been created during the third week in April when six U-boats were operating to the south-west of Ireland and enjoying remarkable success against shipping. Duff's reason for expecting an attack from the south was doubtless based on losses and on two signals intercepted from *U-84* and *U-60* on April 20. These submarines were apparently homeward-bound from the area, and it could be expected that at least four more, known from signals to be operating to the southward, would enter it on their way northward.

Other attempts to catch the homeward-bound U-boats were made by British patrol submarines. On April 30 in the northern North Sea *J-6* unsuccessfully attacked the homeward-bound *U-53* and *U-61*. The next day, when *E-54* sank *U-81*, British submarines also attacked *U-82* west of Ireland and *U-58* to the south. *U-62* was also attacked on May 3. It should be added that the large minefields deposited in the Bight late in April were directed not only against *UC-30* but against other returning submarines as well. In spite of this effort, only *UC-30* was prevented from reaching her base.

C. Signals and Sinkings May-December 1917

For the first fortnight of May the French records contain signals intercepted from only three U-boats. One came from a mysterious UB-boat of the Flanders Flotilla, and her call sign could not be identified. On May 9 at 2200 she was off Ushant. Twenty-four hours later she was twenty miles north of La Hague. Four hours after that, she was twenty miles south-south-east of St. Catherine Point on the Isle of Wight. Evidently she was moving slowly homeward, and the French analysts believed that she was a boat which had been operating in the waters north of the Spanish coast. A check of the German records reveals that only one UB-boat can have been in the Channel on the three days in question. She must have been *UB-39*, out from Zeebrugge on April 23 for the western Channel and the Bay of Biscay. We conclude that she must have made these signals, and that Spindler was doubtless right when he suggested that she was responsible for an explosion east of the Straits of Dover on the night of May 14-15.

In his book on the High Seas Fleet Admiral Scheer gives excerpts from the Fleet war diary for the period May 9-17, and the radio messages included in it suggest that the boats were reporting only from within the North Sea. The signals were made by one U-boat outward-bound in the Bight (*U-30*) and by seven submarines returning through the Bight (*U-58, UC-51, U-62, UC-75, UC-40, U-21* and *UC-49*).[1] None of these signals occurs in the French records, and Scheer himself does not mention a signal made by *UC-44* near the Casquets on May 16. It was intercepted and clearly suggested that the U-boat had just reached the Channel after passing through the Straits.

On May 18 the regular process of interception was resumed when *U-30* made a signal north-west of Ireland; she was actually returning because of leaking oil tanks. The next day *U-49* could be identified out in the Atlantic off Tory Island. She was returning to the north, as was evident on May 23 when she made another signal north of the Dogger Bank. *U-48*, west of Fastnet on the 19th and off the Hebrides on the 24th, was evidently following her. On the 27th *U-46*, homeward-bound, appeared in the North Sea, and *U-30* arrived there two days later.

Toward the end of the month there was some confusion about the call letters of the UC-boats from Brunsbüttel (I Flotilla). *UC-41* was located in the North Sea on May 25 and in the Channel two days later; the signals were actually made by the homeward-bound *UC-33* and the outward-bound *UC-45*. Later on the 27th, however, and again on the 28th, *UC-45* was correctly identified in the Channel approaches and off Fastnet. On the 29th a Flanders UC-boat called 'UC J' was heard from, south of Belle Isle; this was actually *UC-72*.

The French records show that late in May and early in June intercepted signals indicated that several large new U-boats were undertaking maiden voyages. The new *U-88* made herself heard when north of Ireland on May 26, south of Fastnet on May 31 and June 1, and back to the north, west of the Hebrides, on June 5. *U-95* was outward-bound in the northern North Sea on the 2nd, while *U-87* was north-west of the Hebrides on the 6th. *U-70*, between the Faeroes and the Orkneys on the 1st, was south-west of Fastnet on the 8th and in the Channel approaches on the 13th. On June 12 three U-boats formed an arc about Ireland: *U-66* to the north-west, the old *U-24* to the west, and *U-55* to the south. The next day it was clear that *U-50* was west of Brest.

Under these circumstances a British anti-submarine patrol was undertaken to the north of Scotland between June 15 and 24. 'The tracks which the larger U-boats followed', writes Newbolt, 'were, by then, known with tolerable accuracy'. No fewer than thirty-four destroyers and fifteen submarines took part in the operation, but it was a complete failure. The only semblance of success was achieved in the Fair Island passage on June 16, when the British submarine *K-7* fired two torpedoes at the homeward-bound *U-95*. Both hit the target and both failed to explode. The plan to trap the

36

1 *Germany's High Sea Fleet in the World War* (London, 1920), pp. 28s-86. I have corrected the errors in the account.

larger U-boats on the northern route was a sound one, but signals intercepted later in June showed that they were not being impeded. On the 23rd *U-60* was in the western Channel approaches, while on the 28th *U-62* and *U-84* were west of Brest. Signals from *U-94* placed her north-west of the Hebrides on the 27th and near the Shetlands two days later. To intercept signals was one thing; to sink U-boats was another.

Radio interception had a role to play, however, in the sinking of *U-44* early in August. She had been heard from on July 24 as she arrived in her operations area west of St. Kilda, and on August 5 she escaped from the decoy *Chagford* only by making a crash dive, which let water into her batteries. Three days later she met *U-84* west of the Hebrides and reported that during her cruise she had met nothing but decoy vessels. Chlorine gas was keeping her from remaining under water for any length of time. On the evening of the 11th, just west of Utsire Island on the Norwegian coast, she tried to establish radio contact with her base, but the message did not get through until 0200 on the 12th. She was in '096 alpha IV' (5915/0430E.) and expected to reach Lyngvig Light at 0600 on the 13th; she had sunk 6,400 tons of shipping.[1] The British picked up her signals and thereupon alerted the 3rd Light Cruiser Squadron off Norway. At 0600 on the 12th the destroyer *Oracle* sighted a strange ship on the horizon, in 5851/0420E. Two minutes later the ship hoisted a sail, but in three minutes more *Oracle* could make out the bow and stern of a U-boat, which soon took in the sail and dived. After ten minutes she broke surface three miles from the destroyer and hastily dived again; after another two minutes she came up once more. *Oracle* cut through her hull and, as she passed over, let go a depth charge. Three feet of *U-44*'s bow momentarily appeared at a 45-degree angle, but then nothing but oil and pieces of wreckage, including large curved pieces of cork from the hull lining, remained on the surface.

From the position of the encounter it seemed likely that *U-44* was the submarine sunk, but the fact was confirmed by further signals made to her and about her. Three and a half hours after she was sunk, she was told that with *U-60* she would be met by torpedo boats the next morning. At 2031 she was ordered to report her position, and the next morning the torpedo boats went out. That evening a half-flotilla of torpedo boats was sent to search for her - without result. At 0845 on the 14th she was again ordered to report. When no answer was heard, the Zeppelin *L-23* undertook a reconnaissance flight to the north of the Bight, but found nothing.

L-23 herself perished on August 21 after sighting the 3rd Light Cruiser Squadron making a sweep off the Jutland coast. One of the cruisers was

1 This total was not correct; *U-44* had sunk *Thorsdal* (2,200 tons), *John Hays Hammond* (137 tons), and *Chagford* (2,095 tons), and had damaged *Solglimt* (1,037 tons), a total of 5,469 tons. In any event, she did not sink

Belgian Prince (4,765 tons) and drown survivors, as was supposed at the time. This sinking was due to *U-55* (Spindler, IV, p. 249).

carrying a small aeroplane on a platform over her forward guns, and a surprise attack by this plane brought *L-23* down in flames.[1]

On September 12 the British submarine patrol north of Ireland enjoyed one of its infrequent successes when *D-7* torpedoed and sank *U-45*. Because of heavy sea she was able to pick up only two survivors, but they provided a good deal of information. *U-45* had left Heligoland on September 5, and that evening three trawlers escorted her through the swept channel off Norderney (Frisian Islands) along with *U-54* and another U-boat whose number they did not give.[2] As night came on the three submarines separated and headed to the north, sometimes submerged and sometimes on the surface. East of the Orkneys on the 7th, *U-54* radioed good wishes and *U-45* replied by using signal flags. That evening she passed between Fair Isle and North Ronaldsay, submerging only for an hour in order to avoid a patrol destroyer; she then proceeded with a series of broad zigzags to the north of Scotland and outside the Hebrides. Off St. Kilda she again sighted *U-54*, though at a great distance. On the 9th she arrived at the entrance to the North Channel and began her patrol. For three days nothing was sighted. On the afternoon of the 12th she was zigzagging on the surface, using only one engine, when she sighted a submarine she presumed to be *U-54*. Her first radio signal was not answered and after half an hour she made another. At this point the other submarine disappeared. A few minutes later a torpedo struck just before the conning tower and she sank immediately.

The survivors described the white ring painted on their deck plates as a recognition mark for German aircraft and stated that they sent as few radio messages as possible so that their location would not be given away. On their last cruise (June 26-July 29) they had reported their arrival on station at the entrance to the North Channel. Ordinarily, they said, they would not report again until they were in the North Sea on their way home.

Analysis of the interrogation must have revealed that the last statement was false, since on July 20 a signal from *U-45* had been intercepted from waters south-west of Ireland. She had been operating in that area since *U-87* had informed her (on July 12, with a signal also intercepted) about the location of the Allied steamer route.[3] At the very least, however, the statement showed that every signal could prove to be worth reading.

The interrogation clearly revealed how dangerous it was for U-boats to operate in the same area, and it suggested that such operations were, and would remain, unusual.

The French records of radio intercepts for September are very meagre, and indeed contain only the signals picked up from U-boats, which had

1 D. H. Robinson, pp. 243-44.
2 The other submarine was not identified as *U-88* until July 1918. Presumably she was not mentioned because her commander had sunk the *Lusitania*. Radio interception had given her number, however.

3 See Spindler, IV, pp. 266-67.

passed through the Straits of Dover (*U-19* and *U-62* on the 1st of the month) or intended to pass through but ran into trouble (*U-70*, three signals on the 27th).

For October, however, they list 20 signals picked up from ten U-boats. Four of the submarines were arriving or on station in their operations areas; one of these made a further signal upon leaving one operations area for another; five signalled their departure from the area homeward-bound, and one - *U-53* - announced a safe transit through Dover Straits westward on the 10th, return eastward from the Channel on the 17th, and arrival east of the Goodwin Sands on the 19th.

During November this pattern was somewhat modified. Fifteen signals are noted for eleven submarines. *U-67*, out in the North Sea on the 7th, passed through the Straits to her operations area and was heard from again, east of the Thames, on the 29th. *U-82*, east of the Firth of Forth on the 7th, arrived in an operations area west of Ushant on the 18th. *U-95*, homeward-bound, was east of the Scottish coast on the 18th. Almost all the other signals came from U-boats in the Channel or to the west after they had passed through the Straits of Dover, where, the German command suspected, the British were about to lay an extensive new mine barrage. These signals came from *U-58* on the 16th, *U-90* on the 18th, *U-53* on the 22nd, *U-96* on the 24th, and *U-57* on the 27th. *U-53* had certainly passed through the Straits, for she had made a signal in the southern North Sea on the 21st - the day on which minelaying began.

In December most of the 36 signals intercepted from 21 submarines had to do with transit routes. Three U-boats announced that they were returning through the Straits. These were *U-84* on the 2nd (southern North Sea on the 6th), *U-96* on the 3rd, and *U-97* on the 5th (southern North Sea on the 7th). On the 3rd, *U-82* - off the French coast on the 21st of November - made a signal west of the Hebrides and was obviously taking the northern route. Signals from *U-57* on December 6 and 7 showed that she was in the Channel approaches but was going to head north because of engine trouble. On the 6th the most interesting signal was one made en clair to the station at Lands End by a U-boat which identified herself only as UZAG. The signal read as follows: GLD DE (the shore station) UZAG JACOBS JONES TORPEDOED 4925 0622W SURVIVORS ON BOARD THREE RAFTS STILL AT LARGE 2006. This signal was made by *U-53*, actually asking assistance for the survivors of the American destroyer she had torpedoed.

On December 8, early in the morning, a significant message was picked up from *U-96*, now in the southern North Sea. It revealed that off Cape Barfleur she had accidentally rammed and sunk the Flanders minelayer *UC-69*, with the loss of the latter's watch officer and ten men. Naturally the strictest secrecy was observed in regard to this intercept, and it was not until

39

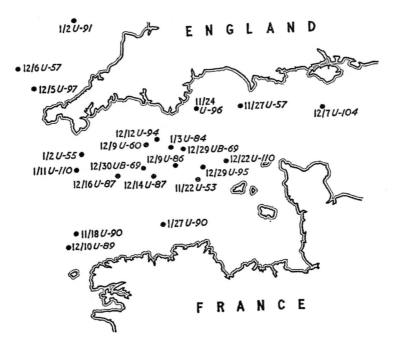

WESTERN ENGLISH CHANNEL - BRISTOL CHANNEL APPROACHES
French Radio Interception, November 1917-January 1918

the third quarter of 1918 that the Admiralty lists noted the cause of the sinking of *UC-69* - by that time confirmed by prisoners.

Finally, on December 20 *U-94*, operating in the Atlantic west of Ushant, reported that she had obtained secret orders giving the route to be followed by steamers bound for America. Since she radioed exact information about the route (evidently derived from the steamer *Bristol City*, sunk four days earlier), it is not altogether surprising that *U-43*, to whom the German command then sent the details, was unable to score any successes.[1] The commander of *U-43* was severely criticized for his failure, but it was doubtless not all his fault. Presumably the route was immediately changed.

D. Interceptions, Prisoners and Wrecks 1918

Most of the nineteen signals listed in the French records for January 1918 have to do with transit routes. We shall consider those related to the

1 Spindler, IV, pp. 4 18-19.

40

Straits of Dover in a subsequent chapter (III). Here we note only that an increasing number of U-boats were taking the northern route. *U-91*, off the Bristol Channel on the 2nd, reached the northern North Sea eight days later. *U-61*, south of Ireland on the 7th, also headed north and was in the North Sea five days later. *U-19* was homeward-bound in the North Sea on the 20th, *U-92* off St. Kilda on the 23rd. On the last two days of the month signals were intercepted from three U-boats heading north in the North Sea.

On February 10 at 0400 a similar signal was picked up from *U-89* and located a hundred miles east of Kinnaird Head, Scotland. This signal, received at home, gave the U-boat's position as '156 beta III', about seventy miles east of Peterhead, and stated that she had sighted a large convoy, escorted by ships of the line, proceeding outward (from the Firth of Forth). Two days earlier a signal not noted in the French records had given her position off Lindesnes. These two signals were the last heard from her. At 2330 on February 12 the British cruiser *Roxburgh*, on convoy escort duty, rammed and sank her off Malin Head, Ireland. Two months later the Allied picture of her cruise was rounded out when French Intelligence sent the Americans 'very reliable' information to the effect that she had headed northward in the Aarosund, east of Denmark, on February 6 with *UC-58*. The reliability of the information, we may add, was due to its having come from the log of *UB-21*.

During February, March and April the number of signals intercepted - and noted in the French records - remained fairly constant, while the proportion clearly related to transit routes steadily declined, from 22/34 to 18/33 to 12/27. Not all the signals are recorded. On February 19, for example, the Admiralty informed Sims that *U-96* had been obliged to return to port because of a broken coupling. This statement was obviously based on a signal intercepted and read, for the abortive cruise of *U-96* lasted from February 14 to 21. (It is not mentioned by Spindler.)

A good deal of information was acquired soon after March 15, when *U-110* was sunk to the north-west of Ireland and the survivors were interrogated. Some of the information was concerned with the IV Flotilla, to which *U-110* had belonged. It consisted of eleven submarines, although several boats had been lost, such as U-28, *U-84* (Roehr), and *U-106* (Hufnagel); in addition, *U-93* (Gerlach) and *U-95* (Prinz) had recently disappeared, and *U-109* was overdue when *U-110* sailed. The survivors described their recent cruises in considerable detail.

The previous cruise had begun on December 20 when the U-boat left Emden and was escorted for six hours by three destroyers. After passing Terschelling, she had lain on the bottom east of the Straits of Dover for four hours, waiting for darkness and high tide; she then crossed the barrage on the surface. In her operations areas, the Irish Sea and the Bristol Channel, she sank two steamers before returning to Germany. Again she rested on the

41

bottom for four hours before attempting passage of the Straits, and she reached Emden on January 16.

Her final cruise began on February 26 after a delay due to an accident in port. After taking the Kattegat route out, she headed north of Scotland for the Irish Sea, where on March 9 she was bombed by an aeroplane as she was diving. Her aft diving rudders jammed and she hit bottom in seventy metres, bending the outer doors of the bow torpedo tubes, which had been left open. On March 15 U-110 torpedoed the steamer *Amazon* but without sinking her immediately. The commander ordered another torpedo fired, but half an hour was spent in moving a torpedo to No. 4 bow tube, the only one usable. By that time she sighted a destroyer on the horizon and, without firing, dived to forty metres. After another half hour the U-boat lost trim and was sighted for a moment on the surface. As she went back down, several depth charges went off nearby; she was severely shaken, and the motor controlling the aft diving rudders was knocked out. The commander ordered a transfer to manual operation, but it took too long and U-110 went down, with her bow down at a 45° angle, to 102 metres. At this depth a stream of water nearly two centimetres in diameter jetted into the control room; it was entering through the studs connecting the water-pump discharge pipe to the hull. After the crew were ordered astern and tanks were blown the submarine rapidly came to the surface, then dived again but could not maintain trim. With no compressed air left, the commander decided to try to escape on the surface. There he sighted two destroyers heading for him, only three miles away, and he ordered the crew on deck with life jackets. The submarine sank almost at once. Only four survivors were rescued; the commander was not among them.

On April 11 the Admiralty told Sims that three submarines - U-19, U-67 and U-53 - were off the North Channel entrance, and it was thought that the last two were homeward-bound. None of the signals on which this information was presumably based are to be found in the French records, which list eleven signals from the Channel approaches and the waters to the west. One of these must have been especially significant. On the evening of April 28 the American destroyer *Porter* sighted a periscope in 4907/0553W. and dropped twenty-three depth charges in the vicinity. From a summary of the episode the Admiralty concluded that the submarine was 'probably seriously damaged'. An additional note stated that 'from chart evidence it appears that this attack caused the S/m to cease operating and return to her base'. The chart evidence must include the signal, listed in the French records, which was intercepted from U-108 at 0300 on April 30; her position was approximately 4900/0650W. Another signal which she made on May 4 showed that she had reached the northern North Sea.

Also during the month of April three U-boats provided survivors for interrogation; these were UB-55, sunk in the Dover Barrage, UB-85, belonging to the V Flotilla, and *U-104*, sunk by the British sloop *Jessamine* in St. George's Channel on April 25. There was one survivor from *U-104*, and he had been in the water for three hours before he was picked up.

U-104 had left Wilhelmshaven on April 11, heading out to the north-west across the North Sea and sinking three sailing vessels on her way. She passed Muckle Flugga and St. Kilda and was on the surface at ¾ speed when a British submarine north of Ireland missed her with four torpedoes. After going west and south-west of Ireland and briefly up into the Irish Sea, she returned to St George's Channel, where her periscope was sighted by the American destroyer *Cushing* about noon on April 23. Diving deep, she moved away at half speed, and *Cushing's* six or seven depth charges exploded about a thousand metres away.[1]

Early on the morning of the 25th she was making between ten and twelve knots on the surface when she sighted *Jessamine* only a quarter of a mile away. The alarm was sounded and the U-boat quickly reached the depth of thirty metres to the keel. *Jessamine* dropped two depth charges. The first lifted the stern of the U-boat but did not damage her. The second, half a minute later, exploded precisely on the s tern. Just afterwards the prisoner, who was in the bow torpedo chamber with ten other men, noticed that the boat was lying at an angle of 30° and that the depth gauge registered fifty metres. Water began to pour into the motor room; the motors short-circuited and went dead. Air pressure in the bow increased so that breathing became difficult. The watertight door had been closed, but water was coming in through pipe fittings. After a minute's interval, another depth charge exploded and forced the U-boat's bow up to a depth of 36 metres. At this moment the men in the torpedo room tried to blow the tanks. Those aft had evidently been crushed by the explosions, and only the tanks forward could be emptied. Ten metres of the bow came up above the surface, and the men rushed to open the torpedo hatch. As *U-104* went down again for the last time, the hatch blew open; the prisoner, who was clinging to it, was the only one to escape.

He explained to his interrogators that *U-104* was surprised on the surface because of the poor watch-keeping of a Bulgarian sub-lieutenant in training for submarine duty at home. In the German casualty list, however, this man is mentioned only as a 'U-Matrose' or sailor.[2] And we know that the prisoner was not altogether accurate in some of his statements. In prison camp he told other prisoners that most of the crew of *U-104* had gone down with the submarine but that a few survivors swimming in the water had been shot by the British. (Conceivably he was confused by an account like the one in the hands of some survivors from *U-103*). After the war he more

1 This statement differs from one from American sources which I published in U.S. *Naval Institute Proceedings* 64 (1938), pp68-69.
2 For the list see Spindler, V, p. 405.

correctly informed the German naval authorities that *Jessamine* had made every effort to find more survivors.

E. The U-Boat Concentration against Convoys

During the first week of May no signals were intercepted from the western Channel approaches; at any rate, there is no French record of any. At 2030 on May 9, however, *U-70* evidently announced her arrival to the west of the Scillies; at 2100 on May 10 *U-103* was heard from near Lands End, and by 2200 the following day she had moved south and east to 4842N./0500W., evidently in search of convoys. Six hours later she was rammed and sunk by the transport *Olympic*, and an hour after that the British submarine *D-4* was able to find *UB-72* in Lyme Bay, where she too had been awaiting the arrival of transports.

During the next few days increasing radio activity revealed the presence of further U-boats in the area. On the afternoon of the 12th two more signals were intercepted from *U-70*, which had encountered a large convoy during the morning but had been unable to sink any ships. On the 14th further signals showed that *U-43* was heading southward in the hope of establishing contact, while *U-70* and *U-92* were remaining on watch in the area where the convoy had been sighted. On the 15th it was clear that *U-43* was still moving southward; *U-70* and *U-92* had proceeded about one degree of longitude to the west. On the 16th *U-70* and *U-92* moved somewhat to the north-east,[1] and that evening signals revealed the presence of *U-55* and *U-94* in the northern part of the area. Evidently a concentration of U-boats was building up against the convoys.

Further reinforcement was on the way, as could be ascertained on the 16th when a German submarine appeared off St. Kilda, west of the Hebrides, and proceeded to fire 72 shells at the radio station and its environs. Before the station was destroyed, a distress signal was made to the base at Lochboisdale on South Uist, but the submarine escaped from hunters and headed southward. She was *U-90*, on her way to the Channel approaches.[2]

On May 17 *U-43* made a signal in the Channel approaches, while *U-55* and *U-94* were in communication in the same area. Early the next morning *U-94* found a convoy to which *U-55* had directed her and was able to sink *Hurunui* (10,644 tons), while *U-55* herself torpedoed *Scholar* (1,635 tons) and *Denbigh Hall* (4,943 tons). These were the only sinkings achieved during the concentration. During the day other signals were picked up from *U-46*, *U-70* and *U-43*.

1 Off Penmarch that day *U-43* asked the French fishing vessel *Petite Marie* if she had sighted any U-boats and exchanged four boxes of preserved meat and vegetables for three baskets of fresh fish.
2 See Spindler, V, p. 34; also J. A. McKay, 'St. Kilda in the First World War', *Journal of the Royal Artillery* 87 (1960), pp94-98.

The concentration lasted for five days more, but without any result. On the 19th signals were intercepted from *U-46* and *U-70*, as well as from *UB-118*, apparently operating independently to the south-west of Ireland (she was announcing her homeward voyage). On the 20th there were signals from *U-43* and *U-46*. One from *U-94* (actually calling *U-55*) was immediately followed by a call from *U-101*, evidently arriving in the area and communicating with her. On the 21st *U-55* was in the western Channel, about to head homeward, while *U-70* was already south-west of Fastnet, homeward-bound. *U-101* signalled the location of a convoy. On the 22nd *U-43* made a similar signal, and messages were also picked up from *U-46* and *U-101*. Only *U-46* and *U-101* seem to have made signals in the area on the 23rd, although another was intercepted from *U-90*, off Fastnet and perhaps homeward-bound.[1]

By this time the concentration was breaking up. On May 24 only *U-94* was heard from, apparently signalling her departure, while *U-90* was apparently reporting on a convoy south of Ireland. On the last day of the month signals came in from the homeward-bound *U-98* (not part of the concentration) and *U-101* west of Ireland and from *U-46* to the north-west.

By this time *U-90* was operating far to the west of the concentration area, and she achieved her only results after the ill-defined group broke up. On May 29 she sank two steamers and two days later was able to find and sink the westward-bound American transport *President Lincoln*, whose destroyer escort had left her twelve hours earlier. A signal on June 1 must have announced her success.

At the end of May French Intelligence summarized what was known of the concentration. At least seven large U-boats had taken part in it.

> To our knowledge this is the first time that the enemy attempted such an operation in compact formation. The objective seems to have been to intercept convoys with American troops and supplies and thus to strike some sensational blow likely to disrupt these military transports.

The results, however, had been insignificant.

> Not only did these successive waves of submarines in close order fail to hinder the arrival of the convoys in any way whatever, but also the units in question were immobilized, so to speak, and completely wasted for two weeks, since in these waters, where traffic was very heavy, they succeeded in torpedoing only three steamers.

1 Some of these signals are not listed in the French records but are inferred from charts 25-27 in Newbolt, *Naval Operations V (Maps)*.

The failure was explained partly in relation to the signals made by the U-boats. It was supposed that they were constantly on watch for Allied submarines and therefore constantly exchanged messages. This supposition was quite wrong. Most of the messages dealt with the location of convoys, though they dismally failed to lead to success.

The orders issued to *U-103* on May 2 specifically instructed her not to name grid square locations in radio signals, but it would appear that she actually did name them, as did the other U-boats involved in the concentration. These locations seem to have proved more valuable to the Allies than to the U-boats, which experienced grave difficulties in finding the convoys in the area.

In the French view, it was unlikely that the Germans would undertake another concentration like this one, although the operations of individual submarines would be linked by exchanges of information. This prediction turned out to be correct. The only exception was provided by the unique, and unsuccessful, concentration of U-boats at the end of the war.

The British view was expressed by Newbolt, who wrote in 1931 but relied on earlier appreciations. The concentration was 'the most methodical and elaborate attempt that the German Staff had as yet made to interfere with the convoy system'. It coincided with a series of German victories on the western front. Because not enough U-boats were involved and because the Intelligence estimates were inadequate, it failed even to slow down the continuing arrival of American troops in England and France. Moreover, during the operation no fewer than183 vessels in convoy arrived safely.[1]

One further detail may be mentioned. The frequent signals made by *U-101* suggested to the French analysts that she might have been in difficulties, and they concluded that while passing through the Irish Sea on her way to the area she had been depth-charged by the American destroyers *Allen* and *Patterson* and the British patrol boat *P-62*. Actually, however, *U-101* was west of Ireland on the afternoon of May 19, when the attack was made, and her signals were chiefly concerned with convoy movements. The submarine in the Irish Sea was probably *UB-119*, out from Germany on April 27 and probably sunk at this time.

Beginning with the reports for May 1918, the French documents contain much less complete accounts of information received and they have to be supplemented by accounts published elsewhere. Considerable information, however, is still provided. Thus we learn that the prisoners taken from *U-103*, sunk in the Channel approaches on May 12, gave some account of previous cruises. The fourth cruise of this U-boat began on March 4 and she went out through the Sund and the Skagerrak, then north of Scotland and west of Ireland, into the St. George's Channel and to the southern Irish Sea.

1 *Naval Operations*, V, p. 282.

1. (a) *U-41* photographed from the steamer *Urbino* off the Scilly Isles, September 24, 1915. While the U-Boat was occupied with *Urbino*, the Q-ship *Baralong* approached.

(b) The end of *U-41* in a cloud of smoke and steam, under gunfire from *Baralong*.

2. Stern and bow views of the salvaged wreck of *UB-110*, in dry-dock at Newcastle-upon-Tyne, October 7, 1918.

In twelve days she sank three steamers of 4,148 tons and damaged one of 6,042 tons. Her attacks were hindered by calm and clear weather and by the watchful patrols. On one occasion more than 50 depth charges were dropped, 20 of them in less than an hour. (Probably this refers to an attack by the American destroyer *Downes* on March 16.) Finally she returned through the North Channel, west of the Hebrides and past Fair Isle, where at periscope depth she steered between two British submarines without being observed, and reached Wilhelmshaven about March 30. Her homeward course thus confirmed the identification of two radio signals intercepted on March 24 and 28. On May 3 she had sailed again, this time to operate in the Channel approaches from May 10 to 12, and achieved no results before being sunk. Off the Scillies on the 10th she had been attacked by a seaplane whose bombs exploded close to her but did no damage. Two days later she was sunk.

Later the same day, *UB-72* was sunk off Start Point. The survivors described the cruise during which she was lost; it had begun on April 27. She had operated in the North Channel May 3-6 and had reached St. George's Channel on May 8, where she fired a torpedo at a vessel under escort (*Quito*). Since she was leaving an oil track, she was chased and depth-charged several times as she was passing through, but she was able to reach the Channel approaches and patrol there from May 9 until she was sunk.

Further details from the interrogation were provided by Doughty.[1] 'On May 7 and 8 a total of 51 depth charges were dropped on *UB-72*. The first three were from a dirigible, and apparently caused no damage. Next, she was pursued for two hours by a destroyer, which dropped 23 depth charges, opening up a leak in an oil tank and causing her to leave a track of oil in her wake. Next day the submarine was again trailed by a destroyer, which dropped 20 depth charges, shaking up the boat considerably and extinguishing 5 lights. Later in the day, a patrol boat dropped 5 more charges on her.' Doughty comments that she provides an 'example of the amount of punishment a submarine can stand from depth charges'.

The interrogators were impressed by the survivors' loyalty to their late captain. They said he had only one fault - 'he would stay on the surface as long as he possibly could, and when at last he did submerge he always wanted to keep within periscope depth so that he could always see what was going on around him'. The interrogators' comment on this is succinct. 'As this habit led to all their troubles and their eventual destruction, he must have had some very good points in other directions.'

One of the survivors asked his captors why they had been rescued. 'He said that the crews of all German submarines had been informed that it was no use to surrender as the British hung all the survivors of U-boats as pirates

1 L. Doughty, Jr., in U.S. *Naval Institute Proceedings* 61 (1935), p.356.

after they got them ashore.[1] A similar point was made, with more detail, by one of the prisoners from U-103. He stated that crews had standing orders not to swim towards British destroyers, since they never took prisoners. According to the officially circulated story, he said, a Flanders U-boat had been on the scene when U-84 was sunk by a British destroyer in November 1917, and had observed the event through her periscope. Rifle and revolver fire from the destroyer had accounted for the entire crew of U-84 as they struggled in the water. The British comment on the story ran as follows. 'Like many other German official lies, this one is spoiled by the wealth of corroborative details. The weak points in the particular story are:

(a) U-84 was not sunk until January 1918.
(b) She was sunk in an area in which Flanders submarines never operate and from which, according to prisoners, they are excluded by their standing orders.
(c) Submarine was destroyed by a patrol boat, and not by a destroyer.
(d) So far from survivors coming to the surface to be shot, it was not until the wreck was located some time later that H.M. ship concerned claimed more than a "possible" sinking.'

As the British suggested, the story was obviously concocted in order to discourage U-boat crews from surrendering. The Germans actually had no idea as to the circumstances of the loss of U-84. It is interesting to note that those who interrogated survivors from U-103 were aware that at first they were not getting much information from them because so many prisoners had been taken. Those who might have talked were rather fearful of the consequences from other crew members. It was never suggested, however, that survivors should not, if possible, be picked up.

Conceivably the specific reference to U-84 was planted just because the cause of her loss was unknown, and the Germans hoped that the British might issue an official denial in which some facts would come to light.

F. Interception June-October 1918

According to the French records, twenty-eight signals were intercepted during June. Four of them came from the southern North Sea and had to do with the homeward voyages of Flanders submarines. The remaining twenty-four were made by only eleven U-boats - ten of them by U-53 and U-105, looking for convoys west of the French coast between June 25 and 30. Three messages were sent by U-111, out on a fruitless Channel-approaches cruise marked by arrival on June 6 and departure ten days later; on the 18th the

1 W. G. Carr, *By Guess and By God* (New York, 1930), p. 255.

50

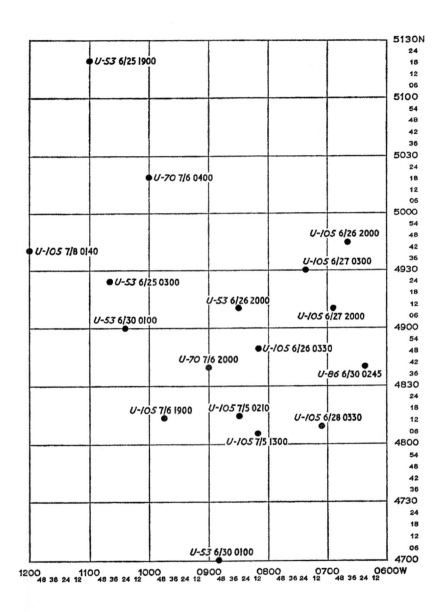

FRENCH RADIO INTERCEPTS, WEST OF BISCAY, JUNE-JULY 1918

Admiralty informed Sims that she was homeward-bound. Two signals on the 8th and the 11th marked the arrival of *U-96* in St. George's Channel from the Irish Sea and her departure homeward. There were also two from *U-19*, but one was clearly mislocated: she was placed west of Ireland on the 19th, when she was actually north of the Shetlands. The other signal was correctly placed in the Atlantic west of Ireland on the 24th.

Single signals from other boats accounted for the rest of the interceptions. *U-62*, far west of Ireland on June 1, was obviously returning after her rather disastrous cruise off the Azores. *U-82*, in the western approaches on the 1st, was appearing again after her previous cruise in April. '*UB-120*', eighty miles south of Fastnet on the 2nd, was misidentified; she must have been *UB-103*, out to the western Channel on May 28. *U-100*, west of Ireland on June 22, was signalling her encounter with a convoy the previous day as well as her return because of low fuel supplies. On the 24th *U-107* also announced her return, as did *U-53*, because of engine trouble, on the 30th. On the latter day *U-86* was heard from in the Channel approaches; she had just sighted a convoy.

The forty July intercepts noted in the French records in part reflect the same pattern and in part indicate a change. During the first fortnight of the month eleven signals reflected the kind of patrol against convoys previously undertaken by *U-53* and *U-105*. *U-53* (misread as *U-55*) was north-west of Ireland on the 4th when she signalled her continuing return, but *U-105* remained in the Channel approaches until July 8, making five signals before she departed homeward. Two signals on the 6th showed *U-70* heading into the centre of the attack area, but that evening - whether or not the signal was intercepted - she announced her return. The next morning *U-19*, far west of Ireland, also stated that she was homeward-bound. A few hours later '*UB-132*' revealed her presence in the Channel approaches; this was actually the new *UB-118*, giving the location of a convoy she had met and apparently also making the 'homeward' signal, for she reached Wilhelmshaven nine days later.

Several boats arrived on the scene soon afterwards. On the 9th *U-92* signalled that she had met convoys in the western approaches, and two days later she informed her base that though she had been damaged by a steamer she was continuing on cruise. On the 14th, however, she sent a 'homeward' message. These three signals, and another on the 17th, were intercepted. *U-108* was outward-bound north-west of Ireland on the 12th. She evidently remained on patrol for about ten days before signalling her return south of Lands End on the 23rd and south of Ireland on the 25th. *U-55* was north of the Hebrides on the 13th. Five days later she made a signal about a convoy and her own successful torpedoing of the *Carpathia* (13,603 tons); she followed the convoy westward on the 19th and 20th, then evidently running low on fuel. *U-60*, arriving in the area on the 18th, began her return only five

52

days later. On the 27th three signals from the Channel approaches pointed to the homeward journeys of *U-91*, back from the Azores, and *U-98*, which had arrived on the 18th, and to the arrival of *U-101*. Since the last submarine also made signals on August 1 and 3, evidently announcing her impending return (actually because of engine damage), it was supposed that she had been damaged by the decoy vessel *Stockforce* on July 30. This supposition was wrong, for *Stockforce* encountered *UB-80*.

Far to the north some significant signals were being intercepted. On July 15 *U-54* was west-north-west of Ireland, and the next day *UB-124*, also outward-bound, was north of the Shetlands. On the morning of the 17th UB-124 exchanged signals with *U-92* west of the Hebrides, and on the morning of the 20th, in the North Channel approaches, she made a signal intercepted by the British but not received at home. Later in the day she was sunk.

The survivors from *UB-124* provided a complete account of their own cruise, the first undertaken by their new submarine. They discussed the movements of other submarines with considerable freedom, as well as the future movements of U-boats from the Mediterranean (*U-47* would return) and to the Flanders Flotillas. *U-140*, a new cruiser, had sailed for American waters on June 20; though the date was twelve days too early, the fact was correct. They themselves had participated in the sinking of the *Justicia* (32,234 tons), although five other U-boats were in the general vicinity - *U-43*, *U-54*, *UB-83*, *UB-90* and *UB-126*. Presumably this information was helpful in identifying signals later made by some of these boats. The French records mention signals from *UB-90* in the North Sea on July 23, *UB-64* in the North Channel approaches on the 29th, and *UB-126* north-west of Ireland the same day. One more signal, intercepted from the waters east of Scotland on July 22 and ascribed to '*UB-131*', was evidently misread. *UB-131* was commissioned only on July 4; the boat in question was probably *UB-87*.

According to the French records only half as many signals were intercepted in August as in July. The seventeen signals listed came from twelve U-boats, some reporting the presence of convoys to the west of the Channel approaches, others announcing their departure homeward. A few signals indicated different situations: on the 6th *U-157* was out in the Atlantic, and on the 19th the old *U-22* was off the Portuguese coast.

Not all the intercepted signals appear in the French records, however. During July there was an important exchange between *U-86*, damaged in the Northern Barrage off Norway, and *U-53*, which came to her assistance. In August a call for help under similar circumstances was made by *U-113*, and it was picked up and read. On August 20 the Admiralty informed Sims that calls had been made to *U-157* although she had not answered them. At the end of the month British interceptors were quite busy. On the 27th the Admiralty informed Sims that there were two U-boats south-west of Ireland, one of which was *U-53*. (They may have read the signals exchanged by *U-90* and *U-53* west of Ireland on the 24th.) On the 30th their statement was more explicit. *U-105* was south-west of Fastnet; *U-53* was off the Scillies; and *U-67* was in about 46°N. and 13°W.

The quota of intercepts for September was back up to nearly forty, though the French records do not include at least eight signals which the British detected from the 'cruiser' submarines. At the beginning of the month, as was to be expected, there were several signals from the Bay of Biscay and westward, exchanged by *U-53* and *U-105* (and with *U-67*, though her presence is not noted in the records). On August 30 and 31, American destroyers and submarine chasers had left Plymouth in order to hunt for these three U-boats, and on the latter day *U-53* sighted the task force, which dropped five depth charges on her without effect. The only other encounter seems to have taken place on September 2, when the American destroyer *Parker* depth-charged a submarine thought to be *U-53* (she was actually *U-82*). According to Sims, *U-53* had been severely damaged. 'For several days afterward the radio operator could hear German submarines calling across the void to the *U-53*, but there was no answer to the call.' About a week later a signal indicated that she was 'off the extreme northern coast of Scotland' - homeward-bound.[1] This last signal seems actually to be the one which *U-53* made on the 11th when she was north-west of Ireland. Her previous silence was due not to damage but to the malfunctioning of her radio.

The arrival of *U-82* became known on September 3, when she made a signal from the waters west of the Channel approaches and repeated it at noon the next day. She was actually reporting that she had discovered the location in which convoys assembled, and by proceeding eastward she was able to meet and damage the westbound transport *Mount Vernon* (18,372 tons) the next morning. She called U-boats in the vicinity to aid in the attack; these were apparently not intercepted, but in any event they were fruitless. *U-105* signalled that she would try to make contact, but she was unable to do so; both *U-53* and *U-67* were too far from the scene. Other U-boats to the north of the position were not involved. An intercepted signal from St. George's Channel on the 5th was tentatively ascribed to '*UB-123*', but it was actually made by *UB-125*, now homeward-bound. Two more signals from that area on the 6th and the 8th were ascribed to '*UB-131*'; they really came from *UB-87*, which on the 7th torpedoed and damaged the transport *Persic* (12,045 tons) with 2,800 American troops on board.

As early as September 2 the Admiralty picked up a signal from the new minelayer *U-118*, which was heading down the Irish coast. Two days later another signal showed that she was entering the Bay of Biscay, and it was thought likely that she would lay her mines between the Gironde and the Spanish frontier; information dated August 23 showed that the enemy

---

1 *The Victory at Sea*, pp. 222-24.

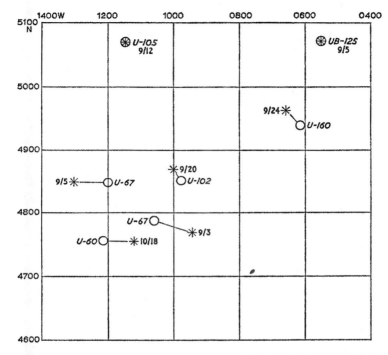

GERMAN CHART-AREA 'OTTO' with sample French intercepts (*), September-October 1918, along with U-boats' actual locations. Note that error increases with the distance from direction-finding stations to the north. (not to scale)

believed that American troops were landing at Bordeaux as well as at St. Nazaire. On the evening of the 8th a signal was intercepted off Belle Isle, and further signals on the 11th showed that the U-boat was moving north-west. It was concluded that she had laid her mines off Bordeaux. In actual fact, she had originally been ordered to lay them off Bordeaux, but on the 6th a signal from Nauen had ordered her to report on observations of traffic in the Biscay area and presumably - since she laid her mines off St. Nazaire and Belle Isle on the 7th - not to operate off Bordeaux. By the 16th she had moved westward and a signal from her was intercepted after she had encountered a convoy and had sunk the steamer *Wellington* (5,600 tons). Nothing more was heard from her, and the French assumed that she reached her base at the end of September. When *Arca* (4,839 tons) was sunk north-west of Ireland on October 2, her loss was ascribed to an unidentifiable UB-boat. The submarine responsible was actually *U-118*, which reached Brunsbüttel only on October 14.

In mid-September only a few U-boats made their presence known from signals in the Channel approaches. *U-111* evidently arrived on the 10th, making signals that day and the next, and presumably announced her departure on the 19th. *U-82* signalled the discovery of a convoy on the 11th; *U-105* started homeward on the 12th. *U-102* was south of Ireland on the 14th and the 18th and still farther to the south on the 20th, when she evidently began her return. Only the last signal was received at home.

A little later, a series of signals began coming in from *U-160*, also south-west of the Scillies but gradually moving to the north-east. Each day from the 22nd to the 26th messages were intercepted from her, and the British concluded that she was in damaged condition. In fact she was first reporting her arrival, then announcing that because of engine trouble she was heading for home. Four more signals were made by *UB-91*, operating south of Ireland, in the Irish Sea and in St. George's Channel. On the 20th *U-54* made a signal south-east of the Shetlands after sighting destroyers and patrols in the western section of the Northern Barrage. Four days later came the first of an almost incessant stream of signals (September 24 and 26; October 1, 2, 3 and 4) as she came south of Ireland and into the Channel approaches - without achieving any results. *U-161* also operated fruitlessly, making her presence known to the south-west of Ireland by signals on September 29 and October 2. On the latter date she was in radio contact with *U-46*, following a convoy about which *U-46* had made a signal the day before. *U-55* was in the vicinity; signals on October 1 and 10 marked her arrival and departure.

Not all the signals intercepted around this time are listed in the French records. On October 11 the Admiralty informed Sims that no fewer than eleven positions, occupied by five or six U-boats, had just been estimated by direction-finding at the north entrance to the North Sea; but none of these occurs in the French lists and charts.

Leighton states that toward the end of the war 'the presence and exact position of the majority of submarines at sea was learned every night by an elaborate system of radio stations along the coast'. He mentions particularly the stations at Lands End, Milford Haven, and Queenstown. The example he gives is not quite correct. A destroyer, he says, attacked a U-boat off Bantry Bay at 1152 on October 17; five minutes later the U-boat made a signal which was intercepted from exactly the same position.[1] Unfortunately this signal is listed in the French records, and it was made by *U-91* at 0045 on the 17th. This error does not change the fact that at the time the Admiralty was making the fullest possible use of interception.

1 Leighton, pp. 103-5.

G. Investigation of Wrecks

During the year 1918 the wrecks of many U-boats were investigated by divers, and useful discoveries were often made. Most of the wrecks were found in the Straits of Dover and will be discussed in the chapter on the Dover Barrage. Here we deal only with other localities.

Our first example, unfortunately, provides nothing but a false lead. The records tell us that on March 10 several vessels were searching for a U-boat active off Trevose Head on the Cornish coast. When the Spanish steamer *Cristina* was torpedoed the group proceeded to drop depth charges; oil and air bubbles came up. The next day dragging operations began, and by March 15 two wrecks had been encountered. On the 20th divers found 'the possible wreck of a submarine'. In his book *Submarine and Anti-Submarine* Newbolt provides further graphic details. On March 25 an officer diver found a submarine 'lying on her port beam ends in twenty-four fathoms'. She had 'a large fracture in the hull, on the port side amidships', and her conning tower was 'practically blown off'. [1]

Oddly enough, this submarine is not included in the 1918 official list of submarines destroyed, and we must conclude that the account is incorrect. In addition, Spindler states that *U-55* was active in the area for several days but headed for home after sinking *Cristina* with her last torpedo. [2] No U-boat was sunk in this area at this time.

Off the East Coast on June 7 a somewhat more significant discovery was made when the destroyer *Quail* saw small oil bubbles on the surface. After she dropped a depth charge at their source, large quantities of oil came up, rising throughout the next day. Divers were sent down, and what they found was the wreck of *UC-39*, sunk in February 1917 but now, though covered with barnacles, emitting oil and air. Later in the month divers found the wreck of *UC-11*. Her commander had been picked up after she was sunk on June 26; the next day divers found his submarine with her mines still in their chutes.

More significant results were obtained after July 19, when the new *UB-110* was sunk off the Yorkshire coast and thirteen survivors were picked up. Divers were soon sent down to recover documents, among them the log book of the submarine. She had left Zeebrugge at 2250 on July 4 for the East Coast, and the log gave her noon position for each day until July 15. On October 4 the wreck was finally raised from the bottom and towed to Newcastle. Photographs taken in dry dock showed how extensively she had been damaged.

In the same approximate area three more U-boats were sunk, later in July and during August. The wreck of *UB-107*, sunk on July 27, was not

1 Newbolt, p. 192.
2 Spindler, V, p. 14

found, and it was not until the end of the war that her loss could be classified as 'known'. On the other hand, off Whitby on August 17 divers identified the wreck of *UB-30*, sunk four days previously, and on September 14 they found the wreck of *UC-70*, sunk on August 28. On October 18 the Admiralty informed Sims that 'search is being made for the hull of a submarine believed to have been sunk off the East Coast of England'. This was probably *UB-115*, sunk off Blyth on September 29. On October 1 sweepers had located an obstruction from which oil was still rising.

The last U-boat to be visited by divers in northern waters was also the last to be sunk. This was *UB-116*, blown up by mines in the approaches to Scapa Flow on October 28. The wreck was investigated by divers the next day. They found three bodies in the conning tower and then, getting into the boat through the fore hatch, cleared the way aft through two compartments to the control room bulkhead. Their way was blocked especially by two torpedoes which had been slung up on purchases, ready to reload the tubes. At the control room bulkhead a diver finally found the door partly off its hinges and jammed. 'After digging away the bedding and debris from around the door he found the forearms and hands of a man thrust out through the crack at the lower part of the door seating', but 'his body was the other side of the jammed door in the collapsed and inaccessible control room'. Rumour later had it that the submarine's crew consisted of nothing but officer volunteers. In fact, as Spindler points out, the only volunteer was a reserve lieutenant who was a friend of the commander. 'Die Tat' - an attack on the Grand Fleet at Scapa Flow - 'ist nicht weniger gross, weil die Männer nicht eigenem Antrieb, sondern der Pflicht gehorchten'.[1]

The log book of *UB-116*, recovered on November 4, reflected the circumstances of her sailing. On the 22nd she had fitted a new periscope; the next day she had taken on torpedoes and prepared for sea. On the 24th she had proceeded to Heligoland and prepared the torpedoes for firing, placing them in the tubes. On the morning of the 25th she had headed out to sea, 'proceeding with escort, course 310°, Heligoland abeam'. There the log book ended.

According to Gröner the wreck of the submarine was raised during 1919, but this idea is incorrect. Naval Historical Branch has stated that 'bodies were recovered in 1919 but otherwise the wreck remained undisturbed and was resurveyed by the Survey Ship *Challenger* in 1940'. The precise location is 585007/030406W.

1 Spindler, V, p. 317.

III

BOTTLING UP THE U-BOATS

FROM NOVEMBER 1914, when the British laid mines off the German held port of Zeebrugge, Belgium, to October 1918, when the last lines were laid in the North Sea fields, the mine was viewed as one of the most significant anti-submarine weapons. For the British it was almost always a weapon of the offensive. Only one major field was laid, and that toward the end of 1918, in order to protect a shipping route. The mine was intended to prevent the German submarines from leaving their bases. For this reason most of the mines were laid (1) off the Flanders coast, (2) in the Bight of Heligoland and the Kattegat, (3) in the Straits of Dover, (4) across the Straits of Otranto, and (5) across the northern North Sea between Norway and the Orkneys. Smaller fields were laid in the English Channel, off the East Coast, and in the North Channel in order to trap U-boats at specific points usually related to their navigation problems. Obviously the use of the mine was defensive as well as offensive. U-boats kept out of the Atlantic or the Mediterranean were certainly prevented from attacking Allied and neutral shipping. But the main purpose was to destroy or damage them before they could get far from their bases.

It is clear that the closer the mines were laid to the bases the more likely it was that they would be swept up by enemy minesweepers. In waters under Allied control there was little likelihood of sweeping, and for this reason the fields in the Dover Straits, the Otranto Straits, and the northern North Sea resembled walls, intended to keep invaders out. The situation was quite different off the Flanders Coast and in the Bight of Heligoland. In these areas surprise was of the essence, and it was absolutely necessary to have exact information concerning the routes the U-boats took, and concerning whatever defensive minefields the enemy himself might have laid.

Such information was provided by two means: (1) investigation of wrecks and interrogation of prisoners, and (2) interception of enemy radio.

A. Against the German Bases: Zeebrugge and Ostend

After the collapse of Belgium in the early months of the war, and the capture of the ports of Ostend and Zeebrugge on the Belgian coast, the German command undertook studies of small coastal submarines which could be employed from these ports; on October 15, orders were given for fifteen small 'UB-boats', and on November 23 similar orders were placed for fifteen small minelaying 'UC-boats'. They were built so rapidly that six of the UB-boats actually undertook cruises during the following April, while two of the UC-boats laid mines near the Sunk and Kentish Knock Light Vessels during June.

Before that time, however, several of the larger boats had been stationed temporarily at Ostend and Zeebrugge, and in December 1914 two of them fell victim to British minefields. *U-11* left Zeebrugge for Dunkirk and Calais on December 9 and did not return. Presumably she encountered one or another of the British minefields laid to the north of Zeebrugge and Ostend during October and November.[1] *U-5*, out on a patrol off the Belgian coast on the 18th, also vanished, probably for the same reason.

Within a very short time the British were aware of these losses, but none of the minefields subsequently laid east of the Dover Straits seems to have produced any results during the following year. In part this failure was due to the almost total inefficiency of the British mines available at the time. In part it was due to the locations of the fields.

What seems to have led to the destruction of several Flanders U-boats was the surrender of *UB-26* off Le Havre on April 5, 1916. The French had been expecting the arrival of German submarines in the area since March 27, when an agent had sent word that large submarines were preparing to lay mines 'as near Le Havre as possible'.[2] Eight days later *UB-26* was off Le Havre; the next day she came in close, bumped a steamer with her periscope, and thus alerted the patrols. Soon afterward she got tangled in a net and went to the bottom to wait for darkness in order to escape. Depth charges dropped by the destroyer *Trombe*, however, damaged her battery. Her commander, out on his first cruise, surfaced and surrendered. *UB-26* then sank but was raised by the French on April 14. Documents found in this U-boat gave 'the position of the mines and buoys laid by the Germans off the coast of Belgium' and also 'the supposed positions of minefields as laid by the Allies, together with the British net barrage'.[3]

It can hardly be a coincidence that on April 24 and 28 and on May 15 and 26 the British minelayers were active off the Belgian coast. By the latter date, indeed, 'about forty miles of double lines of deep contact mines and fifteen miles of mined nets had been laid at a mean distance of thirteen miles from a strongly defended enemy coast.'[4]

The largest field consisted of 1,445 mines. It was laid to the north and the north-west of Zeebrugge, to the south of the Thornton and Rab Banks, on April 24. The minelayers were sighted by *UC-1*, *UC-5* and *UC-10*, out that morning from Zeebrugge, but though all of them reported their observations

1 Chart in Spindler, II, p. 61.
2 A. Chatelle, *Le base navale du Havre* (Paris, 1949), p. 204.
3 E. K. Chatterton, *On the High Seas*, p. 213.
4 Cowie, p. 54.

the news came too late for *UB-13*, out the previous evening for the East Coast. She undoubtedly encountered the mines on her way home. *UC-5* freed herself from the nets and returned to Zeebrugge. On the 26th, after minesweepers had cut a path through the nets, she set out again but stranded on Shipwash Shoal. There a British destroyer captured her, and later on, practically intact, she was towed to Harwich.

British minelaying activities continued on May 26 when to the southeast of Rab Bank they laid no fewer than 750 mines. *UC-1* found the minefield the same day, but not in time to warn *UC-3*, sunk soon afterwards. On July 3-4 they set two fields of 96 mines apiece to the south-east of the Thornton Ridge. On July 5 the submarine *UB-12*, on picket duty to the west of Bligh Bank, sighted a U-boat steering eastward from North Hinder. She was indubitably *UC-7*, which had sailed on the 3rd to lay mines to the north of the Downs. She did not return and must have encountered the new fields.[1]

The Admiralty estimates as to the losses of these submarines show how difficult it was to assess the effect of minefields. It was rightly believed that *UB-13* encountered the mines in about 5133/0245E. On the other hand, it was wrongly supposed that *UC-3* blew up in mine nets on April 23 and that *UC-7* was depth-charged off Lowestoft on July 6-7. Obviously the Admiralty had no access to the records of the Flanders Flotilla.

During the first six months of 1917 British minelaying off the Flanders coast was highly sporadic - and ineffective. No U-boats were sunk by the mines, although on June 5 *UC-70* was severely damaged during a bombardment of Ostend. On June 25 a German torpedo boat hit a mine near Middelkerke Bank, but apparently it had not been laid recently. In July, however, the minelayers moved in much closer to Zeebrugge and achieved instant success.

The first field to be laid consisted of 160 mines only four feet beneath the surface. This field, placed in '065 beta', was not discovered until August 21, when a torpedo boat was damaged. Since it was laid on July 14, it almost certainly accounted for the loss of *UC-1*, out on the morning of July 18 to lay mines off Calais. She did not return and nothing was ever heard from her.

On July 25 a field of 120 mines was set in '059' and '060 beta' at a depth of 25 feet. That day the Germans sighted a British force of two light cruisers, twelve destroyers, and a monitor in the area, but three days later *UB-20* proceeded out of Ostend for diving trials (she had been slightly damaged by an air attack on June 17) and did not return. If she practised to the north of Ostend she must have bit these mines. If, on the other hand, she headed west she must have encountered one of the two other fields (96 mines apiece) laid on July 25 to the south-west of Middelkerke Bank. The corpse of her commander came ashore on the Jutland coast in early September. Prisoners

1 Spindler, III, pp. 184-86.

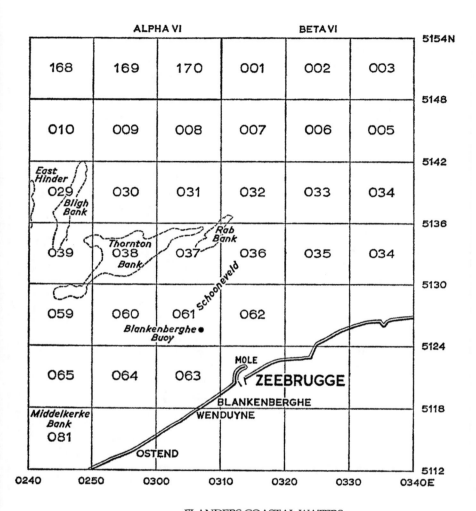

FLANDERS COASTAL WATERS

62

3. Submarine shelter at Bruges, with a six-foot reinforced concrete roof for protection against aircraft, photographed by the author in July 1938. The shelter was obliterated during the Second World War.

4. The salvaged wreck of *UC-44*, on the beach near Waterford, Ireland, in the autumn of 1917. Note the net-cutter teeth on bow. Photograph reproduced by permission of David Masters.

5. Views of the interned *UC-48* and the Spanish *Torpedo Boat No. 2* in dry-dock at Ferrol, Spain. These photographs were taken by an Allied agent.

from several U-boats sunk in the autumn of 1917 reported that she had been sunk, and it was learned that several guests of the commander had been on board. In July 1918 these guests were identified as two naval surgeons and two or three nurses.

From July 30 to the end of the year minelayers began to work close to Zeebrugge, precisely on the U-boat route. The date suggests that the British were relying on information acquired from *UC-61*, out from Zeebrugge on July 25 and stranded near Gris Nez the next day. During August three fields of 40 mines were laid, roughly eleven miles to the north and north-west of Zeebrugge, and on September 22-24 the effort was intensified. Eighty mines were placed in the German squares '037' and '036 beta', and coastal motor boats dropped five more just two miles north of Zeebrugge. On the afternoon of the 24th a British leader with four destroyers and seven aircraft provided a diversion to the north of the Middelkerke Bank.

In consequence, *UC-21*, out for the French west coast on September 13 and due back early in October, did not return, probably striking the mines on her way in to Zeebrugge though she made no radio signal. On October 3 *UC-14* certainly hit the mines just north of Zeebrugge. The detonation that marked her end was observed at 2215. The day before, *UC-16* had sailed for Boulogne, where she probably laid her mines. She did not return, however, and in all likelihood she too encountered the British fields. *UB-32*, out for the western Channel on September 10, may also have bit mines on her return, but it is more likely that she was bombed by a seaplane from Dunkirk on September 22 in 5145/0205E. The seaplane sighted oil and wreckage after its two bombs exploded.

Proof that *UC-14* and *UC-16* were sunk in the southern North Sea was provided when officers' corpses came ashore on the Dutch coast.

Meanwhile a two-day skirmish in the southern North Sea had provided the Admiralty with a great deal of radio-intercept material, as the German command was aware. At 0058 on September 27 the outward-bound *U-70* struck a mine off the Goodwin Sands and soon thereafter was able to surface and radio a report to Bruges (French records give 0030=0130 as the time). German aircraft were sent to look for her, but in the dark they had no success. At 0330 and 0530 further signals showed French radiogoniometrists that she was moving first ENE, then NE by E. At 0745 British ships and aeroplanes arrived on the scene. At first *U-70* supposed that they were from Bruges, but when she picked up a British radio message stating 'Submarine directly beneath us' - obviously from an aeroplane - she dived with considerable difficulty and stayed on the bottom most of the day. The British searchers did not find her; neither did *UC-71*, out from Zeebrugge at 0900 to look for her. At 1430 she made another signal to ask for an escort, to report that her main rudder would not turn and her engines were working badly, and to give her position ('056 beta'), course (40°) and speed (4 knots). Bruges answered at 1600: she would be picked up by an escort at 2000. Unfortunately for *U-70*, two British patrol boats had arrived at 1515. At first she thought they were German submarines and made a recognition signal. Immediately afterward, she recognized them and hastily went to the bottom, surfacing only at 2240 after they had dropped eleven depth charges and then left the area. At this point she received a signal from Bruges, informing her that German torpedo boats were looking for her.

These two torpedo boats had sailed at 1630 to search for her and had then headed for '056 beta' without result. At 2130 they had already been ordered to return to Zeebrugge because of some confusion at Bruges. At 2250 *U-70* spoke again. She 'urgently' requested an escort and was in '041 beta right upper'. The torpedo boats sailed again at 2310, and at 2400 Bruges ordered her to come back across '060 beta', where the torpedo boats would meet her.

At 0100 the U-boat radioed that an hour later she would be in '030 beta middle' and expected her escort to meet her there, but at 0120 the German torpedo boats sighted a destroyer leader and five destroyers in precisely that square. The torpedo boats briefly exchanged fire with the British forces and then headed for Zeebrugge, since it was impossible to pick up *U-70* at the time. The submarine, warned by Bruges that five British destroyers were searching for her, sighted them at 0325 and, before bottoming again, told Bruges that she was in '030 beta right lower' on a course of 190°. At this point the two torpedo boats, reinforced by two more, came back to the area. They searched squares '038' and '060 beta' but found no trace of the U-boat, though British forces fired at them without effect. *U-70* came to the surface at 0440 but had to dive again when she sighted ships in the distance. Possibly, as Michelsen suggested, they were the German torpedo boats.

At 0848 Bruges ordered her to come directly to Zeebrugge. There were no mines on her course except in '037 beta lower'. The torpedo boats had returned to Zeebrugge, but she could expect to meet German aircraft. At 0930 a German aeroplane found her and informed her that it would go back for the torpedo boats.

Twenty minutes later four torpedo boats appeared from the south. To the north, however, six British destroyers were even closer, and out of the sun came an enemy aeroplane, fixing its machine gun and dropping three bombs, one of which exploded in the water close to the conning tower. This time *U-70* stayed on the bottom until noon. When she surfaced, another attack by an aeroplane drove her under and she came up again only at 1600. She then informed Bruges that she would stay on the bottom until 1900, when she expected an escort in '060 beta'. Bruges checked the signal directionally and when *U-70* came to the surface this time she soon found the half-flotilla of torpedo boats, one of which took her in tow. She reached Zeebrugge at 2330.

The escorts had earlier failed to meet her not only for the reason Michelsen emphasizes, that she had wrongly reported her positions in '056', '041', and '030 beta', but - more important - because British forces, acting on reliable information, were constantly on watch.

During wartime British records were not fully correlated, and it was believed that on the morning of September 28 the British seaplane *8676* accounted for a U-boat, supposed to be *UC-6* from Flanders, in the southern North Sea. 'On the morning of the 28th', says the history of *The War in the Air*, 'wireless interception indicated a U-boat near the North Hinder, and a flying-boat took up the hunt. The flying-boat reached the North Hinder at 8 a.m. and then began to search in a southerly direction. After 28 minutes, the wireless operator in the flying-boat reported that he was intercepting signals from some type of enemy vessel less than ten miles distant'. Evidently this was the German aeroplane which had just found *U-70* (0828 British time=0930 German). 'Within six minutes a submarine, in full buoyancy and showing a mast and a gun, was sighted.'

According to the aeroplane's report it then flew straight for the submarine and dropped a 230-pound bomb, 'which was observed to have hit the tail of the submarine, making a large rent in the deck'. The observation was not quite correct, as we have already seen.

At this point the seaplane sighted 'three more hostile submarines.. heading south-west, in line abreast with two seaplanes with three destroyers behind them, all six firing at us'. The three submarines were obviously British destroyers like the other three vessels, and *8676* was lucky to escape. She stayed in the vicinity only long enough to drop another bomb near the submarine, which seemed to be sinking by the stern. 'The whole submarine seemed to quiver and then sank immediately, leaving a large mass of blackish oil, bubbles, and foreign matter.' What actually had happened was that *U-70*, desperate to dive, had flooded her tanks in order to get under as rapidly as possible.

To be sure, *UC-6* was certainly sunk around this time. Actually, however, she had already been destroyed by mines off Kentish Knock.

After the successes of September and October, British minelayers did not return to the Flanders coast at once, but on November 5 *Ariel* laid 40 mines, ten miles north by east of Zeebrugge, and on the 13th and 17th motor boats deposited their cargoes by the Blankenberghe Buoy and a few miles north of the Zeebrugge Mole. On the morning of the 17th *Ariel's* mines accounted for one torpedo boat and damaged another. The outward-bound *UB-40* was immediately instructed to stay out of '036 beta VI', and when another torpedo boat was sunk on November 23 the main U-boat route was changed to 'Weg B', from the Schouwen Bank ('031 beta') to '038 beta', thence through '061 beta' to Zeebrugge or through '060 beta' to Ostend. Signals from and to *UB-56* on the 24th showed the new route in operation. She reported that she was heading for Zeebrugge via the Schouwen Bank and was ordered to keep one mile east of 'Weg 4'- possibly as far east as '033 beta' - and not to go west of it. Further British mines laid during December seem to have achieved no results, and at the end of the month signals showed that 'Weg B' was being used.

On January 14 *UC-17* was told that both 'Weg A' and 'Weg B' were free of mines, but at 0200 on the 15th British destroyers moved in to '036 beta' again and laid a field of 150 mines. By the 20th the British were aware that the new mines had been found. The homeward-bound *UB-80* was instructed to take Routes A or B or keep one mile east of Route 4 (thus *not* taking Route 3) since there was a new field from Buoy 14 to 5135/0316E.

In February the sporadic laying of mines off Zeebrugge and Ostend accounted for one torpedo boat close to Ostend itself, and late in March *UB-59*, back via Middelkerke Bank, was told to keep to the south of '065 beta'. On the 29th *UC-11*, heading back to Zeebrugge from the Thames estuary, asked if she should take Route 4 but was ordered to Route B instead, presumably because B was constantly being swept. Early in April, however, two minelayers homeward-bound from the Channel were given their choice of B, 3, or 4 into Zeebrugge.

On the night of April 11-12 British monitors and motor boats appeared off Ostend and one of the motor boats ran aground after being set afire. In the wreck the Germans found British plans, dated April 9, for an assault on Zeebrugge and Ostend. It is not fully clear what use, if any, was made of them. Some authorities have stated that the capture led to an alert on the Flanders coast. A German intelligence summary dated May 4, however, lists only three items which might have pointed towards an attack. In March it had been learned that the British planned a fleet action against the German coast if the western front crumbled; on April 12 it was learned that British submarines were to lay mines in the Bight; and on April 16 an army agent in Antwerp reported that there would be major naval operations in the near future. There was no indication in these reports that the Flanders coast would be attacked.

On the night of April 22-23, however, British forces with French support struck at both Zeebrugge and Ostend. Following a route already marked by buoys as far as the south-west corner of the German '038 beta', thirteen miles north-west of Zeebrugge, the forces then divided and followed the U-boat routes towards both Zeebrugge and Ostend. Block ships were sunk inside the Zeebrugge Mole at the entrance to the canal to Bruges; an old submarine was blown up at the shoreward end of the Mole itself At Ostend, however, the ships lost their bearings and had to withdraw. By the afternoon of the 23rd Bruges ordered all U-boats to use the harbour at Ostend because Zeebrugge had been mined. Signals intercepted during the following eleven days showed that U-boats were taking Route B to Ostend, and it was not until May 5 that *UC-11* radioed that she was following this path to Zeebrugge. (*UC-17* had actually done so the day before.) The same night, however, *UC-70* proposed to take Route B to Zeebrugge but was ordered to Ostend instead. On May 6 and 7 *UB-103* and *UB-30* reported making fast to the Zeebrugge Mole, evidently waiting for high tide before passing the block ships.

Early on the morning of May 10 British forces raided Ostend again, but without any success. Though Admiral Keyes laid plans for a third assault, the Admiralty instructed him not to carry them out. Intercepts and air reconnaissance proved that most U-boats were passing in and out of Zeebrugge.

Indeed, a signal to *UC-11* on May 14 gave a precise indication of the position of Route B, since it stated that the Blankenberghe Buoy was at the south end of the Schoonveld Bank. The submarine was asked when she expected to reach Zeebrugge and she replied that she was two hours from port. Not surprisingly, on May 21 the British laid a field of 240 mines in '037 beta', just to the north of the Blankenberghe Buoy and extending westward into '038 beta'. The field was not discovered until the end of the month, although several U-boats must have passed through it.

Signals made on May 30 and 31 revealed a good deal about the routes. *UC-64*, intending to take Route B to Zeebrugge, was told to stop and await orders because a mine had been found in '037 beta'. Ten hours later she was ordered to take Route 3 from '032 beta'. The same order was sent to *UB-30*, and this submarine, later ordered to report her position, replied that she was in '061 beta'. The locations of Routes B and 3 were thus clarified, although it may not have been known that Route 3 went far to the east. According to Gladisch a U-boat now had to spend a whole day on the route.

On May 31 *UC-75* was sunk in the North Sea and under interrogation prisoners 'revealed' that when leaving Zeebrugge the U-boats were accustomed to sail due west for three or four miles, then head toward the Straits of Dover. Though she had sailed on May 22, before the route was changed, the statement was evidently intended to mislead the British. In early June several signals showed that Route 3 was being employed, and *UC-11* ordered to Ostend on this route, was told to stay out of '037' and '031 beta', north of Blankenberghe. Between June 17 and 20 German aircraft sighted 'countless' British mines between the Scheldt and the Hinder Bank, and on the 29th a signal to *UC-71* instructed her to steer from '039 beta' via Route 3 to Ostend. Soon thereafter many of the mines in '037 beta' were swept up, but in early July *UC-17* was instructed to take Route 3 from '032 beta' to Zeebrugge; *UB-110* was heading out along the same way. On July 19 *UC-49* was warned that enemy motor boats were off Zeebrugge, and she was ordered to pass far to the east through '003 beta', near the Hook of Holland.

Further signals in July and early August revealed only that Route 3 continued in use, and on the night of August 7-8 the British sent *Abdiel* and five minelaying destroyers to '037 beta'. There they laid a field of 234 magnetic mines. The results were immediate. On the afternoon of the 8th one torpedo boat was sunk and another was slightly damaged. On the 11th another was damaged. It was difficult to clear the field, for British aircraft kept attacking the minesweepers. On the 15th another torpedo boat was lost, and the next day a 'leader vessel' also went down. By the 18th some sweepers were equipped with magnets for detection, and three U-boats sailed from Zeebrugge on the 19th. (Since the 8th only three others had left port.) All U-boats were escorted by torpedo boats with sweeping gear.

Before the new field was located, or indeed was even laid, Johannes Lohs took *UB-57* out of Zeebrugge, sailing at 2330 on August 3 to attack troop transports in the eastern Channel. He was not heard from again until 2215 on the evening of the 14th, when Bruges received a signal located near the Sandettie Bank. *UB-57* was heading for Zeebrugge and had sunk three ships for a total of 15,000 tons. No further signal was received, although an hour later, as well as the next day and the day after, Bruges ordered her to report her position. In London on the morning of the 16th Sims was told that *UB-57* was overdue. Within a month it was learned that corpses of her crew members had been washed ashore on the Dutch coast.

The French records make it possible to reconstruct *UB-57*'s homeward cruise at least in part. At 1750 on August 13 she torpedoed and sank the 7,000-ton *City of Brisbane* off Beachy Head and probably passed through the Straits the next morning. Apparently she lay on the bottom north-east of Gris Nez until the afternoon of the 14th, when a British seaplane sighted her. French patrols from Dunkirk hunted for her between 1800 and 1900, using hydrophones and dropping 24 depth charges in an area nine miles north of Calais. At 2100 she was on the surface again, heading north-east twenty miles north of Gravelines - or approximately in the location from which she made her last signal.

Gröner locates her loss in 5156/0202E., near the Outer Gabbard Light Vessel, but this cannot be right. Corpses came ashore not only in the Scheldt estuary and near The Hague but also at Zeebrugge and Ostend. It is virtually certain that *UB-57* encountered the magnetic mines that sank three other vessels.

Prisoners or charts taken from *UB-109*, sunk off Folkestone on August 29, indicated that on July 28 this submarine had left Zeebrugge and, three hours later, was lying on the bottom in 5142/0247E., or '010 beta', north-west of Zeebrugge. It was also learned that from Zeebrugge submarines were accustomed to steer north-west to the Blankenberghe Buoy (5 miles N. 30°. W. of the Mole) and then proceed for eighteen miles on a course of 285°. true. There was a 'leader cable' from the vicinity of Wenduyne Church, on the coast just west of Blankenberghe, to the Thornton Ridge, where the position was marked by a red conical buoy. Relying on this news, the British laid forty mines off the Hinder Bank on September 6, thus across the route *UB-109* had taken, and eight more on September 18 south of the Wenduyne Bank, where the leader cable was supposed to be. These efforts brought no success, for on September 1 the Flanders submarines had abandoned use of the route through the Straits of Dover and therefore no longer followed what was essentially Route B.

B. Against the German Bases: The Bight of Heligoland

It was important to lay mines off the Flanders bases, close to the British Isles. It was even more important to place mines in the Bight of Heligoland, through which the larger U-boats passed on their way to the East Coast or the Straits of Dover or the waters between Scotland and Norway. Indeed, during the first quarter of the year 1917 almost all British mines laid were deposited in the Bight - without any result except that on April 6 the outward-bound *U-22* struck a mine to the north-west of Horns Reef and was badly damaged. Through April and May the minelaying continued, much of it representing an attempt to trap the homeward-bound *UC-30* in the Bight. During June and July, however, it was greatly reduced, for two reasons. First, Intelligence was aware that their ideas about the German swept channels in the Bight needed correction - in view of the fact that no U-boats had been sunk on British mines since April. Second, the Admiralty were also aware that the British mines were extremely inefficient, and they were waiting for the delivery of the new Mark H2 mine, copied from a German model.

Accurate information arrived before the new mine did, and the old mines were employed in large numbers during August. It is highly probable that the locations were provided, at least in general, by documents recovered from the wreck of *UC-44*, mined off Waterford on August 4 and subsequently salved. One such document, indeed, specifically stated that the route from '003 epsilon' to '061 epsilon' was free of mines. Equally important was a report from the British submarine *E-31* on August 15. She had found the exact location where the German-swept channels, somewhat to the north, came to an end. There were buoys in 5405/051030E., as well as in positions about five miles to the south and west. That same night British surface minelayers moved in to deposit a thousand mines about ten miles to the west of the position given. The ships were sighted by German patrols and even overheard as they laid their mines. The next day British destroyers attacked German sweepers in the area, and on the 21st and the 26th the sweepers found mines belonging to Field 56. The full extent of the field remained unknown.[1] On August 22 another thousand mines were planted off Texel (Field 58). That evening the outward bound *UB-21* had sighted the minelayers heading east, south of the Dogger Bank, and radioed a report to her base. Nothing was done about it.[2]

This inertia was all the more unfortunate because several U-boats were about to sail for the west, hence across Field 56. On August 31 *U-50* was escorted out to '010 epsilon'; she made a signal to her base and then headed north-west under water. Presumably she encountered Field 56 soon afterwards. Nothing more was heard from her. At the end of September her commander's body came ashore in the North Frisian Islands. It is not clear that the loss of *U-66*, out on the afternoon of September 2, had anything to do with the new minefields, but they certainly accounted for another submarine on the 5th. That evening *U-54* and *U-88* left their escort in '166 gamma' and headed under water to the north. An hour and a half later *U-54* scraped a mine cable in '012 epsilon'. After another forty-five minutes she was practically in the middle of Field 56 when she heard a heavy detonation behind and above her; ten minutes later there was another. The next day *U-54* tried to radio her base but could not make contact. News of the presumed loss of *U-88* reached Germany only when she returned to port on October 8.

During September British submarines laid two small fields to the east of Field 56 and two to the east of Field 58. The principal mining effort of the month, however, was made on September 24, when 432 of the new Mark H2 mines were deposited to the west of Field 56. The next morning two outward-bound submarines passed through the field under water. After *UB-64* came to the surface, she made a signal to report mine explosions, which had caused a small leak. The portion dealing with the location was garbled, and on the 26th she was ordered to make a fuller report. There was no reply, and the first details were obtained only on September 30, when *UB-34* returned to Bremerhaven.

The new *U-106* had sailed on September 8 for the waters west of the Hebrides and the Irish coast. In early October the Admiralty expected her and several others to return to base, passing south between 0030E. and 0300E. and also between two minefields east of the Dogger Bank. Just to the south of latitude 5600, ten miles of mine-nets were laid on October 1, and for ten days they were patrolled by destroyers, trawlers and submarines. No definite results were achieved, but at 0530 on October 5 a signal was picked up from the homeward-bound *U-106*. She had sunk 10,000 tons of shipping and would meet her escort at 0600 on the 7th.

The next morning she repeated the signal and gave her location. The German records give her position as '026 epsilon V', but this would place her

1 Gladisch, VII, pp. 24-28.
2 Ibid., p. 21. For the significance of August 22.

100	125	132	62 157	164 012	60 017	59 032	037	050	055	068
101	124	133	156	56 165	011	018	031	038 73 049	056	067
102	123	134	155 67	166 65	64 010	019	030	039 048	057	066
103	122	135	154	167	009	020	029	040 047	058	065
104	121	136	153	168	008	021	028	041 046	059	064
105	120	137	152	169	007	022	027	042 045	060	063
106	119	138	151	170	006 50 49	026	043 044	061	062
107	118	139	150	001 005 51 68	024	025	AMELAND
108	117	140	149 61 002	71 52 70 004	TERSCHELLING
109	116 58	63	148 003 66	VLIELAND
110	115	147 54
111	114	143	146	TEXEL
112	113	144	145

54°N ... 53°N

4°E 10 20 30 40 50 5° 10 20 30 40 50 6°

BRITISH MINEFIELDS OFF THE WEST FRISIAN ISLANDS, 1917

to the east of Spurn Head off the Humber, a rather unlikely location, and it was therefore corrected to '026 gamma V', just off St. Abbs Head, Scotland. The British located the U-boat in 5446/0108E,. equivalent to the German '010 beta V'. Something was evidently wrong with the signal. In any event, *U-106* expected to reach '018 epsilon', off Terschelling, on the 7th.

Proof that the French, or British informants, read part of this signal is provided by their October report, in which *U-106* is credited with two ships for a total of 11,079 tons. Since the ships were actually sunk by *U-67* and *U-82*, they were evidently assigned to *U-106* in an effort to give her about the 10,000 tons mentioned in the signals.

Wherever *U-106* may have been on the 6th, that day she was somehow delayed. At 0200 on the 7th she made a signal to state that she would not arrive until 0600 the next day. During the next few hours the German command finally realized that the approaches to '018 epsilon' were full of mines, and at 0407 *U-106* was ordered to take the route close to the Dutch coast. An escort would meet her in '003 epsilon'. Evidently this order was transmitted in a new cipher and *U-106* did not have a key to it on board; she replied, 'Not understood'. The new cipher must also have been used for another signal transmitted at 0711. This time *U-106* was ordered to take the more northerly route but enter it somewhat to the south, through '167 gamma'. The same reply came back: 'Not understood'.

The old cipher, at any rate, was being read by the British, for precisely on October 7 the submarine *E-51* deposited twenty mines just to the west of quadrant '018 epsilon' on what British records describe as 'the route most used by the enemy at the time'.

According to the German records, *U-106* tried to communicate with her base at 1830 on the 7th. Nothing could be made of the message.

Early on the morning of October 8 German escort vessels left Borkum with orders to pick up two homeward-bound U-boats in '018 epsilon'. As the sky lightened they could make out *U-8* in '032 epsilon', and soon after 0800 she was picked up at the rendezvous. Nothing was seen of her sister submarine. During the day escort vessels were on watch for *U-106*, but when she did not appear they were recalled. The next day escorts were sent to both the 'Weg Gelb' and the 'Weg Schwarz', but to no avail. The British intercepted a signal stating that she had not arrived at 'Point Q' on the 'Weg Gelb'.

On October 10 a signal from the Chief of U-boats informed submarines that to the west of the 'Weg Gelb' there were apparently deep mines and mine-nets and that these had probably accounted for *U-88*; the fate of *U-106* was open to question. By this point the command was also aware that *U-50* had perished, for her commander's body had been washed ashore on Amrum, off the Danish coast, on September 23.

Late in November prisoners taken from *U-58* and *U-48* confirmed these losses. Those from *U-58* stated that Schwieger had been lost in September when *U-88* struck a mine. Their own boat had been in radio contact with *U-106* on October 8 - a contact not mentioned in the log of *U-58* - and was to have accompanied her to Heligoland the next day. Nothing was heard from her on the 9th, however, and since there were no decoy vessels in the vicinity it was presumed that she had struck a mine. The prisoners from *U-48* said that both *U-66* and *U-106* had struck mines, while *U-50* must have been lost near the German coast since her commander's body came ashore on 'the island of List' (doubtless List on Sylt) on October 8.

Presumably it was this erroneous date which led the Admiralty to assign the sinking of *U-50* to the October anti-submarine operation. Another error was also due to testimony from *U-48*, for prisoners stated that *U-88* had sunk after her conning tower was hit by gunfire. The encounter was identified as one between the decoy *Stonecrop* and a submarine on September 17, and perhaps it was assumed that the witness to the encounter was another U-boat which sank the decoy the next day. (In actual fact the episodes were quite wrongly identified, for *U-151* escaped on the 17th and *U-43* sank *Stonecrop* on the 18th.) It would have been better to rely on the prisoners from *U-58* and on the intercepts bearing on the cruise of *U-88*. From these intercepts it was known that *U-88* was escorted out with *U-54* on

September 5 and that the German command on October 10 assigned her loss to a mine.

In July 1918 the authentic story was reiterated by a prisoner from *UB-124*. He himself had sailed in *U-54* and had heard the explosions that accounted for *U-88*. The interrogator noted, however, that his story could not 'be accepted without confirmatory evidence'. Perhaps in the hope of obtaining a German confirmation, the Admiralty had his story published in *The Times* on August 10, but the Germans made no reply.

Early in October U-boat Command decided to countermine the 'Weg Schwarz', but on the 17th the route was opened again. The next day, *E-45* arrived on the scene to lay mines in '003 epsilon', and she was followed in by *E-51* on November 18. Two signals which the Admiralty intercepted on November 29 proved that *E-51* had achieved success. At 1023 the first signal showed that four U-boats were being escorted out along the 'Weg Schwarz'. At 2325 the second indicated that *UB-61* and the trawler *Dirk van Minden* had struck mines and sunk in 5325/0458E., or '005 epsilon'. Nine men had been rescued from the trawler, none from the submarine. The escorts had been unable to sweep for mines because of the high wind and sea.

In consequence of these losses, the 'Weg Schwarz' was again countermined early in December; fields 70 and 71, laid by *E-51* and *E-34* in November, were found for the first time. U-boats returning from the southwest used only the 'Weg Gelb'. This fact was known to the British because signals intercepted on December 6 and 8 showed that *U-84* and *U-96* expected escorts to meet them in '010 epsilon'. In addition, a petty officer taken off the wrecked *UB-81* on December 2 was carrying a notebook with descriptions of the entrances to both routes. As of November 10, the 'Weg Schwarz' ran from '145 gamma' to '003 epsilon'. The 'Weg Gelb' extended from '102 gamma' to '010 centre'.

On December 12 the British submarine *E-51* therefore laid twenty mines directly across the 'Weg Gelb' (Field 73), and results came immediately. A signal intercepted the next morning showed that *U-75* was proceeding out on this route. That evening she blew up in the field, leaving only nine survivors. The British picked up the news from German radio. Gladisch comments that 'the field lay exactly on the route, and it is certainly possible that *E-51* watched the escorts and then deposited the field'. It is more likely that she had been given precise orders for the location.

These new mines were immediately swept, and during the following fortnight no more were laid, although intercepted signals proved that U-boats were continuing to use the 'Weg Gelb'. In the new year the larger submarines soon stopped passing through the Straits of Dover and the routes off the Dutch islands gradually fell into disuse. It would appear that countermining was finally successful. The British submarine *H-10*, out to the area near Buoy 5 (5355/0350E.) on January 6, did not return; neither did *E-*

50, out on January 21 to 5445/0615E. On the other hand, the sweeper *Senator Westphal* was mined on the 'Weg Gelb' on January 30.

On March 1 the smaller *UB-34* was being escorted out on the 'Weg Schwarz' when four of her escorts fell victim to mines, and soon thereafter these routes were finally abandoned. On April 2, the Germans laid 604 mines north of Terschelling and Ameland, and during May and June no fewer than sixteen minefields were set in the waters from Vlieland east towards Ameland. No U-boats were lost in the area, but the British *E-34* was sunk off Vlieland during July.

Since the summer of 1917 the British effort had been concentrated almost exclusively against the two southern routes, chiefly because the U-boats could thus be deterred from hastening through the Straits of Dover and partly because their information about the routes was so good. To the north fewer mines were laid. On December 30, 1917, however, 339 mines were placed to the north-west of the end of the 'Weg Blau', used by many U-boats at the time, and on the night of January 18 British destroyers laid mines along the 'Weg Mitte'. That night six trawlers and the minesweeper *Doggerbank* escorted *U-71* out along the route but failed to observe the minelayers at work. The next morning they picked up the homeward-bound *UB-78* and headed south-east. Within a few hours *Doggerbank* hit a mine and sank. Their radio report to Heligoland was garbled in transmission, and at the base it was supposed that the mines were farther east than they actually were. No change was made, therefore, in the orders of *UB-22*, out with an escort at 0200. At 1700 the submarine and the torpedo-boat *S-16* struck the new mines. Because of heavy weather there were no survivors from either vessel. The next day two more torpedo boats were sunk.

British listeners followed the episode closely. At 0901 they learned that *UB-22* was being escorted on the 'Weg Mitte'; at 1732 news came in that *UB-22* and *S-16* had struck mines and sunk in 5437/0635E. The next morning the information was passed on to Sims. The losses had included *UB-22*, a patrol boat, two minesweepers, and two torpedo boats, as far as the interceptors could tell.

Further minelaying in these areas resulted in the sinking of minesweepers and torpedo boats but no submarines. It also forced the Germans to make frequent use of the Baltic and the Skagerrak instead of the Bight, and thus added many unproductive days to the U-boats' cruises.

In April a series of incidents indicated how well the British were acquainted with the Bight situation. Off Utsire Island, Norway, on April 24 the homeward-bound *U-19* signalled the presence of eleven old British cruisers. The identification she made was wrong, as both German and British listeners were immediately aware. The cruisers belonged to the High Seas Fleet, which had gone to sea to attack the British-Scandinavian convoy - relying on erroneous information about its sailing dates. The cruisers were now returning home because of an accident to the battle cruiser *Moltke*. At 0815 the next morning they were sighted by the submarine *J-6* in the Bight, and that evening *E-42*, ordered by radio to look for them about forty miles north of Heligoland, fired four torpedoes at a line of ships and inflicted further damage on *Moltke*. Though depth charged, she was able to escape. Thus ended the last sortie of the German Fleet.

The ability of *E-42* to move through the minefields was not due to chance. On April 15 the submarine *E-45* had discovered the German swept channel from near the South Dogger Bank Light Vessel to Heligoland. In addition, of course, the British knew where their own mines were.

Admiral Scheer was dismayed by the attack on *Moltke*. On April 29 he sent a memorandum to German Naval Intelligence. The British Admiralty, he pointed out, evidently possessed an excellent chart of minefields in the Bight, far superior to what the Germans possessed. He supposed that in part it was based on documents recovered from U-boat wrecks. Whatever its sources, Germany needed something equivalent or superior to it, and he urged Intelligence to offer half a million marks for a good chart. A week later, Intelligence sent out telegrams to various German representatives in neutral countries. The emphasis was laid more on economy than on results. The suggested price was only 100,000 marks.

We do not know what the results were. Conceivably Admiral Hall, who had been able to sell a fake plan of a barrage in the Straits of Dover to a German agent for £2,000 (as James reports), was able to meet the demand on this occasion too. On the other hand, German mines laid during June accounted for the British destroyers *Vehement* and *Ariel* off Horns Reef on the night of August 1-2.

Most of the time, however, the British enjoyed total immunity while operating in the Bight. During the year 1918 they laid 21,105 mines there (including 1,222 dummies to mislead the enemy). Obviously the Germans had lost control of these waters.

C. The Dover Barrage

The British had long been aware that the larger U-boats were staying out of the Straits of Dover, in spite of that fact that the route north of Scotland took about ten days away from a cruise lasting three or four weeks and thus meant that only ten to fifteen days were profitably spent. On September 1 they intercepted two signals from boats which had just passed through the Straits, one from the old *U-19* at work in the Channel, the other from *U-62* which because of lack of fuel had taken the shorter route and was now in the southern North Sea. Such passage remained unusual, however, and a whole series of signals on September 27-28 made it possible to search for *U-70*, damaged by a mine off the Goodwin Sands but finally able, in spite of attacks by destroyers and aircraft, to reach Ostend. On October 10 *U-53* announced her arrival in the Channel after passing through the Straits. A week later she reported from the Channel again. She was about to return eastward, and the next morning she was east of the Goodwins. Evidently she was testing the route and further use of it could be expected.

In November the larger U-boats began to pass through the Straits in increasing numbers. On the 16th *U-58* reported her arrival in the Channel, although the next day she had to surrender to American destroyers off Queenstown. Between the 18th and the 23rd she was followed by *U-90*, *U-53* and *U-96*. On the morning of the 24th the outward-bound *U-48* ran aground to the north of the Goodwins, and at daybreak three drifters began attacking her. The submarine returned their fire, but when the destroyer *Gipsy* began shelling her, explosive charges were fired and the crew abandoned ship. Twenty-four prisoners were taken, and they revealed that the Straits route was now being enforced. (Even in February the top of the conning tower could still be seen at low water, but the wreck could not be salved.) The same morning signals were intercepted from *U-94*, which had grounded near the East Goodwin Light Vessel and was returning to port. These misadventures did not keep U-boats out of the Straits, however; on the 27th *U-57* signalled her arrival in the Channel and on the 29th *U-67*, homeward-bound, reached the southern North Sea.

On November 21 the first lines of mines had been planted in the Straits of Dover, and by the end of the month about 2,300 had been laid between Le Colbart and Cape Gris Nez, on the French side of the Straits, at depths between 40 and 100 feet. During December 420 more were laid in this area, 314 between Le Colbart and the Varne, and 1,065 from the Varne toward the British coast. Naval Intelligence eagerly awaited news of results.

The mines had no effect whatever as far as the intercepted signals showed. On December 6 it was learned that *U-57* would have to return home, but her return was due to a broken dynamo shaft. On the 8th *U-96*, just back through the Straits, reported the loss of *UC-69*, which she herself had rammed off Cape Barfleur in the Channel. During the month, however, eighteen large U-boats made signals revealing that they were taking this route. (Signals from *U-84*, in the Channel on the 14th and the 16th, were not received at home, and since she did not return the German command remained in the dark about her route.)

At Dover Admiral Bacon was extremely reluctant to illuminate the barrage at night, for he thought that lights would invite attack by German destroyers. On the 18th, however, he was summoned to London and explicitly ordered to patrol the deep minefield night and day. Flares and searchlights were first employed on the evening of December 19.

Shortly before midnight the destroyer *Gipsy* was shaken by a violent explosion in the minefield, and after half an hour's search she heard voices calling and saw men struggling in the water. She put out a boat, but they had gone down before it reached them. To starboard, voices were still calling, and the boat headed for the spot where two men could be seen. Only one could be picked up, and an hour later he died on board the destroyer. His clothes, marked 'Bleeck', showed that he was an engine-room petty officer, but they did not serve to identify the U-boat. It had certainly been sunk, for during the following month oil came up sporadically from the location. At the end of January prisoners taken from *UB-35* stated that in December *UB-56* under Hans Valentiner had been lost, and proof that she was the submarine in question was given when the British read the *Preussische Zeitung* for January 28. It contained the casualty list for Valentiner's submarine.

As the new year began, the U-boats' signals indicated no interruption to their passage through the Straits of Dover. On January 1 both *U-89* and *UB-35* signalled their arrival east of the Straits in the southern North Sea; on the 4th they were followed by *U-94*, on the 14th by *U-110*, and on the 21st by *U-55*. Other U-boats were heading westward through the Straits, although only one signal is recorded from a large U-boat just reaching the Channel. This signal was made by *U-84* on January 3, although it was not received at home. Evidently *U-84* continued to try to communicate with her base, for Spindler relates that on the 6th a garbled message was received from her by *Rugia* at Emden; the submarine had reached the western end of the Channel - and was sunk in the St. George's Channel on the 26th.

On January 8 the drifter *Brothers Jem*, on watch in the Straits, felt a heavy explosion nearby, and she soon found a large quantity of oil and dead fish. Because of bad weather she was unable to investigate further, and the explosion was listed as 'unclassified'. It is highly probable, however, that it marked the destruction of the Flanders minelayer *UC-50*, which had sailed the day before and was not heard from thereafter.

The next episode occurred on January 19, when, as the Admiralty informed Sims, 'a minelaying submarine was forced to dive into the minefield in the Straits but escaped damage'. It was later reported that there had been an explosion in the barrage that night, though its effect remained uncertain. Admiral Keyes correlated the two events and concluded that the submarine, probably sunk, was the homeward-bound *U-95*.[1] This conclusion was not correct since the U-boat in question, sighted by the destroyer *Mermaid*, dived towards the west and therefore was not homeward-bound. Actually she must have been the outward-bound *U-90*, which passed the Dover-Calais line at 2045, was depth charged by a destroyer at 2159, and was

---

1 Keyes, pp. 171-72.

five miles off Gris Nez at 2305. No submarine was actually sunk at this time.

Six days later a German submarine east of Portland stopped a small Greek steamer but had to leave two crew members behind in a boat when a patrol vessel came on the scene. The next day the destroyer *Leven* depth-charged a submarine north of Calais after sighting a periscope moving in a north-easterly direction. Seven men appeared on the surface as the fourth and last depth charge exploded, but only one could be picked up; he died some time later. The wreckage included a cap marked 'Mahlmann' and a letter addressed to 'Petzolt'. These items were shown to the prisoners taken in the Channel, and they recognized them as belonging to comrades aboard *UB-35*, now sunk on her homeward voyage.

On January 27 Sims was given current information about three U-boats of the IV (Emden) Flotilla. *U-93* and *U-95* were now overdue; the former had been at sea for twenty-nine days, the latter for thirty-one. In addition, the large new *U-109* was now heading outward through the northern North Sea, closer to the Scottish-coast than usual. She had refused to sail with an escort of only five destroyers and had demanded nine. Presumably this information was derived from calls sent out for *U-93* and *U-95* and from signals from and to *U-109*. This submarine was actually off Gris Nez on January 26 - two days out from Emden - when she was sighted, heading west on the surface, by the drifter *Beryl III*. Gunfire forced her to dive into the minefield. The men aboard the drifter who saw the submarine reported that she had two deck guns and resembled U-boats of the U33-36 class. Keyes had them examine U-boat photographs and silhouettes; they reported that 'the conning tower and bridge was in a single vertical line instead of in two steps. . and that her sheer forward was higher'. He concluded that she belonged to a higher-numbered class. In his memoirs he says that divers identified the wreck as *U-109*.[1] Evidently they did not do so before March 1, for on that date Sims was told only that *U-109*, now out for thirty-five days, might have been sunk at the beginning of her cruise.

Meanwhile the German command was finding the Straits losses incomprehensible. It was concluded that four large U-boats - *U-87*, *U-84*, *U-93*, and *U-95* - had simply disappeared while passing through the Straits. This conclusion was not altogether correct. A garbled message had come in from *U-84* in the Channel approaches on January 6, and *U-95* had signalled a safe transit. In addition, *U-87* had made two similar signals, although neither was received at home. But though the conclusion about current losses was not quite correct, the decision based on it - to use the route north of Scotland after February 1 - was probably justified. Losses in the Dover area were going to increase.

The French analysts were aware that the smaller U-boats were continuing to pass through the Straits. During January *UB-35*, *UB-55*, and

1 Keyes, p. 172.

UB-80 had definitely been at sea. This conclusion was based on statements by prisoners from *UB-35* and on Nauen propaganda communiqués describing cruises made by Wenninger (February 6; *UB-55*) and Viebeg (January 27; *UB-80*). Five or six UC-boats made cruises: these were *UC-75* and 'UC x 5' (actually *UC-17*), back from cruises begun in December; 'UC y 1' (*UC-64*), laying mines off Plymouth and Falmouth; 'UC y 2' (*UC-71*) off the Royal Sovereign Light Vessel, the Nab, and the Owers; and *UC-31* (I Flotilla), which made a signal in the southern North Sea on February 5 after laying mines off Queenstown.

During January British Intelligence also provided information about the German destroyers which were expected to raid the Straits. On the 14th Keyes was alerted by the Director of Naval Intelligence.[1]

> Towards nightfall I received information from Admiral Hall, which pointed to a strong force of enemy destroyers being at sea. He told me that he thought they probably included the powerful destroyers, which were being built in Germany for Argentina, but were taken over by the German Navy when war broke out. These were generally led by Commander Hennecke, who had attacked and destroyed a Norwegian convoy, escorted by the *Pellew* and *Partridge*, only a month previously.

The raid - presumably predicted from intercepted signals - was actually directed against Yarmouth and Southwold; for the moment the patrols waited in vain.

Early in February, it was believed, two more U-boats perished in the Straits. The first sinking supposedly took place at 0530 on the 4th when the destroyer *Zubian* sighted a surfaced submarine off Dungeness and proceeded to depth charge it, assisted by other destroyers and patrol boats later in the morning. Large quantities of oil came up, and according to Keyes 'later a diver was sent down, and *UC-50* was found there'.[2] Admiralty records, however, indicate that the submarine was identified because *Zubian* identified her as a large minelayer and because prisoners later reported her loss. Since *UC-50* sailed on January 7 she was due back about three weeks later and should not have been involved. In fact, the minelayer in question was *UC-79*, homeward bound off Dungeness at 0630 (German time) when she made a crash dive before destroyers. The first depth charge exploded when she had reached 15 metres, and later thirty more were dropped. One fuel tank and several ballast tanks were opened up, but she got home.[3]

The second sinking (actually the first) took place on the night of

1 Ibid., pp. 174-75.
2 Ibid, p. 173.
3 Some details in Spindler. V, p. 89.

February 8, when the drifter *Gowan II* saw a surfaced U-boat cross the beam of a distant trawler's flare, apparently heading west-north-west. Alter twenty minutes' search, the drifter was shaken by a very heavy explosion. This marked the end of *UB-38*. The Germans knew of her loss because she had met *UB-33* west of the minefield earlier that day; the British learned of it from prisoners taken later.[1]

On February 14 Keyes received another telephone call from Hall. 'A submarine, commanded by a very determined German officer, was homeward-bound, and would probably pass through the patrol that night, and might well try to do so on the surface.' Presumably a signal had been picked up from *UB-57*, commanded by the 'very determined' Johannes Lohs; she was about to pass through the Straits on her way back from a cruise around the British Isles. She actually passed through that night, and at the same time German destroyers made a raid on the patrols, sinking a trawler and seven drifters and damaging five drifters and a minesweeper.[2] On the night of the 15th, the outward- bound *UC-56* arrived off Dover and fired 22 shells into the town. As she headed westward she deposited mines near the harbour entrance, evidently in the hope of trapping the destroyers she expected to follow her. The destroyers, however, were at sea and the mines were discovered and swept up the next morning.[3]

The French summary of Flanders U-boat operations for February was based partly on Nauen communiqués (*UB-59*, *UB-57*, *UB-80*) and partly on the mines laid by the few UC-boats on cruise. 'UC z 1' (*UC-79*) laid mines off the Pierres Noires and operated briefly in the Bay of Biscay, while 'UC z 2' (*UC-56*) laid mines in the Firth of Clyde and 'UC a 3' (presumably *UC-48*) was also at sea.

Towards the end of February the American Naval Planning Section in London tried its hand at showing how to achieve 'denial of English Channel to enemy submarines'. Perhaps the most important part of the memorandum lies in the information it reflects.

Normally about 10 big submarines per month use the Channel for passage, going past Dover as a rule on the surface at H. W. slack, and during darkness. Lately the number has decreased, probably due to the increased efficiency of the Dover Barrage. They usually keep to the deep gut [between Le Colbart and Gris Nez] so as to facilitate diving. There are generally 3 or 4 small U.B. or U.C. submarines from the Flanders Flotilla operating in the Channel; principally against overseas through-channel traffic, which normally brings them nearer to the

1 For the discovery of the (unidentified) wreck, see later in this chapter.
2 Keyes, p. 176.
3 In discussing this cruise Spindler (V, p. 86) does not mention the episode.

English than the French coast. In bad weather they usually bottom in Lyme Bay, the Plymouth Bight, or other bights where sea is smooth. At night they probably cruise slowly at from 1 to 2 knots.

This information, reliable except as to the route through the Straits, pointed towards reinforcement of the Dover Barrage.

A month later the Planning Section was given further information from I.D.25, concerned with radio interception. This report clearly demonstrated both the efficiency of interception and the declining use of the Straits of Dover by the Germans.

		North about	*Dover*
December	out	10	25
	Home	13	13
January	out	12	8
	home	7	9
February	out	18	5
	home	11	7
March 1-15	out	7	6
	home	14	2

Obviously the report could not include all transits, but the information provided made clear what the trend was. Another table, compiled on a somewhat different basis, made the same point.

	Boats	*Passages*	*North about*	*Dover*
December	21	42	17	19
January	13	26	18	5
February	21	42	39	1

An additional note stated that 'no large submarines are believed to have passed through Dover Straits since the 18th February'. Henceforth only the Flanders boats would try to get through.

No sinkings took place in the Straits, however, between February 8 and March 10, although the patrols reported explosions in the minefields on February 13 and March 1. Three explosions near the Varne Light Vessel early on the morning of March 10 led to a search by the patrol vessel *P-24*, and after two hours she came upon a large pool of oil containing small bits of wood, some fresh loaves of bread, and papers including a battery log and details of the trials of *UB-58* at Bremen on August 1, 1917. That evening Admiral Keyes instructed coast watchers 'to look out for wreckage, documents and papers washed ashore, especially those covered with oil'.

The only additional evidence, however, consisted of three gloves, which had been picked up shortly after the explosion.

Further explosions took place the same day, as well as on the 13th and the 19th. On the last date oil came up from 0615 to 1515, and some papers in Norwegian print and one bearing a Hamburg stamp were picked up shortly after the explosion. Keyes was convinced that a U-boat had been sunk, and the Admiralty concurred. We shall later see that *UB-54* must have been sunk at this time.

At the end of March a Zeebrugge minelayer disappeared. This was *UC-79*, out on March 20 to lay mines off Brest and operate in the Bay of Biscay. The British were not at once concerned with the loss, since they thought she had been sunk in October. The Germans naturally knew better. On March 23 the radio station at Bruges was able to intercept signals from French vessels off Brest in pursuit of a U-boat which must have been *UC-79*. She almost certainly laid her mines, for the French records state that eleven were swept up off Brest during March.

What happened to her is a matter of conjecture, though it was claimed that she was sunk in the Dover Barrage. Keyes ascribed her loss to a mine explosion on April 19 in 5101/0117E., though he had to admit that no wreck was ever found. Laurens asserted that she was mined on April 27, but the explosion on that date occurred in 5102/ 0116E., and no wreck was found there either. Both dates are too late for the sinking, since *UC-79* should have passed eastward through the Straits by April 10. In addition, during April U-boats usually headed homeward through the 'deep gut' between Le Colbart and Gris Nez; neither of the explosions occurred in it. A more plausible setting is given by Gröner, who says that she probably struck a mine west of Brest in 4817/0516W. during April. Unfortunately he gives no reasons for his statement, and we can only conclude with Spindler that the loss remains unexplained'.[1] We should add, however, that there is no reason to suppose that *UC-79* was sunk in the Straits.

Around this time the British were well aware that the Straits had not been closed. 'An enemy submarine', writes Keyes, 'escaped through the patrol on the 31st March, and one or more submarines were very active to the westward of the Barrage during this anxious period, but were well hunted; some mines were laid off Boulogne but were swept up and we suffered no damage.'[2] The homeward-bound *UB-57* crossed the minefield on the surface during the night of March 31-April 1, and the minelayer in question was *UC-78*, off Boulogne on March 31.

A definite sinking took place, however, at 1800 on April 11, when the drifter *Ocean Roamer*, on patrol between Le Colbart and the Varne, sighted a violent explosion to the south-west. A thick column of smoke and water

1 Keyes, p. 260; Laurens, p. 296; Gröner (ed. 2), p. 374; Spindler, V, p. 90.
2 Keyes, p. 245.

showed the whole drifter division where to go, and on the spot they found a large pool of oil with wreckage in it. At nightfall oil was still coming up, and *Ocean Roamer* marked the location with a buoy. On May 6 divers finally found the wreck of *UB-33*; a fortnight later they removed the corpse of Gregor, her commander, from the conning tower and also recovered a steel box with codes and signals.

It is something of a mystery why *UB-33* was in the Straits of Dover on this date. She had left Zeebrugge only on April 6 with orders to attack shipping in the Channel as far as the western approaches, and Spindler states that on the 8th she probably sank a small steamer off Berry Head in Lyme Bay.[1] We must probably assume that she had experienced engine trouble and that she was the U-boat, carrying a sail, which the patrol vessel *P-59* sighted in the Channel (501930/0032W.) late on the afternoon of the 10th. As *P-59* approached, the submarine dived, and four depth charges followed her down; she broke surface and then went under again, accompanied by three more depth charges. Oil and air bubbles came to the surface as *P-59* and *P-16* dropped further charges. Evidently she was already homeward-bound; the next day she perished in the barrage.[2]

No questions arose regarding the sinking of *UB-55* near the Varne on the morning of April 22, for eight survivors were picked up. They stated that she had left Zeebrugge the previous morning and after a trial dive headed for the Straits, operating on the surface until 0400. Near the Varne Buoy the commander had ordered a dive to 12 metres. As the boat took this depth a net or mine scraped along the hull, exploding violently at the stern. Water poured in and the stern went down. The crew were ordered forward to restore trim, but the motor room was soon full of water. The ballast tanks aft could not be blown, although the engineer officer was able to set the boat level on the bottom in 25.3 metres. Water leaked into the control room, however, and the batteries were emitting chlorine gas. As the air pressure increased, several men committed suicide by stuffing their mouths and nostrils with wadding and putting their heads under water. Others tried to shoot themselves, but the damp cartridges would not fire. Finally two men got out through the conning-tower hatch and twenty more through the bow torpedo hatch. The change of pressure as they ascended killed most of them, but after an hour and a half in the water a patrol drifter, searching for oil and wreckage, picked up the commander and seven others.

Wenninger, the commander, provided little information. He knew of special navigating apparatus for use with a leader cable, though he stated that *UB-55* had not been equipped with it. He had seen the new *Magnet-Zunder* or magnetic pistol for torpedoes but had never used it. He was

1 Spindler, V, p. 115.

2 The submarine attacked off Boulogne on April 7 by the airship *Z-1* and patrols *P-12* and *P-75* was probably *UC-78*.

willing only to confirm the British notion that the commander of *UB-80* was Kapitän-Leutnant Viebeg, nicknamed 'Maxe'. Even this insignificant detail, however, was later used by Intelligence.

For April the French records mention *UB-55* and four submarines identified from Nauen communiqués: *UC-71* (Warzecha, Nauen April 22), 'UB a 3' (Steindorff, Nauen May 1; actually *UB-74*), *UB-80* (Viebeg, Nauen May 8), *UC-75* (Schmitz, Nauen May 13), and *UB-57* (Lohs, Nauen May 14). Other minelayers were thought to be 'UC x 1' off Boulogne (*UC-78*), 'UC x 2' off Dieppe (actually *UC-71*), 'UC x 3' off Le Havre (*UC-77*), and 'UC x 4' off Falmouth (*UC-17*). This analysis was remarkably accurate.

During May the U-boat losses sharply increased. On the 2nd the homeward-bound *UB-31* was destroyed not far from Folkestone. After her periscope was sighted moving east-north-east, drifters dropped two depth charges and the U-boat probably struck a mine. Though no wreck was immediately found, she was certainly sunk. That same morning, only a few minutes later, drifters stationed toward the Gris Nez side noted the explosion of six mines and soon sighted oil coming to the surface. During the day several depth charges were dropped in the vicinity, and later the Admiralty decided that the explosions had accounted for *UC-78*, on her way out to the Channel. This identification was certainly wrong. First, *UC-78* did not leave Ostend until 0247 GMT on May 2 and could not have reached the vicinity of Gris Nez five hours later. More important, the mines she had been ordered to lay were found off Boulogne on May 4 and off Newhaven on May 8. She evidently survived her westward transit of the Dover Straits. Most important of all, the submarine actually on the spot (505645/012315) on the morning of May 2 was the homeward-bound *UC-17*. When she reached her base she reported that five depth charges had been dropped on her by a patrol boat. What she heard must have been the exploding mines.

It might be supposed that *UC-78* was responsible for oil and air bubbles observed in the Straits (5101/0118) on the afternoon of May 11, or for the explosion of five mines that evening (5101/0120), or for another explosion two nights later (5056/0119). According to Keyes, the detonations on the evening of May 11 meant that 'a submarine was unquestionably destroyed'. He tries to prove his case by arguing that 'two months later, while searching for another submarine, a second one was found with her stern blown off, which could not be identified'. He suggests that the 'second one ' was sunk on May 11 and that she was *UB-119*. Unfortunately his account is highly confused. The search took place in August, not in July, and it resulted in finding the wreck of *UB-55*.

There is therefore no reason to suppose that *UC-78* was sunk on either May 11 or May 13, though she was certainly sunk during the month of May. We shall later indicate the reason for supposing that she hit a mine off Gris Nez and that her unidentified wreck was found there.

On April 20 the first lines of shore-controlled mines had been laid off Cape Gris Nez, and at 2325 on May 3 the hydrophone station picked up the sound of U-boat motors to the north. By 2353 the U-boat was in the minefield and the mines were fired. Three hours later she was heard again, this time to the south, and it was supposed that she had got away.

The submarine in question was *UB-59*, which was severely damaged and therefore proceeded to the Vergoyer Bank, south-west of Boulogne, and lay on the bottom all day. That evening she surfaced and headed for the Straits, an hour later being forced under and depth-charged by patrols, and then heading for the Varne Bank. At 0215 (German time) motor boats attacked her west of the Varne. She escaped by crossing the bank on the surface and then heading to the north-east. Four and a half hours later she was on the surface and informed Bruges that she had been badly damaged by a mine off Gris Nez and would have to enter dry dock. She reached Ostend that evening. That night the Bruges radio warned U-boats about enemy submarines off Beachy Head and south of the Sandettie Bank. In addition, 'off Cape Gris Nez are deep anchored mines', and U-boats were advised to pass the Straits by the English coast.

UB-59 entered dry dock on May 6, but ten days later British aircraft dropped about forty bombs in the vicinity. One of them set fire to an oil tank of *UB-59*, and the flames were extinguished only after an hour's efforts. At the time when the Germans evacuated Flanders she was still undergoing repair, and she was blown up on October 5.

Another Flanders submarine perished on the evening of May 26, this time in Lyme Bay where the yacht *Lorna* sighted a periscope only 150 feet away and was able to ram the conning tower before dropping two depth charges. Four survivors appeared on the surface and *Lorna* dropped another depth charge in order to finish off the U-boat. One man was picked up, along with a cap marked 'Unterseebootsabteilung'. Three hours later he died of injuries, after stating that he belonged to *UB-74* under 'Ober-Leutnant Schtiendorf', a week out of Zeebrugge and with three ships to her credit. (There is a discrepancy between this statement and what Steindorff told *U-101* off Ushant on the 25th: he had been out for a fortnight and had sunk one steamer. This was either *John G. McCullough*, 1,985 tons, sunk on May 18 off the Ile d'Yeu, as Spindler suggests, or *Skaraas*, 1,625 tons, sunk on May 23 near the Lizard. French records ascribe the latter sinking, which Spindler does not mention, to *UB-74*.) Later on the log book of *UB-74* was recovered by divers. She had sailed on the night of May 11-12 and had passed through the Straits on the surface. On the evening of the 13th she was rammed by a steamer off Beachy Head. The log ended on May 16, and up to that date the U-boat had sunk nothing. Also recovered were lists of officers and crew for December and January, but these provided little of value.

On the last day of May *UC-75* was sunk in the North Sea. Her presence off Flamborough Head had been established by directional interception on the 29th, and she was sunk while trying to attack a convoy. The survivors described two earlier cruises to the Channel with considerable accuracy, though they claimed one steamer actually torpedoed by another submarine. They also gave details about passage through the Straits. After leaving Zeebrugge U-boats were accustomed to steer west for three or four miles. They then shaped their course, usually on the surface, to pass outside the sandbanks until they picked up 'No. 4 Buoy' off Dover - apparently the British No. IIA. Their hour of departure was set so that they could pass through the Straits at dusk or during darkness, if possible with the tide. The commander had heard of old mine-nets off the Belgian coast but apparently was unaware of any newer ones. (Previously intercepted signals showed that he was well aware of mines and swept passages off Zeebrugge.) He regarded the net barrage between the Goodwins and Dunkirk as harmless, since it could be crossed on the surface. Though he knew of the deep mines in the Straits, he had no clear idea as to their position or extent. He had been ordered not to dive in the area where they were supposed to be. He and his crew knew that there were drifters with flares on patrol in the Dover area. One man thought that they were intended to force U-boats to dive, while others regarded them as simply revealing their presence. In any case, there was little difficulty in slipping past them on the surface at full speed, at distances from 250 to 400 yards. Perhaps the U-boats would encounter more difficulties if the craft with searchlights were faster and if there were more vessels without lights.

The survivors provided a few bits of information about U-boat losses, such as the facts that *UB-17* had been lost two or three months earlier and that *UB-78* was overdue on May 19, when they had sailed. They were impressed by what their interrogators told them. The corpse of Gregor had been recovered from the wreck of *UB-33*, and four other submarines (*UB-55*, *UB-54*, *UB-58*, and *UC-79*) had recently been sunk by 'twin magnetic mines' in the Straits. This statement obviously consisted of a judicious mixture of fact with fiction: the British had no idea as to how *UB-54* had been sunk, and they were also guessing about *UC-79*. There were in fact no magnetic mines in the Straits.[1]

The French summaries for May reflect little definite information. *UB-74* and *UB-78* had been sunk, while a cruise of *UB-57* was inferred from a Nauen communiqué of June 6. 'UC x 4' (*UC-17*) returned from a cruise; *UC-56* was interned; and *UC-71* laid mines off Dover (Nauen, May 29).

During June one U-boat was sunk in the Straits on her way to the Channel. This was the minelayer *UC-64*, out from Ostend at 2120 on June 18.

---

1 By the end of September, when Wenninger of *UB-55* was able to transmit word about the 'twin mines' to Germany, the information was useless because the Straits route had been abandoned completely.

Just after she sailed the Commander of U-boats, Flanders, radioed to ask if she had on board the report of *UB-80* on Channel conditions. Nothing more was heard from her. Early on the morning of June 20 drifters dropped six depth charges on a U-boat in the barrage and drove her into the minefield. The wreck, which we shall later describe, was found on July 6 in 5058/0123E.

In the French records for June the activities of Flanders U-boats are described a little more definitely than before, and intercepted signals are listed as made by four homeward-bound U-boats, all east of the Dover Straits. These came in from an unidentified UB-boat (*UB-103*) on the 13th, from *UB-80* on the 16th, from an unidentified UC-boat (*UC-49*) on the 20th, and from *UC-71* on the 29th.

Keyes reported to the Admiralty on June 29 that in his opinion four submarines had been destroyed in the minefield. The records of the Dover Patrol show that he thought U-boats had definitely been sunk on June 7, 12, 20 and 23. Of these cases, however, only the one on June 20 really resulted in success.

He was also convinced that a submarine blew up in the barrage on July 10, and when it was learned that *UC-77* had been lost around this time it was concluded that she was sunk in the barrage. Since *UC-77* left Zeebrugge at 2356 on July 10, however, she was certainly not responsible for the explosion. Observation of British radio signals led the command at Bruges to conclude that she laid a minefield off the Nab, as Spindler points out, and probably she then headed westward. She may have struck deep mines off Portland. Alternatively, she may have caused explosions in the Dover Barrage on July 14 in either 505630/0131E. or 505520/012810E. A periscope was sighted in the latter location, but no wreck was found in either place.

For the month of July the French records list only one intercepted signal; this was made by the homeward-bound *UB-103* on the 24th. They also note that *UC-71* was on cruise, perhaps because mines were swept up off the Royal Sovereign Light Vessel, near which she often deposited her cargo. At Dover Keyes was offering rather precise information (though based on conjectures) to visitors. At the end of the month two American captains, Knox and Yarnell, paid him a call and he showed them a chart 'giving the location of 22 submarines which he considers as practically certain of having been destroyed since June 1'. His own records show that they misunderstood him; he had in mind the period from January 1 to the end of June. He went on to say that 'a number of these have been visited by divers'. The number, as we shall presently see, was three.

He also told his visitors that

a searchlight patrol is now maintained on both sides of the deep minefield, and has replaced to a considerable extent the use of flares. Submarines occasionally manage to slip through the Straits, one having recently passed through the Folkestone Gate. Their passage is usually known to the authorities there.

The Folkestone Gate was on his mind because since early June he had been laying shore-controlled mines in it. Thus far the only result had been damage to the drifter *City of Edinburgh* on July 6, while more than one U-boat had managed to get through without difficulty. It was not until the next month that results were achieved.

A signal intercepted from *UC-71* at 0935 on August 13 did not come as a complete surprise. The submarine, in the southern North Sea, stated that she was proceeding in, apparently after striking a mine in the Channel. Nearly an hour later Bruges informed her that five German seaplanes were on their way to protect her. What had happened was that the U-boat was at 14 metres in the shipping channel close to Folkestone when the shore hydrophone station picked up the sound of her motors. Half an hour later, at 0447 German time, a line of mines was fired. The submarine continued eastward, but in all likelihood she had been damaged. By the time the Admiralty briefing was over that morning Sims could be told that 'a Flanders submarine reports that she struck a mine in the Channel and was badly damaged'.

Meanwhile an aeroplane from Dunkirk found the submarine, heading north-east on the surface to the north of the Straits, and dropped two bombs, forcing her to dive. Later in the morning the submarine was able to drive other aeroplanes away with gunfire, and in the afternoon she reached Zeebrugge, where she remained under repair until she was sent to Germany at the end of September.

During the day the Bruges radio sent out a warning: 'Mines in Folkestone Gate'. It was not received by *UB-109*, north of the Azores; in May her radio masts, which made her top heavy, had been taken off at Ostend. It may have been received by *UB-57*, which apparently passed through the Straits the next day near Gris Nez. These were the only two Flanders boats west of the Straits on the 13th.

By August 29 the British had captured a carrier pigeon which, they told Sims, was to have informed Bruges of an impending arrival. Presumably it had flown eastward from *UB-109*, sunk by electrically controlled mines early that morning.

The survivors were fairly talkative. Their boat had been under repair for three months before sailing, at 0100 on July 28, for an experimental cruise to the Azores. By 0400 she had reached 5142/0247E. and lay on the bottom the rest of the day. By about 2200 she had reached No. 15 Buoy in the Straits when she was forced to dive by a drifter which dropped four depth charges on her track. Soon thereafter, however, she surfaced and thus crossed the lines of mines. On her way out to the Azores she attacked no shipping, although far to the north of them she had sunk a steamer on the 17th. Back in the Channel on the 25th she had been able to sink two small ships, but later attempts had been unsuccessful. During a cruise of 32 days she had sunk only 6,353 tons of shipping.

The navigating warrant officer described the Flanders Flotillas as 'the Drowning Command for Navigating Warrant Officers', and added that commanders had a healthy respect for the Dover Barrage because its contents and limits were unknown. Most of them believed that it could safely be crossed at 15 metres depth. He did not agree, however, although he had been at 15 metres and had just gone to 12 metres when the mines exploded.

Most of the information supplied about Flanders losses was correct, although one prisoner added the graphic detail that the barracks room in which the crew of UB-112 kept their gear had been officially sealed. This action indicated that she was overdue and presumed lost. In fact, UB-112 had reached Flanders only on July 21 and did not sail until August 13.

After the loss of UB-109 only one more Flanders U-boat tried to pass through the Straits. This was UB-103, depth charged off Gris Nez on the afternoon of September 16.

By the time UB-103 was sunk the Flanders Flotillas had outlived their effectiveness. Indeed, Captain S. W. Roskill has argued that they never were remarkably effective, and that the Admiralty pressure for an attack on land which would lead to the capture of Ostend and Zeebrugge was quite mistaken; the whole campaign known as 'Third Ypres', with its incredible losses 'in Flanders Fields' was unnecessary. Only a third of the tonnage sunk by U-boats - in northern waters - was due to submarines from Flanders, and their activities should have been halted, as they were in 1918, by mines and raids.[1]

During the year 1918, however, these submarines were still able to sink nearly half a million tons of shipping, according to Spindler's narrative, and they did so under extraordinarily difficult circumstances. Not all the commanders composed verse, but it is worth recording the Wagnerian lines which one of them created.[2]

> Wem weist die Walküre den Ehrensitz
> In Walhall nach Walvaters Wille?
> Den Recken, gefallen in Donner und Blitz,
> Von der flandrischen U-Boots-Flotille.

1 S. W. Roskill in *Journal of the Royal United Service Institution* 104 (1959) pp. 440-42.
1 'Das Wort einer Dichter-Kornmandanten', cited by O. Steinbrinck in E. v. Mantey (ed.). *Auf See Unbesiegt*, I (Munich, 1922). p. 208.

DIVERS AND WRECKS IN THE STRAITS OF DOVER

It was one thing to sight U-boats and observe explosions or oil on the surface of the Straits. It was another to prove conclusively that a U- boat had been destroyed. Much of Admiral Keyes' correspondence with the Admiralty in London had to do with questions of evidence for the sinking of U-boats, for when one was sunk the Admiralty awarded £1,000 for distribution among the crews involved. Proof could be provided by prisoners, wreckage, or even the failure of a U-boat to return to her base. Keyes was an optimist and an excellent Vice-Admiral of the Dover Patrol. By the end of the war, he believed, twenty-six U-boats had been sunk in or near the Folkestone-Gris Nez barrage. The true figure, in our opinion, was fourteen.

The *Operation Packs of the Dover Patrol* contain records of most of the U-boat wrecks found in the Straits during 1918, and from these records the losses of most of the U-boats can be confirmed. To be sure, there are no records in regard to the wrecks of either *UC-50* or *U-109*, both of which, according to Keyes' memoirs, were found. We have already seen that the wreck of *UC-50*, supposedly depth charged by *Zubian*, could not have been found. It remains possible that divers did visit *U-109*, although in Admiralty records a post-war note by Captain Dewar says there was 'no absolute proof'. Perhaps her wreck was found but not positively identified.

Divers certainly found and identified the wreck of *UB-33*, sunk on April 11. At the location drifters picked up a bucketful of oil and some wood wreckage with an acid-proof coating. On the 27th sweepers found the wreck, and on May 6 divers first went down to it, returning on the 21st to bring up the commander's corpse from the conning tower and a steel box with codes and signals from inside the hull.

The wreck of *UC-64*, sunk on June 20, was found on July 6 but at first could not be identified. Sims was told that she 'had all the bottom blown up from the conning tower forward to such an extent that the forward compartment was filled up to the upper deck with a mass of debris consisting of batteries, hammocks, bodies of men, and so forth'. The divers used explosives to clear the interior and later identified the wreck as *UC-64*.

Another wreck was found in July while divers were searching for a U-boat wrongly supposed to have been sunk on June 27. The location was 5058/0122E., where they found 'a small UB which had been down for some time'. Three 'small UB' boats were sunk in the Straits, but *UB-33* had already been found and identified and the unidentified wreck of *UB-31* was to be found off Folkestone. The submarine in question must have been *UB-38*, mined in approximately the location mentioned.

On August 7 Commander Damant was off Gris Nez when he found a UC boat with two screws and two rudders, much damaged by mine

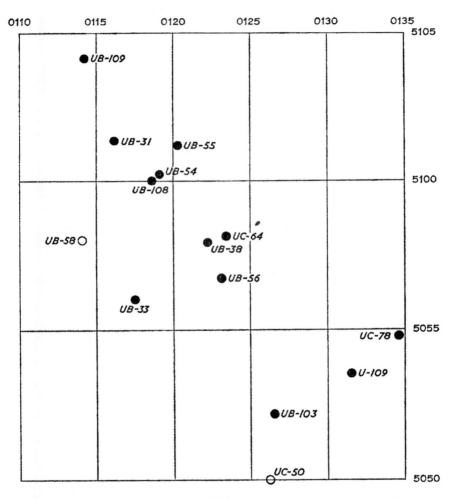

WRECKS (●) AND EXPLOSIONS (○) IN THE DOVER BARRAGE, 1918

explosion under gun. Crushed and folded in neighbourhood of officers' quarters. There is marine growth and some barnacles on gun. Don't yet know if any mines are in tubes or not but owing to crushing I think prospects of recovering anything bad. Have opened conning tower. No body visible inside, and nothing by which to identify boat. Depth 18 fathoms.

Some 'organisms attached to a piece of tin' were brought up and sent to the British Museum (Natural History) for examination. There the authorities concluded that the sinking took place before June. We conclude that the submarine can only have been *UC-79* (March-April) or *UC-78* (May). Since there is no reason to suppose that *UC-79* was sunk in the Straits, she must have been *UC-78*.

The next day Damant moved on to a position 'close to No. 13 Buoy in the minefield'. He received an unexpected reward: there were two wrecks on the bottom, 'one of them old and covered with barnacles, the other much more recent'. He reported that 'large pieces of hull of the older boat were seen and two plates and chain cable of the newer boat were actually in contact with the old wreckage'. On the 11th divers went down again.

The remainder of the hull of the more recent case was found; the fore part of the hull up to the gun appeared to have been blown off by an internal explosion. There was a moderate amount of marine growth, but it did not appear to have been there long.

On the 12th the submarine's 105-mm deck gun was brought to the surface and found to bear the date '1917'. The location was 5100/011845E.

At the time no attempt seems to have been made to identify the two submarines by number. As for the older of the two wrecks, Keyes thought that it was that of a U-boat which had struck mines in the vicinity on March 19. There is no reason to question this conclusion. The wreck must therefore have been *UB-54*. which disappeared after sailing for the Channel from Zeebrugge on March 1. On a previous Channel cruise she was at sea from January 18 to February 5, a period of approximately three weeks. There is every reason to suppose, therefore, that she was homeward-bound in the Straits on March 19.

Keyes thought that the newer wreck had been sunk on April 22, a few hours after the mining of *UB-55*. This guess was incorrect, for no other submarine was sunk on that date. The calibre of the deck gun proves that the boat belonged to the UB-III class (UB48-132), and five boats of this class had been lost in or near the Straits by the beginning of August. It is clear that four of them can be excluded. (1) *UB-56* was sunk in a different location, and as we shall see her wreck was later found though not identified. (2) We have just accounted for the wreck of *UB-54*. (3) Though the wreck of *UB-58* was not found, she was sunk in a location considerably to the westward of the wrecks the divers found. (4) We shall presently see that the wreck of *UB-55* was located in another position. This means that the only submarine which the divers can have found was *UB-108*, out from Zeebrugge at 2300 on July 2 and not heard from thereafter. The records of the Dover Patrol show that a submarine was attacked in the Straits on July 4 and that oil continued to come to the surface for two days. The position was 5101/0117E. We conclude that the two positions agree, as Hall commented in another instance, 'as nearly as could be expected', and that *UB-108* was therefore sunk in the Straits on July 4.

On August 12 another UB-boat was found, this time in 505645/0123E. Her stern was blown in and she was full of sand. Evidently she had been on the bottom a long time. Keyes claimed that she had been sunk in the second of the two encounters on May 2, but we have already noted that this encounter was with *UC-17*, which was not sunk. There is every reason to suppose that the boat in question was *UB-56*. To be sure, when the destroyer *Gipsy* was shaken by the explosion marking the end of *UB-56* she was in 5058/0121E. The submarine was not sunk in that location, however. When *Gipsy* hoisted her boat after picking up one survivor she was in 505630/0I22E., and the tide was setting strong to the south-west. We conclude that the old UB-wreck was that of *UB-56*. since it was found a short distance to the north-east of *Gipsy's* last position.

A letter of August 14 to Admiral Keyes states that this wreck was 'the eighth submarine on to which diver has been at present'. Our figures, allowing for the undescribed discovery of *U-109*, agree with this number.

On August 14 yet another wreck was found, and the next day Keyes informed Hall that 'the wreck of the submarine sunk in position 510115N./012010E. was examined by divers yesterday'. Eight days later Hall replied.

With reference to your letter of 15 August, from an ink impression on one of the scraps of paper forwarded, the submarine has been identified as *UB-55*, sunk on 22 April 1918. This is confirmed by an entry in the note-book recovered subsequently and sent up yesterday by hand.

By this point, then, nine U-boat wrecks had been found in the Straits of Dover. Only three of them had been definitely identified, but an analysis of dates and places now makes it possible to identify all of them.

Later in August, it would appear, a tenth wreck was found, for Keyes stated that in the area off Folkestone where a U-boat was depth charged and probably mined on May 2, divers found the wreck of a UB-boat. Though it was not identified, the submarine was undoubtedly *UB-31.*

There could be no question about the sinking of *UB-109* on the morning of August 29, and divers were sent down at once. That morning they found the wreck, buoyed it, and shackled it with wires. Commander Damant's report deserves full quotation.

At this time the water inside her was quite hot, presumably from mixing with the sulphuric acid of the batteries. She is lying in fourteen fathoms on a sandy bottom, heading NE, 30°. list to starboard. Fore hatch and conning tower open, no buoyancy remaining, about twenty feet abaft conning tower the damage begins and from there aft the vessel is shapeless wreckage. The damage is far more severe than that generally met with in deep minefield cases. The forepart of the boat is quite intact, for instance the large mirror on door of captain's wardrobe is not even cracked. For this reason and because the depth was moderate I decided to work aft from the fore hatch without cutting any plates by explosives. Owing to muddy water it is generally quite dark on the highest parts of the wreck. While inside it is of course always so and all work must be done by touch and hand lamp. To get to their objective divers had to negotiate a chain of five narrow apertures: (1) fore hatch, (2) WT door in fore bulkhead of officers' quarters, (3) partition between officers' and captain's quarters, (4) WT door in fore pressure bulkhead of control room, (5) door of WT cabinet. Between 4 and 5 are the awkward obstacles formed by compass and steering pedestals in control room. P.M. on day of sinking fore hatch was cleared of bodies, bedding, etc., and some personal material sent to the Admiralty. On the 30th and 31st much important material was recovered though weather only allowed work on one tide. Diver had by now got as far as control room. On 1st September again only one tide could be worked but the control room was passed, the WT cabinet entered and much valuable material found. Sept. 2nd and 3rd weather remained unfit but on the 4th a whole day's work was got in completing first part of the programme. I do not propose sending men inside during spring tides but there is work outside the hull which can be done then. The inside divers - Leading Seaman E. Blackford and Able Seaman T. Clear - have shown much skill and determination in squeezing through these narrow places and making such a cool and thorough search.

As early as the 31st Sims was told that the divers had brought up a chart which traced the cruise of *UB-109* from the Channel to the Azores, south of

Gibraltar, and up the coasts of Spain and France to the Channel again, along with 'other valuable charts'.

It is a question whether or not the wreck of *UB-103*, the last submarine sunk in the Straits, was actually found. Two days after patrols dropped depth charges on a pool of oil in 505215/012640, a drifter with search gear thoroughly investigated a square mile around the position but found no trace of a wreck. No information about divers is provided in the *Operation Packs*, but on January 4, 1919, the Admiralty made a £1,000 award. It was stated that the oil and bubbles observed on September 16 'probably came from *UB-103* sunk by striking a mine, and the destruction of this submarine is therefore regarded as "Known". ' One might suppose that this conclusion was based on German records showing that *UB-103* did not return and on the lack of evidence for any other encounter with a homeward-bound U-boat at this time. On the other hand the official history of British minefields states that 'during further search *UB-103* was located', and we must therefore assume that the divers' reports are simply absent from the *Dover Packs*.

Of the fourteen U-boats sunk in the Straits of Dover, it is now evident that no fewer than twelve were found by divers, even though during the war, and afterwards, five of the wrecks were not identified. The only boats whose wrecks were not found were *UC-50* and *UB-58*. No search was made for *UC-50* because the date and place of her sinking were wrongly assigned. Papers and wreckage from *UB-58* made it unnecessary for divers to look for her wreck.

D. The Northern Barrage

By late winter in 1917-18, as the French summaries show, the Germans were known to be feeling the effectiveness of the Dover Barrage. In November the Straits route was reported as 'habitual and familiar to the large U-boats', and in December the situation was the same. In January, however, at least eight identified U-boats took the northern route. 'It even appears that some of them went via the Skagerrak and the Sound, since many movements of submarines leaving or returning were signalled along the Norwegian and Danish coasts.' During February, it was concluded, 'only *U-90* and *U-53* came back through the Straits; all the other large submarines passed north of England both out and back'. By March only the Flanders U-boats were still making use of the Straits.

It was therefore time for the Allies to complete plans begun during 1917, and during the spring agreement was finally reached in regard to the extent, location, and composition of minefields to be laid between the Orkney Islands and Norwegian waters. The Americans were to employ new mines with long antennae, while the British would use their new contact mines which had achieved success in the North Sea and the Straits of Dover. Both British and American mines would be laid at the eastern end of the barrage, while only American mines would be laid in the central area. For the time being, the waters off the Orkneys were to be left free. An Admiralty memorandum stated that 'the navigation of Pentland Firth by submerged submarines is considered impracticable'.

Mining began on June 8, but for some time no results were achieved. At 0520 on July 8, however, a signal was intercepted from *U-86*, giving her location in 5938/0420E. and reporting that she had struck a mine. Half an hour later *U-53* was heard from. She was proceeding to the aid of the damaged submarine, and at 0906 she reported meeting her. Though *U-86* could not dive she still had enough fuel to reach Skagen, where she expected an escort. The two U-boats would steer close to Norwegian territorial waters. Further signals from *U-53* were located by directional interception, but although British forces were sent out to look for both boats they were unable to intercept them. Another signal, this time from *U-60*, provided some details about the explosion. It had occurred when *U-86* was a considerable distance away from a glass ball she had observed, and the mine could therefore be regarded as deeply submerged. A further signal from *UB-90*, outward-bound on July 11, showed that British submarines were in the Kattegat and outside the entrance to the Skagerrak. They waited in vain, however.

Analysis of these signals must have confirmed the Allied suspicion that the antennae of the American mines were too long. Originally planned to extend a hundred feet, they had already been shortened to seventy feet and it had already been planned to reduce the length to fifty-five feet. After *U-86* was damaged they were finally shortened to thirty-five feet.

The next episode was announced at 0120 on August 13 when *U-113* made an 'urgent' signal to her base. She had suffered slight damage from a mine but could still dive. Her speed was twelve knots. She expected to meet an escort probably on the 13th. About noon she added that her battery was very low, but she would get to Skagen at 2300, heading thence to Laeso Rinne. At 1803 she was told that destroyers were moving out from the Little Belt to Laeso Rinne, where they would pick her up. A Nauen signal on the 14th showed that she had reached port and that she had sighted glass balls both to the north-east and to the south of the new barrage. Obviously the mines to the north-east, almost within Norwegian waters, had accounted for the damage.

Analysis of communications and reports by agents, indeed, indicated that between July 11 and August 2 no fewer than eight U-boats had passed through Norwegian territorial waters when homeward-bound, and one more - *U-113* herself - had passed through them on her way out on July 20. She had been sighted both from land and by the patrol submarine *J-3*.

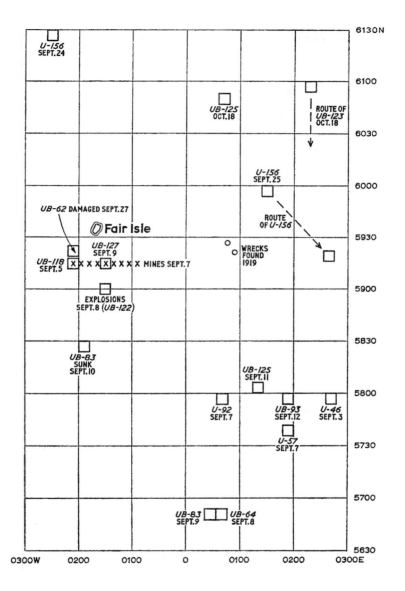

U-BOATS IN THE NORTHERN BARRAGE, SEPTEMBER - OCTOBER, 1918

During the month of August, it was observed, nearly all the U-boats outward-bound passed through the Fair Isle passage, and it was therefore decided to lay mines in Area B, east of the Orkneys. During the first week of September shipping was secretly directed to avoid the area, while on the 6th an elaborate patrol was set up in order to keep U-boats from observing the laying of the mines. On the 7th, American forces laid six lines of surface mines across the area; the British laid one line parallel to them. The field thus constituted was located in approximately 5910N. and ran from 0210W. to 0050W.

No U-boats, it appeared, had passed through the area or, indeed, through the northern North Sea in the first four days of September. On the 5th *UB-118* went through on her way home and was sighted by the patrol; on the 6th both *U-46* and *U-102*, outward-bound, came through Area B but were not sighted. It could be expected that more U-boats would soon attempt the Fair Isle passage, and on the 7th three of them were heard from. At 1630 *UB-127* was in 2537K, to the north-west of Heligoland; at 2100 *U-57* reported from 1757E; and at 2146 *U-92* revealed her presence in 1400E. These boats would probably pass through Area B.

The British estimated that *U-92* would reach the Fair Island area at about 1800 on the 8th, and it is therefore significant that *UB-122*, about 25 sea miles south of Fair Isle in very heavy weather, not only observed the constant detonation of mines in the new field but also was shaken by a violent explosion which threw up a column of water at 1440. Her commander noted that this was not just a mine explosion. Spindler was therefore probably right when he suggested that it marked the end of *U-92*, not heard from thereafter. During the day *U-57* passed north west from 865E. to 400E. and observed mines floating at 5900 latitude. At 2100 the outward-bound *UB-64* revealed her presence in 1389E. and reported 'Nothing special'.

Early on the morning of September 9 several signals showed that U-boats were about to pass through Area B. One of them led to a good deal of confusion in the records; it was from 1329E. at 0110 and reported 'Nothing special'. It must have been wrongly enciphered, for the call sign was identified by the German command as '*U-92*' (though with the notation 'uncertain') and by the British as '*UB-92*'. Presumably it was made by *UB-83*, which from exactly the same location made the same signal at 0200, directing it to the Chief of U-boats and to III Flotilla.

At 0936 this submarine, presumably identified by recognition signals, was sighted by *UC-58* in about 5800/0000. At 1100 a large UB-boat, presumably *UB-104* heading north from Flanders, was sighted from Fair Isle.

That evening at 2000 a signal came in from *UB-127*. She was in 753E. just south of Fair Isle, and reported 'Nothing special'. The signal was seemingly undramatic. The location, however, was in approximately 5915/0130W., or almost precisely in the lines of mines laid on September 7.

Indeed, within a very few minutes she must have encountered the mines. On the 20th, during a minelaying expedition a few miles to the north, a destroyer sighted the floating body of a sailor with a German life preserver. The location, given as 'about midway between the ends of the previous field', almost certainly proves that he came from *UB-127*. During minesweeping in June 1919 an obstruction was found in the same spot, and a large oil patch came to the surface.

Meanwhile *UB-83* had still not passed through the minefield, and at 0620 on the morning of the 10th the kite balloon towed by the destroyer *Ophelia*, on patrol to the south of Fair Isle, sighted a U-boat's conning tower in a small oil patch about two and a half miles away. The submarine dived, but the destroyer soon reached the position and dropped three depth charges, set to explode at two hundred feet. Four minutes later another explosion brought thick oil to the surface; it kept rising until noon, though no air bubbles or wreckage were observed. At 1240 *Ophelia* dropped four more charges on an oil patch in 5836/0228W. This patch, however, cannot have been due to *UB-83*, which must have been sunk in the first location. Conceivably the pool of oil first sighted by the kite balloon had been caused by damage sustained in an earlier attempt to pass through Area B.

Three U-boats perished, therefore, in the waters adjacent to Area B during the first three days after the new field was laid. On the 10th, however, *UB-122* warned the homeward-bound *UB-93* of the inexplicable explosion she had observed south of Fair Isle. On the 12th *UB-93* passed the information on to her base, and many U-boats avoided the area thereafter.

On September 20 American and British forces returned to Area B. The American forces sighted a U-boat (probably *U-91*) off Stronsay Firth and attacked her with depth charges; they then proceeded to an area north of the minefields laid on the 7th and proceeded to deposit 5,520 mines in a little under four hours. The British squadron laid a line of 1,300 mines to the north of the new American lines.

A signal from the cruiser *U-139* on the 16th had shown that she passed around the western end of the barrage by night, but it could be expected that other U-boats would encounter the mines. After all, as the Admiralty informed Sims on the 17th, neither *U-92* nor *UB-92* had been heard from since signals from them were picked up on the 7th and the 9th. As a matter of fact, five outward-bound submarines were now heading for the area, and on the 19th signals had been intercepted from two of them. *U-54* sent observations on British cruisers and destroyers east of the Firth of Forth, while *U-161* simply noted her own position farther to the east. The German station on Borkum tried to make contact with *U-55*, apparently without success.

The German records show that precisely on the 20th and the 21st three boats passed northward through both fields in Area B. East of the Moray

Firth on the 20th, *U-161* noted first three destroyers, then another two; she also heard depth charges exploding in the distance. The next day she passed through both fields without incident, although she sighted many antennae. *U-54* apparently submerged in the field to the south, with Fair Isle ahead, and then headed to the north-west. At 0300 on the 21st, north of Scotland, she reported that south of Fair Isle there was a weak patrol; she had passed through at periscope depth and had noted no nets. *U-55* passed around the western edge of the minefields after observing a heavy explosion south of Fair Isle.

It was not until September 27 that the new field achieved a definite result. At 0657 that morning the outward-bound *UB-62* had already crossed the southern minefield in Area B when, east of North Ronaldsay, she was badly damaged by a mine at the western edge of the northern field. Continuing on in a north-north-easterly direction, she was forced to dive by a destroyer, and when she surfaced she found that her radio was useless. Fortunately for her, she was sighted by the homeward bound *U-98* and could inform her that though damaged she would return through the centre of the barrage. The next evening *U-98* radioed the news that *UB-62* would return from 1357E. to 1590E. This route was extremely dangerous. *UB-62* did not actually take it, though other U-boats must have done so around the same time.

A few days earlier the homeward-bound cruiser *U-156* was lost in Area A, but we shall discuss her fate in dealing with cruisers at a later point. Here it is enough to say that two other submarines must have perished in Area A within a few days' time.

The first of these was *U-102*, whose cruise had been followed by means of eight signals she made when west and south-west of Ireland between the 8th and the 20th of September. On the latter date she announced that she was heading for home, but this was the last news received either from or concerning her. It is quite probable that her wreck lies in 592030/0055E., where sweepers found an obstruction during the summer of 1919; it 'was thought to be the *U-102*'. In 1474E., the wreck lay on the route which *UB-62* intended to take. The date would be about September 28.

The second was *UB-104*, which we believe left Lyme Bay on the night of September 23 and was lost in the Northern Barrage towards the beginning of October.

Since the signal about *UB-62* clearly showed that submarines were still taking the route close to the Orkneys, on October 11 the British laid two relatively short lines of surface mines in the south-western part of Area B. No results were obtained, for after *UB-62* was damaged few U-boats took this route.

Towards the middle of October several signals revealed that the German command was much concerned with finding safe routes. On the

10th the homeward-bound *U-118* reported that patrols were using hydrophones to the east of the Shetlands. The next day, *UB-94* was in that area when she signalled her position and added that she was with *UB-92*. Two hours later she was a little more explicit about her activities. She had crossed the barrage somewhat to the eastward of the locations given in her orders. Presumably the U-boats were testing the barrage for gaps in it. Proof that they were doing so was supplied on the 13th, when Nauen ordered three submarines - *U-60*, *U-119*, and *U-122* - to report on the route they had just taken. *U-119* replied immediately, but her garbled message remained unclear until she repeated it on the 17th. Then it could be known that she had passed glass balls along the track from 1893E. to 1836E. to 1901E. *U-60* answered on the evening of the 14th, although apparently the British could not read her message. She had gone from 619E. to 389E., then to 1363E., 1369E., and 1072E. On the 14th *UB-90* also contributed information about the old route from 1720E. to 1953E. ; there were many 'ball buoys' but she encountered no mines. On the 17th *U-55*, also homeward-bound, reported drifting glass balls in 1479E. and 1771E., as well as a strong patrol east of the Shetlands.

The cruise of *UB-90* was especially meaningful to the interceptors. At 0600 on the morning of September 27 she was in 1814E., south of Area A, and she was heard from again on October 5, though her signal could not be read. Apparently neither signal was received at home. On October 12 she was north of the Shetlands when she explained her difficulties in a signal fully picked up only by the British. Both sides read that she had not reached her operations area in the Bristol Channel but had made repairs to her propellers and a diving rudder off the Faeroes on the 11th. At 7 knots on the surface she expected to operate off Peterhead for three days. Only the British learned that she had sunk 3,575 tons in October and had broken off her cruise on October 3. The damage, it could be inferred, was somehow related to her torpedoing the 3,575-ton steamer *Eupton* off the mouth of the Shannon on that date. A further signal, stating that she had passed through Pentland Firth on the night of September 28, was received only by the British.

On the 14th she spoke again. Her information about the Northern Barrage was not received at home, but both sides read her location, in 2130E., and her request to be given an escort on the 18th.

Thus forewarned, the British submarine *L-12* was patrolling underwater on the afternoon of the 16th, fifteen miles from Skagen, when she sighted the conning tower of a U-boat heading eastward. After a twenty minute chase *L-12* fired four 21-inch torpedoes. One and a half minutes later there was a violent explosion, and the British boat could find only a great pool of oil and small bits of wreckage. The commander believed he had sunk an ocean-going type like *U-110*. His target was actually *UB-90*.

Two days later, signals provided more information. At 0200 the outward-bound *UB-125* announced her location north-east of the Shetlands. She had crossed the barrage on the surface but had sighted only the usual buoys and glass balls. Nearly six hours later the nearby *UB-123*, heading south, began transmitting a request for a route through the barrage, though her sister submarine did not pick it up until 0910. At 0924 she replied, instructing *UB-123* to head for 1910E. and then proceed south. This was the route she herself had just taken, but for *UB-123* it proved fatal, either that day or the next.

Also on the 18th a signal from Nauen was picked up, with orders for all U-boats. They were to pass the Skagen Light Vessel at not more than six miles distance (because of the loss of *UB-90*). They could cross the middle of the barrage by day on the surface, and were not to employ the Fair Isle passage. Pentland Firth, they were advised, was open.

Since the end of September several U-boats had been exploring the possibilities of Pentland Firth as an alternative to passage through the minefields. A signal from *UB-126* on September 30 described British and American warships in the area, and another from *UB-77* on October 10, apparently not intercepted, stated that the Pentland Firth light was not burning. On the 12th and the 14th the homeward-bound *UB-90* described her transit on September 28. There were no lights, and she had been forced to submerge because of motor boats on patrol. These signals were not received at home. On the 18th, however, *UB-126* reported that Pentland Firth was safe for passage because there was no patrol there. On the 21st the homeward-bound *U-91* took this route, and soon afterwards, according to Spindler, *UB-96* also went through. A signal from *U-90* on the 28th reported destroyer patrols in the area.

U-boats continued to pass through the centre of the Northern Barrage. A signal from *UB-89* on October 19 showed that she had encountered no obstacles while crossing on the surface from 1479E. to 1711E. Nothing could be done about this route, however, since it lay between two groups of mines in Area A. The last minelaying excursion, completed on October 26, was therefore intended to close a gap about six miles wide between Area A and Area C. Another excursion was planned for early November but, as the American official history states, 'further mining would have been an unnecessary waste of time, effort, and material'.

During the year 1918 there could be no question of sending down divers or using sweeps to search for wrecks in the storm-tossed and mine-infested waters of the northern North Sea. In the following summer, however, the fields were swept up, and at that point sweepers encountered one 'certain' U-boat wreck and two other 'probables'. The first, as we have seen, must have been that of *UB-127*, sunk in Area B on September 9. The other two obstructions were found in 592030/0055E. (=1474E.) and

592930/0044E. (=1415E.). If these were U-boat wrecks, as they almost certainly were, they can be identified. Both of them lay in Area A.

Six submarines certainly or almost certainly perished in the Northern Barrage, and one more may have done so. (1) *UB-127* has already been accounted for. (2) *U-92* must have been sunk in Area B, and if *UB-113* was sunk in the Barrage at all, she was lost in the same area. (3) The routes taken by *U-156* and *UB-123* led them to the east of the locations in which the obstructions were found. (4) This means that the two obstructions can only have been the wrecks of *U-102* and *UB-104*. Accepting the Admiralty's identification of the wreck in 592030/0055E. as *U-102* (a point stated in the American official mine history), we are forced to conclude that the other one must have been *UB-104*.

IV

U-BOAT OPERATIONS

A. Minelayers Westward

'AT THE END OF February, 1917', writes Admiral Jellicoe in *The Crisis of the Naval War*, 'it was estimated that the enemy had a total of about 130 submarines of all types available for use in home waters, and about 20 in the Mediterranean. ... Of this number some 50 per cent were vessels of the mine-laying type.' It was obvious that the unrestricted campaign against British and neutral shipping would be carried on by the minelayers to an extent unheard of before. Such, indeed, was the case. During the month of April no fewer than 515 mines were swept up off the British coast, but at the loss of one minesweeper almost every day. April marked the peak of the minelayers' activity, and thereafter it declined almost steadily. The decline was due almost entirely to the effectiveness of the anti-submarine campaign and the consequent losses of the minelaying UC-boats. Sixty-three U-boats in all were lost during the year 1917, and of these thirty-two were UC-boats - almost all of them sunk in the waters around the British Isles.

The first minelayer sunk in the year 1917 was *UC-46*, homeward-bound on February 8 after laying mines in the Bristol Channel. She made the mistake of surfacing east of Dover when only half a mile away from the destroyer *Liberty*, which immediately worked up to 24 knots and rammed her just forward of the conning tower. When the destroyer docked it was clear that she had cut into the submarine's hull to a depth of four feet. She cannot have made any signal, and the note in German records to the effect that about three hours later she was 'proceeding in via Middelkerke Bank' must be based on confusion with her sister submarine *UC-26*.

Another minelayer perished later the same day. This was *UC-39*, engaged in shelling a steamer off Flamborough Head when the destroyer *Thrasher* came on the scene. The U-boat dived, but a depth charge brought her to the surface; under gunfire she stopped and surrendered. Three officers, twelve men, and two British prisoners were rescued. The destroyer tried to take her in tow, but she subsequently sank. The surrendered log book contained little of interest; it ended with *UC-39*'s attack on *Ida* on the morning when she was sunk. (For the later discovery of her wreck, see Chapter 2).

During the rest of February scraps of information could be pieced together in regard to several other minelayers. A signal intercepted from *UC-24* in the Channel on February 2 could be related to the sinking of *Ellavore* and *Havgard* four days later: survivors observed that the U-boat was marked '*UC24*'. The dossier was completed on the 9th when off the Portuguese coast a submarine stopped the steamer *Eldrid* and gave her master a certificate signed 'K/L Willich'. Since Willich was known to be in command of *UC-24*, it was fairly clear that this submarine was bound for the Mediterranean. Another U-boat could be identified on February 15, when submariners used the boat of *Marion Dawson* in order to place time bombs on board ship. They left a light bulb with the following mark in the boat.

UC-21

13

Signals intercepted by the French were incompletely identified. It was wrongly supposed that *UC-41* made a signal in the Channel on the 11th (the submarine was *UC-33*) and that *UC-36* (actually *UC-17*) was off Boulogne on the 25th. The reconstructed list of call signs was not quite correct. On the other hand, *UC-65*, north of Dunkirk on the 19th and evidently returning to Zeebrugge, was identified.

More important was a violent explosion off Sunderland on the evening of February 23. An examination vessel picked up the commander of *UC-32* and two of his crew, and three days later divers found the wreck. Fourteen mines were still in the tubes. The divers brought up one of the torpedoes.

Radio interception during March provided a little information about the minelayers. *UC-44* was in the western Channel on the 4th, back in the North Sea nine days later; an unidentified UC-boat (*UC-21*) was off Cherbourg on the 9th, Ushant on the 17th, and east of Dover on the 19th. Off Muckle Flugga in the Shetlands, *G-13* was on patrol on the 10th when she was able to torpedo an unidentified submarine at a range of 2,300 yards. Her commander saw the torpedo hit just forward of the conning tower. All that was left of the submarine was a square mile of oil on the surface, along with a few pieces of broken planking. She was later identified as *UC-43*. Three days later another UC-boat blew up on her own mines off Start Point in the Channel. The Admiralty apparently learned of her loss, like that of *UC-43*, from interrogated prisoners. They then ascribed the sinking of *UC-68* to an attack made by the submarine *C-7* off Zeebrugge on April 5. They were not in a position to know that this attack was actually made on *UB-10* and that it had no effect.

Significant information about a minelayer was finally acquired early in April, and the series of subsequent events led directly to her destruction.

On the evening of April 4 the steamer *Hunstanton* (4,504 tons) was off Bishops Rock in the Channel approaches when she was suddenly shaken by a violent explosion. As she gradually began to sink, her crew took to the boats, and as they pulled away they could see a German submarine emerging out of the darkness and coming close to the stern to read the ship's name. At the top of the conning tower of the U-boat there were glowing flames like a volcanic eruption, presumably coming from a fire below. The next morning, when the boats were brought in to port, the Admiralty were immediately informed.

Intelligence had already been analysing a signal which the submarine *UC-30* had made at 2200 that evening, only half an hour after *Hunstanton* was torpedoed and in approximately the same location. It is not clear whether or not the signal could be read; it was certainly received at home and gave a location 25 miles south-west of the Scillies. Because of severe engine damage *UC-30*, which had just come out through the Dover Straits, was heading for home.

British listening stations picked up another signal from her at 0600 on the 5th and this showed that she was heading north toward the Irish coast. By noon the next day she was south of Fastnet, evidently taking the northerly route home. During the following week nothing was heard from her, but on the morning of April 13 the station at Barra Head at the southern tip of the Hebrides picked up her call letters again. She had taken a week to sail about five hundred miles and was therefore making about three knots. That evening at 2140 Barra Head intercepted another signal, this time a rather lengthy one made by *U-50*. The message, at least partly deciphered by the British, read as follows: '062 beta IV West Coast. Have sunk 1,460 tons. This morning met *UC-30* homeward, west of St. Kilda, because of engine damage can make only three knots. Took provisions on board. *UC-30* did not lay mines ...*U-50*.'

In his log Berger of *U-50* recorded his meeting with *UC-30* after the exchange of recognition signals. The minelayer was operating on only one engine, badly damaged; the other was completely useless and neither could be repaired at sea. Stenzel, her commander, assured Berger that he would get home, however. He had enough fuel and oil for twenty days, though he needed provisions, which *U-50* supplied, and asked Berger to inform Heligoland that he had not laid his mines.

The intercepted signals suggested to the Admiralty that it would take *UC-30* about another week to reach the northern North Sea, and they eagerly watched for the signal which would announce her arrival and her request for an escort through the Bight minefields. On the evening of the 18th their patience was rewarded, and that night surface layers deposited 235 mines directly across the 'Weg Blau' which U-boats took when passing near the Danish coast. The next night *UC-30* was still in the North Sea, finally

6.The rudders and propeller shafts of *UC-48* being dismantled at Ferrol, Spain.

7.The interned *UC-48* being towed out of dry-dock at Ferrol.

8. Views of the interned *UC-56* at Santander, Spain.

establishing radio contact with her base from a location 75 miles west-south-west of Lindesnes. She had not laid her mines but had sunk one steamer of about 3,000 tons and one sailing vessel. She expected to meet her escort on the 21st.

Because of bad weather the British minelayers had been unable to operate on the night of the 19th, but on the night of the 20th they laid no fewer than 1,308 mines, in a highly irregular pattern, just to the south-west of the previous field. Another field of 235 mines was laid to the north on the night of the 22nd. UC-30 did not meet her escort on the 21st nor did she answer the radio calls made to her. The only trace of her that was ever found consisted of the corpses of two of her crew, washed ashore on the Danish coast in June. Evidently she struck the new mines along her route homeward.

Within a month or two the Admiralty obtained 'information from German sources' which indicated that about April 19 UC-30 'struck a mine in the North Sea and was lost'. Indeed, the fact of her loss was already evident from the radio calls made to her and from a signal made by U-62, outward-bound on April 22 and reporting not having sighted UC-30. Echoes of the loss were heard in the report of a prisoner taken from UC-29 in June. He said that all engineer officers had been ordered to check their Diesels' cylinders because a U-boat had failed to return after all twelve cylinders stopped. It was evident that the missing boat was UC-30.

Gröner gave the location of her loss as 5725/0434E. There were no mines in this location; he must have relied on the grid square from which she sent her last message. Post-war British analyses more probably place the spot in 5519/0710E. - in the minefield laid on April 20 and on the route from which U-62 reported.

The German command was so strongly impressed by the loss of UC-30, and also by the discovery of further British fields in the Bight, that in mid-May they laid two defensive minefields near Horns Reef on the Danish coast. The result was disastrous. In heavy fog on the night of May 14 U-59 was being escorted out when she lost her bearings, ran on to the German mines, and went down with most of her crew. This news too reached London at once, for German records include signals from German minesweepers reporting the event.

On May 8 another minelayer was sunk, this time off Calais as she was heading for Zeebrugge on the surface. The two survivors who were picked up provided details about her sinking and about her final cruise.[1]

The UC-26 was sighted at 0100 by three British destroyers, and on account of her slowness in diving she was rammed by H.M.S. *Milne* just forward of the conning tower. Water entered, but not very rapidly, and

1 L. Doughty, Jr., in *U.S. Naval Institute Proceedings* 61 (1935), p. 354.

no gas was noticed. She sank to the bottom in 150 feet of water. Soon afterward a depth charge exploded near by, extinguishing all the lights. An effort was made to blow the tanks and come to the surface, but the attempt failed. Whether this failure was due to the damage caused by the ramming or the depth charge was not determined. The water rose inside the boat, and the crew turned to efforts at escape. Attempts were made to open a hatch, but the pressure of water outside prevented. The captain then said, 'It is no good', and ordered three cheers for the Kaiser, which were duly given. A petty officer meanwhile had the more practical idea of turning on compressed air into that compartment. This soon raised the pressure inside to equal that outside, and the hatch was opened without difficulty. A number of the crew managed to get out and reach the surface, but only two survived, both of whom had ascended slowly. The death of the others from excessive air pressure in their lungs was probably caused by too rapid an ascent or too slow venting of the air in their lungs.

A diary carried by one of the prisoners revealed that *UC-26* had left Bruges at 1845 on April 30. The next morning she had been bombed by French planes west of Berck, while on May 2-3 she had laid her mines off Le Havre, Ouistreham and Cherbourg. During her cruise she had sunk one small steamer and damaged two others off Le Havre, but much of the time she had been lying on the bottom in the Seine estuary. On May 7 she began her return.

During June the cruise of the minelayer *UC-75* could be rather clearly delineated from intercepted radio signals. She was first heard from at 0700 on the 6th in the eastern Channel, evidently reporting a safe passage westward through the Straits of Dover. Her next signal, at 0200 on the 9th, showed that she was continuing westward, presumably towards the Irish coast; a new field was due off Queenstown about then. On the 12th she laid her mines off Queenstown, and they were promptly swept up. Later the same day the decoy sailing vessel *Prize* was able to attract her attention but could not damage her with gunfire. On both the 12th and the 13th *UC-75* observed many American destroyers on patrol but easily avoided them, making another signal from the Channel approaches at 0230 on the 15th. Soon afterwards she had exhausted her torpedoes and began her return, signalling from the Channel at 0400 on the 21st and, after negotiating the Straits, at 0400 on the 22nd. That day she sighted three submarines in the southern North Sea. Presumably they had been sent to intercept her, but they had no success.

Meanwhile on June 7 the decoy steamer *Pargust*, on watch west of Dingle Bay, Ireland, where German mines had recently been found, was torpedoed by a U-boat which finally surfaced in order to interrogate the crew. Under heavy gunfire from the decoy, the submarine tried to escape on the surface, but soon rolled over and sank, leaving two survivors. The watch officer spoke English but would give no information; a machinist's mate had little English but talked rather freely. *UC-29* had left Heligoland May 29 and was due back about June 19. She had sunk two sailing vessels, using a torpedo on one of them. Her second torpedo had passed under a British destroyer, while the last one had damaged *Pargust*. The U-boat had dived in order to escape, but a 'false move' had brought her to the surface again.

The prisoners also stated that *UC-29* had come out from Germany to the north of Scotland and had not laid her mines. The first statement was suspect, in view of radio intercepts from other minelayers; the second was obviously false, since three of the mines laid by *UC-29* were swept up in Dingle Bay six days later.

The machinist's mate must have been the prisoner who reported that the larger UC-boats were experiencing a good deal of engine trouble. During May he had been ordered to inspect the cylinders with care after another boat had failed to return: all twelve of her cylinders had failed. (The interrogators rightly concluded that the boat in question must have been *UC-30*.) In addition, a radio report from Bruges had just indicated that in port *UC-70* had been damaged by gunfire. Obviously this information was related to the monitor attack of June 4-5.

More significant for Intelligence was the grounding of *UC-61* near Gris Nez in a thick fog on July 26. After demolition charges were fired, the wreck and the crew were captured by a detachment of Belgian cavalry under French command. The French Intelligence report is reproduced by Newbolt in slightly paraphrased language.[1]

UC-61 was commissioned in December 1916 at the Weser Yard, Bremen, but her trials and preliminary cruises were not completed until two months later. On February 25 she left Heligoland for Zeebrugge and Bruges. After this she made four cruises and was lost during the fifth. The first cruise was made without mines,[2] off the Dutch coast, and was simply a trial trip. The second took place about the middle of March, but lasted only seven days on account of serious damage incurred in running wildly from a British destroyer. At the moment when the chase began the stuffing-boxes of the U-boat's two crankshafts were not tight, and were leaking considerably. To dive in this condition was dangerous, but she had no choice.... Down she went, and in such a hurry that she reached a depth of 197 feet before she could be stopped: the flow of water from the stuffing-boxes increased

1 *A Naval History of the War 1914-1918* (London, c. 1920), pp. 263-66.
2 On this cruise (March 1-6) *UC-61* actually laid mines in '106 alpha VI', although Spindler (IV, p. 241) does not say so, perhaps because they were laid off the Dutch coast.

to a serious extent under the heavy pressure. Another panic rush brought her back to the surface with her bows up at a sharp angle: there she was greeted by a sloop, whose gunners drove her down again with all speed. This time the accumulation of water in her stern rushed forward into her bows as she dived, and her electric motors were completely fused. She rolled about under water till night...; but her commander on bringing her at last to the surface found that the motors were absolutely useless, and all he could do was to take her back to Zeebrugge. As he could not travel submerged, this was a three days' voyage: he had the luck to escape without being further attacked, but his cruise was a dismal failure. He had not fired a gun or a torpedo: he had not even laid a mine.[1]

Repairs at Ostend took six or seven weeks, for one of the motors had to be replaced, while the other was drained after unwinding the armature. Then the third cruise of *UC-61* began. According to the prisoners, 'she was barely clear of Zeebrugge when she damaged her rudder so that she had to return at once and go into dock at Ostend again'. The actual fact, however, was that she proceeded to lay mines off the Needles and Portland on April 30-May 1 and then cruised in the Channel before returning to port on May 15. The fourth cruise (June 23-July 8) was described more accurately, as were the orders for the fifth and last.

> *UC-61* left Zeebrugge for her fifth cruise at 1 p.m. on July 25. Her orders were to pass through the British barrage as best she could, to lay mines off Boulogne and Le Havre, and then to continue cruising, probably along the Atlantic coast.

The next morning at 0420 she ran aground, and an hour later customs authorities spotted her on the beach. She barely had time to make radio contact with Bruges and report the disastrous mishap, before firing explosive charges.

The prisoners also stated that while at sea the Flanders submarines rarely transmitted radio messages, though they mentioned that *UC-61* had reported her grounding to Bruges. Messages were sent to the U-boats at regular times: orders came from Bruges at 0100, 0500, 1000, 1500 and 2000 Greenwich time, and from Nauen at 2300. The cruiser *Arkona*, stationed at Emden, transmitted information at 1800. Under questioning they provided a list, essentially accurate, of the nine Flanders UB-boats and sixteen UC-boats in service, as well as another list, not quite so reliable, of the nine UB-boats and thirteen UC-boats which had been lost.

By this point it was clear enough that after a burst of activity in March

---

1 Spindler does not mention this cruise to the Channel, which took place March 17-23.

the minelayers were settling down to a rather regular routine. No fewer than 33 mines had been laid off Waterford, Ireland, during March; then the harbour was visited on April 18 and again on June 14-15. Off Queenstown mines had been laid on February 12 and March 6. The lack of a visitation in early April could be explained as due to the vicissitudes of UC-30, but then the schedule resumed with minelaying on May 3, June 12 and July 18.

On this basis it could be expected that an intruder would arrive off Waterford towards the end of July. Meanwhile the British had become aware, perhaps in consequence of the capture of UC-61, that their code for announcing mine-clearance had been broken by the Germans. One of the fields laid on June 14-15 by UC-42 off Waterford was therefore left intact, but it was announced that it had been swept. There was not long to wait. On July 31, UC-44 left Heligoland and, after passing through the Dover Straits, arrived off Waterford on the evening of August 4. She laid four mines at the western side of the harbour and then proceeded to the east to lay five more. Just after the ninth mine dropped there was a violent explosion, and the submarine sank to the bottom in about ninety feet. The commander and two others were able to get out through the conning-tower hatch, but he alone was able to keep afloat until a rowboat from the fishing village of Dunmore picked him up, an hour and a half after UC-44 sank. Soon afterwards, he was sent to London for interrogation by Major Trench at the War Office, then to Colsterdale in Yorkshire.

UC-44 had almost certainly encountered a field laid by UC-42, even though her commander had fixed his position by the lighthouses in the bay and 'during the laying... personally checked the chart work of the Chief Petty Officer Coxswain in the control-room'. During the course of his interrogation he said that he had fixed his position by the lights at Dunmore and Hook Point and then submerged in eleven fathoms. He pointed out the position on a chart in 5207/0659W. He was asked when the loss of UC-44 would probably be known at home, and he indicated that the date would be around August 22, when the submarine failed to communicate by radio. Could he read the British signals showing areas dangerous because of German mines? As an officer, he refused to answer, but the interrogator thought that he probably could.

Divers had meanwhile been rushed to the scene, and on August 6 they located the wrecked submarine. Evidently other crew members had tried to escape from the intact fore-part of the U-boat, for both the conning tower hatch and another before the deck gun were open. Only the stern was badly damaged. The divers also recovered the signal book, orders on the conduct of the submarine campaign, and the U-boat's log book.

The log book revealed that on August 3 she had twice sighted a destroyer in the Channel but had avoided it by diving. She had been able to exchange signals with UC-75 just before the destroyer went after the other submarine. (Therefore the Germans would know that *UC-44* had passed safely through the Straits of Dover.) On the afternoon of the 4th she had pursued a small steamer for a while but then tried to get her bearings for minelaying. After locating Newton Head and Hook Point near Waterford she lay on the bottom and waited for darkness. At this point the log ended.

Salvage vessels finally floated the wreck and beached it near Waterford on September 26. The radio apparatus, though immersed in sea water and oil, was carefully examined; it could transmit on wave-lengths between 300 and 820 metres and was tuned for eight different frequencies within this range.

It remains a question whether *UC-44* was destroyed by a mine laid by *UC-42* or by one of her own. The fact that the mine exploded under her stern suggests that it was one of her own. Other submarines of her class encountered similar mishaps. In any event, the sinking was extremely important not only because of the salvage of the wreck and of the documents we have mentioned but also because there were some indications as to the routes through the minefields in the Bight of Heligoland. In 1918 Admiral Scheer suggested that British minelaying successes there were due to information of this kind.

On August 21 another minelayer was sunk and then investigated, this time off the Scottish coast in the Tay Estuary. *UC-41* was laying her mines under water when three minesweeping trawlers converged upon her. She heard them coming and began her escape, but in her hurry she fouled one of her own mines and the sweepers soon found her. A German mine floated to the surface, and while one sweeper shelled it the others dropped depth charges. Oil, air, and wreckage came up, even though the U-boat's motors could be heard running for another two hours. Divers went down and explored the wreck, bringing up the deck gun and the hydrophone equipment.

In September German minelaying off Waterford and Queenstown practically came to an end, although *UC-33* laid mines off Queenstown on August 11 and to the east of Waterford on September 23. She did not return to port, for on the 26th a patrol boat rammed and sank her in the St. George's Channel. She was unable to dive rapidly because of engine trouble incurred in a net east of Waterford. Her commander, the only survivor, told his captors that he had laid his mines in the Irish Sea. He was impressed by the extent of their information. They had a list of all the U-boats and their officers, and in their conversation with him they made only one mistake. They informed him that *UC-33* had spent some time at Hamburg. Actually only the commander himself had been there, and he concluded that British agents checked hotel registers in the port. During October he was able to send a letter to Germany, but the only news he conveyed was that his boat had been sunk at the end of September - thus indicating that he had laid his mines - and that he himself was the only survivor.

As for Queenstown, large quantities of oil were sighted off the Daunt Rock Light Vessel on October 31, and two patrols dropped depth charges. Two days later divers went down and found the wreck of a submarine with the stern blown off. One of them brought up the U-boat's starboard sidelight with the number '42' on it. On the 13th a diver finally identified the submarine as *UC-42*. She had evidently laid three mines, for her forward chute was empty while the others were full. Her bow lay at the depth of 78 feet, the stern at 92 feet. All the hatches were open, thus showing that her crew had evidently tried to escape. The log indicated that she had perished on September 10.

It is highly probable that *UC-42* fouled one of her own mines and was thus blown up. It is just possible, however, that she encountered one of the mines laid by *UC-33* on August 11 in approximately the same location. We do not know that all of them were swept up. In mid-December prisoners taken off the American destroyer *Jacob Jones*, out of Queenstown, informed their interrogators that a minelaying U-boat had been depth-charged at the end of October; there were no survivors, but divers had found the wreck. Since no minelayer operated off Irish ports during October, this information, while correct, remained incomprehensible to the German interrogators.

At the end of September the British successfully played a variation on the theme which may have accounted for *UC-44*. Since February, small minelayers from Flanders had been actively fouling the waters of the Thames estuary, but occasionally, it could be observed, they would proceed a few miles to the north and lay their mines fairly close to the Kentish Knock Light Vessel. It was clear that this had happened on May 11, June 1, June 22, July 26 and August 14. On September 27 new mine-nets were laid about ten miles to the south-south-west of the Light Vessel, and that afternoon she heard the faint buzz of U-boat motors, followed by five explosions two hours later. After an hour of silence, 'suspicious sounds' began again; another half hour, and three more explosions ended the mysterious encounter.

In January the nets were endangering shipping, and when they were hauled up they contained three pieces of steel plate and a part of machinery marked 'Schmierröhre Anker Winde' - 'capstan lubricating pipe' - as well as a badly twisted German mine-sinker. Evidently a U-boat had been sunk. At the time it was supposed that she was *UC-21*, since a prisoner from *UB-81* had stated that this submarine had been lost in the southern North Sea during September, and that a headless corpse had drifted ashore from her. Actually, however, she was *UC-6* (also mentioned, though without a date, by the prisoner) - the same submarine which had laid the other fields off the Light Vessel. She had sailed on September 27 and did not return.

The autumn of 1917 brought disaster upon the minelayers from Flanders. By early November the British learned, from survivors of *UC-63* and *UC-65*, that no fewer than three other minelayers had recently been sunk, and early in December they were able to add three more. In September, it was supposed, *UC-72* had disappeared. In mid-October *UC-14* had struck a mine only six miles from Zeebrugge; the explosion could clearly be felt on shore. (Actually the date was October 3 and she hit one of five mines deposited by fast coastal motor boats on September 24.) *UC-16* and *UC-62* had also disappeared in October. To this quota should be added *UC-21* and *UC-6*. Finally, late in January prisoners taken from *UB-35* revealed the loss of *UC-51*, two or three months earlier, *UC-47* (no date), and *UC-69*, in November or December.

Sorting out the causes of these sinkings proved an almost impossible task. Because of the mention of September, it was supposed that *UC-72* had been bombed by aircraft on the 22nd of that month. Only after the war was it possible to assign the sinking correctly - to the decoy vessel *Acton* on August 20. *UC-62* was supposedly torpedoed by the British *E-45* in the southern North Sea on October 19. Actually *E-45* fired at *U-53* but missed, while *UC-62*, after laying mines discovered off St. Alban's Head (Channel) on October, perished on her way to Portland, presumably in a field of deep British mines. *UC-21*, as we have said, was thought to have been sunk off Kentish Knock; actually she disappeared after leaving Zeebrugge for the Biscay area on September 13. It was wrongly supposed that *UC-6* had been bombed by a British seaplane near the North Hinder on September 28. The loss of *UC-51* was ascribed to the destroyer *Firedrake* in the North Sea on November 13, whereas actually she was blown up by British mines off Start Point (Channel) on November 17- a sinking which was thought to be that of *UB-18*.

It is odd that the prisoners taken in January were the first to reveal the loss of *UC-47*, for after a U-boat was sunk to the east of Flamborough Head on November 18, divers were sent down and they recovered sea charts marking the minefields which *UC-47* had laid off Guernsey on July 16 and off Cherbourg on September 24. It is likely that these prisoners did not provide the first news of the sinking of *UC-69*. This submarine was on her way to Cherbourg on the night of December 6 when the eastward-bound *U-96* accidentally rammed and sank her with the loss of eleven men. A radio message from *U-96* must have been picked up by the British and was probably deciphered.

During the autumn of 1917 the British acquired considerable information about other minelayers from the survivors of various U-boats. Prisoners from *U-48*, sunk at the end of November, informed their captors that *UC-76* had blown up at Heligoland on May 14 and had been salved. The fore compartment had been destroyed by the explosion, but the main part of the hull and the engines were not damaged. The location of the explosion clearly showed that her cargo of mines had been involved. In addition, they stated that *UC-45* had been lost off Heligoland on September 18 and that her wreck had been found in about 22 fathoms; conceivably she had already been salved. (Actually it was not raised until April 11, 1918.)

On September 29 *UC-55* was about to lay mines off the Shetlands when she lost trim and had to be brought to the surface. As British destroyers arrived on the scene and opened fire her crew scuttled her. The prisoners taken from her insisted that their submarine had been sabotaged, for the tanks used to compensate for mines laid were already full of water. Apart from this claim, they supplied the information that during their cruise they had learned by radio that a U-boat had struck a mine near the Flanders coast but was able to make port. The news obviously referred to *U-70*.

The next loss of a minelayer took place about a month later after Admiral Bacon had sent the British submarine *E-52* out on patrol on the U-boat route north of Le Sandettié Shoal. At 0112 on November 1 she was heading west-south-west on the surface when she sighted a U-boat on the opposite course. Two minutes later she fired two torpedoes at the enemy. Both hit, and she then picked up the one survivor. About an hour earlier this submarine, *UC-63*, had informed Bruges of her impending arrival in '069 beta VI', slightly to the east of where she was sunk. When nothing more was heard from her, U-boats were sent closer to the Goodwin Sands - sometimes encountering misfortune there.

The prisoner from *UC-63* listed the units of the Flanders Flotilla and named thirteen of them which had been sunk. He stated that *U-70* was under repair at Bruges and also described the last cruise of his own submarine. She had gone out through the Straits of Dover on the surface, though forced to dive several times because of patrols, and had laid her mines off the Isle of Wight. After cruising in the Bay of Biscay, she had returned through the Straits, this time submerged, and was about sixteen miles east of the Barrage when she was sunk.

Two days later the British submarine *C-15* was on patrol in the Channel off Beachy Head when she sighted a submarine in the distance and submerged. Half an hour later she was able to fire two bow torpedoes, one of which hit the target. Five survivors, including the commander of *UC-65*, were picked up. They stated that they had left Zeebrugge on October 21 and had passed through the Straits on the surface at night, close to the British coast. They had laid mines off Le Havre on the night of October 22-23 (these mines had already been found and swept up). The periscope of *C-15* had been sighted, but Lafrenz, the commander, believed he could avoid a torpedo by zigzagging on the surface.[1] He had just put the helm over when one torpedo passed under the U-boat, scraping the hull, while the other

1 Orders recovered from the wreck of *UC-44* instructed U-boats to head towards enemy periscopes or torpedo tracks.

struck the stern and exploded.

Lafrenz also provided a good deal of information about German minelaying procedures, as American reports make plain. Included in it was his statement that 'there was little danger in laying mines in the same place in which mines had previously been laid, but . . . if he went to the same place a second time he would always make it a point to come in at the high-water mark'.[1] This comment showed that the Germans were unaware of the cause of the sinking of *UC-44* and confirmed the practice she had followed: she had laid her mines in Waterford Bay at high tide.[2]

> The German policy as to minelaying is to sow mines in the vicinity of harbours and in harbour approaches. The object of all mine-laying, as Lafrenz pointed out, is not merely to sink ships, but it is considered just as important to keep enemy mine-sweeping craft so that these vessels are not available for offensive operation. Mines are nearly always laid in slack water and in theory, according to the German officer, it is best to lay four mines off one harbour and then four off another, and so on, as the same sweeping operations are necessary to sweep up four mines as eighteen. In practice, he said that the submarine commanders are usually too anxious to get rid of their mines and so lay them in groups close to one another. It is left to the commanding officer as to where his mines are to be laid.[3]

It is fairly clear that while Lafrenz talked a good deal, he said little that would not have been fairly obvious to anyone dealing with minesweeping. Similarly his statements about the losses of Flanders U-boats provided little new information. *UB-13* under Georg Haag had been lost about Easter 1916; *UB-37* under Paul Günther in January 1917; *UB-39* under Heinrich Küstner in May; *UB-36* under Harald von Keyserlingk in June; and *UB-20* under Hermann Glimpf in July. When the British records state that this information was 'confirmed from a source which must be considered as absolutely reliable' the reference is probably to the Admiralty's own records.

Other prisoners from *UC-65* told interrogators of the losses of other submarines. They said that *UB-32* had been lost in July and mentioned the sinkings of six UC-boats. *U-10*, they said, had been lost on a mine off the Baltic coast of Sweden between March and June 1916. More recently *U-50* under Berger had been mined in the North Sea, and the commander's corpse had washed ashore on the German coast. *U-66* had also disappeared. There was ill feeling in Germany, it was stated, in regard to the sinking of *UC-26*.

1 U.S. Navy Department, *German Submarine Activities*, p. 123.

2. E. Hashagen, *U-Boats Westward* (New York, 1931), pp. 120-21.

3 Navy Department, op. cit., pp. 122-23. As a prisoner, Tebenjohannes believed that *UC-44* had been sunk by her own mine; Arnold (*UC-33*), however, criticized the policy of laying mines in regular patterns and believed that it had been responsible for the loss of *UC-44*. News of this exchange of views reached Berlin in January 1918.

Graf Mathias von Schmettow had been well liked, and it was generally believed in the German Navy that the destroyer *Milne* had intentionally avoided picking him up.

The last point was especially interesting, for it showed that details about the sinking of *UC-26* had somehow reached Germany. As a whole, the interrogation reflected the impression of openness, which Lafrenz was able to convey while, at the same time, providing little information of importance. In any event, by the time he was captured the main thrust of the minelayers' campaign against shipping had been thwarted.

As far as German minelayers were concerned, the new year 1918 opened auspiciously for the British. If their information was as reliable as usual, they knew that for use in northern waters the Germans possessed only two-thirds as many boats as they had had at the beginning of 1917, and progress in new construction was subject to many delays.

For tracing the activities of these minelayers British and French Intelligence had no new methods and could only hope that the Germans would not come up with any new tricks. Their most potent ally was the new mine barrage in the Straits of Dover, which as we shall see began to take an increasingly heavy toll during the summer months, and even earlier had compelled several minelayers to be sent to the North Sea.

It must be said, however, that as far as the Flanders minelayers were concerned the Allies had won the battle already. Three little minelayers continued active in the southern North Sea, but after *UC-50* disappeared, early in January, there were only ten of the larger UC-boats in active service. By September 1, when the Straits route was finally abandoned, there were only four UC-boats left at Bruges, all of them undergoing repairs.

The difficulties involved in tracing the minelayers' activities were considerable. Incomplete and overlapping records of mines swept up off the French and British coasts did not always indicate which mines were new and which were old. By 1918 the UC-boats had learned, and had been ordered, not to make use of radios except in emergencies, and the Nauen communiqués naturally said little about their operations.

In spite of these difficulties, their cruises were charted with considerable accuracy, although after April the French analysts stopped assigning particular fields to particular boats. Presumably they were impressed with what survivors from *UC-75*, sunk on May 31, reported. This U-boat had laid mines off the Isle of Wight, then off Cherbourg, and then off Wight again. Such a procedure made it practically impossible to trace the tracks of individual submarines.

In most areas German minelaying activities were sharply diminishing. *UC-31*, identified by a signal she made homeward-bound in the southern North Sea on February 5, laid mines off Queenstown for the last time on January 25. On February 18 and March 29, *UC-56* laid mines in the Firth of

Clyde, and on March 8 *UC-75* temporarily closed the port of Liverpool, delaying the sailing of the *Mauretania*, which had to leave the port before the transport *Leviathan* could come in. No serious damage was caused by any of these fields, and thereafter the UC-boats were used against ports to the south.

Within particular months, it could be observed; the UC-boats were sent out to the same general areas. Thus in January mines appeared along the British side of the Channel at Plymouth and Falmouth, near the Isle of Wight, and off the Royal Sovereign Light Vessel; on the French side they were found near Brest and off Barfleur near Cherbourg. In February there was a lull and no mines were found, but in March the minelaying started up again - off the Isle of Wight, the Royal Sovereign Light Vessel, Boulogne, Cherbourg and Brest. During April the minelayers returned to Plymouth and Falmouth, to the Isle of Wight, to Dieppe, to Le Havre, and to Cherbourg. May saw them concentrated toward the eastern end of the Channel: mines appeared off Boulogne and Newhaven, off Dover and the Royal Sovereign, and off Dieppe again. The eighteen mines swept up off Brest undoubtedly belonged to *UC-56*; she had laid them before interning in Spain on the 24th of the month. During June a similar pattern was repeated as mines appeared off the Isle of Wight, the Royal Sovereign, Newhaven, Brighton, Etaples, and Le Havre. By July, however, it was evident that few minelayers were still at work: their mines were found only off Le Havre and Cherbourg and, on August 1, off the Royal Sovereign.

It would appear that about 320 mines were laid off the Channel ports during the year. They produced the sinking of only eight ships (17,040 tons) and damage to three more (15,186 tons) - but at the cost of eight submarines, six of which simply disappeared, the other two being interned in Spanish ports. In these last instances the Allies were able to acquire some information.

The first case was that of *UC-48*, which arrived at Ferrol on March 23. She was put into dry dock; her propellers and ammunition were removed; and Allied agents soon provided descriptions and photographs of her (see Plates 6 and 7). There was a two-metre tear in her hull, over which a large steel plate had been bolted, and it was presumed that her commander had beached his boat at high tide in order to make such repairs.[1] Crew members described the U-boat's final cruise. She had left Zeebrugge about March 17 and had laid her mines off the Needles and elsewhere by the Isle of Wight. On the night of March 20-21 a British destroyer had found her in the Channel. Three depth charges had exploded less than fifty metres away; with her fuel tanks opened up she had lost so much oil that she could not return home and therefore headed for Spain. This 'information' was a mixture of

[1] H. Wickliffe Rose, Brittany Patrol (New York, 1937), pp. 198-99.

fact and fancy. *UC-48* had actually laid her mines off Cherbourg and near Barfleur (as the German naval attaché, Madrid, reported on March 28), and the eighteen mines swept up off the Needles after March 23 had been laid by *UC-17*. It was true that the destroyer *Loyal* had depth charged the U-boat, but she dropped two charges, not three, and observed no oil or air bubbles on the surface.

The other interned minelayer was *UC-56*, which put in to Santander on May 24. According to her report to the Spanish authorities, she had suffered simply from mechanical difficulties, which began five days after she left port. She had come in for internment because she was unable to charge her batteries. There was some confusion as to her activities at this point. According to Spindler, her orders were to lay mines off the Loire but she was unable to do so.[1] On the other hand, a Spanish officer who inspected her upon arrival reported that she had no mines on board, and eighteen mines swept up off Brest during May could have been laid by no other submarine.

During the early months of the year the larger UC-boats were sent to the British East Coast only for shakedown cruises on which they did not carry mines. In April, however, *UC-64* laid mines off Cromer and near the Inner Dowsing Light Vessel, and in May *UC-17*, too old for further Channel service, laid fields north of Lowestoft. *UC-75* sailed for the Channel on May 19, returned to Zeebrugge the next day with mechanical difficulties, and headed for the East Coast on the 22nd. After laying her mines off Outer Dowsing four days later, she was rammed and sunk by the destroyer *Fairy* on the 31st.

From January to the latter part of June the small *UC-4* and *UC-11* laid no fewer than twenty-five fields off the Shipwash Sand; the last of these was deposited by *UC-4* on June 25. The next morning the skipper of the lifeboat *Patrick* observed a violent explosion about a mile and a half to the north-east of the Sunk Light Vessel. On the spot he found a large oil patch and one man, who stated that he was the engineer of *UC-11*. His submarine had laid her mines and was homeward-bound. Divers went down the next day and found the wreck with her stern blown off. Her mines were still in the chutes, and the survivor turned out to be her commander. He had actually encountered a German mine.

After this point *UC-4* laid only two more fields before her engines broke down completely. *UB-12* undertook several more cruises but disappeared off the Thames about August 20. *UC-70* probably laid mines before being discovered off Whitby on August 28. She was lying on the bottom, exuding oil, when a patrol aircraft bombed her and the destroyer *Ouse* dropped depth charges. On September 14 divers finally found the wreck of a submarine, only one mile east of Kettle Ness. Thus ended the operations of the Flanders UC-boats.

During the year minelayers of the I Flotilla were fairly active off the Scottish East Coast; four UC-boats undertook a total of eighteen cruises in these waters, with little success but no losses.

Much more important was a special operation for which the larger minelayers were held in readiness after January 20. By March, when the operation began, only U-71 and U-80 were available, though in June U-78 completed repairs and was also sent out. The scheme was to lay an arc of mines with the Bell Rock, in the Firth of Forth, as its focal point. Should a final battle take place in the North Sea, it was expected that the Grand Fleet would have to pass through these fields.

The operation was completely frustrated by the Admiralty. Soon after March 26 a moored mine was reported awash about forty miles east of Montrose, and, after a trawler brought up another, mine sweepers sent to the area were able to destroy thirty-two more. Evidently a large minelayer of the U71-80 class had been at work. The purpose of the minefield remained obscure, but during April two more fields were discovered in the vicinity. As Dorling writes, they 'were duly plotted on a large chart in the Minesweeping Division at the Admiralty'.[1]

The Assistant Director of minesweeping, Commander H.M.J. Rundle, was examining the chart with a pair of dividers when he made a crucial discovery. 'The first three groups of mines were precisely ten miles apart and on the arc of a circle precisely 45 miles from the Bell Rock.' According to Dorling, Rundle exclaimed, 'I'll bet we find the fourth batch of mines ten miles from the third on the arc of the same circle'. He added, 'They'll probably be laid on such and such a date'.

In the May report of the Anti-Submarine Division of the Naval Staff the matter was put more restrainedly. 'This area [east of Montrose] is believed to consist of a series of fields laid by large submarines carrying 36 mines, and it is therefore probable that two cargoes have already been laid, and further additions must be expected till the area reaches the limit at which it will begin to interfere with the enemy's passage to and from his bases.' Seventy-two mines had been destroyed during the fourth week of April, though not all were in these waters.

Late in June 'a further extension - to the southward and eastward - of the field previously laid was located. The enemy appears to be concentrating all his larger minelaying submarines here; 120 mines have been cleared from open waters and about 30 more from coastal areas since the beginning of the operation in December last.' In fact, on June 4 U-80 had returned to the northern end of the arc, while on June 20 and 21 U-71 and U-78 extended the wall to the south. Similarly in July U-80, U-78 and U-71 worked at the

1 Dorling, *Swept Channels*, pp. 131-32. These were the fields laid by *U-80* on March 26 and April 20 and by *U-71* on April 27.

9. The conning tower of *UC-56*, behind is Taileres de Corcho Hijos.

10.*UB-105* stranded on the Danish coast, April 6, 1918. Official U.S. Navy photograph, taken by an Allied agent.

11. View of *U-39* interned at Cartagena, Spain. Official U.S. Navy photograph, taken by an Allied agent.

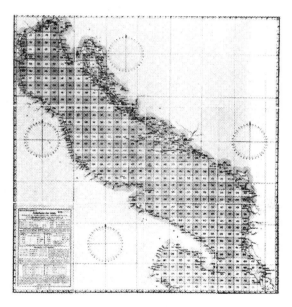

12. German Naval grid chart of the Adriatic Sea, in use before July 1918. Photograph by permission of the Heeresgeschichtliches Museum, Vienna.

southern end of the minefield. *U-71* observed sweepers already at work clearing the field just laid by *U-78*, but apparently she did not suspect how thorough their work was. The British report states that

> the extensions made were across the route of exit and entry for H.M. ships using the Firth of Forth. His policy, therefore, developed in the direction anticipated. A broad channel was cleared for fleet purposes, and the situation was quickly in hand.

In mid-August 'mines were located as expected off the East Coast of Scotland', and the last field was found between October 20 and 26. Meanwhile UC-boats of the I Flotilla were laying further fields to the north-west and the south-west of the great arc - which had ceased to exist.

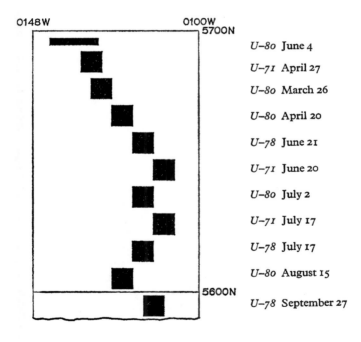

THE BELL ROCK ARC, 1918

Towards the end of the war the only real threat posed by German minelayers was presented by a few submarines operating off the American coast and by a new minelayer or two. The Admiralty were aware that one of these, *U-117*, had been sent to American waters, and they closely followed the movements of her sister, *U-118*. As early as September 2 they picked up a signal from her as she headed south along the Irish coast. Two days later another signal showed that she was entering the Bay of Biscay, and it was thought likely that she would lay her mines between the Gironde and the Spanish frontier. Information dated August 23 showed that the Germans believed that American troops were being landed both at Bordeaux and at St. Nazaire. On the evening of the 8th a signal located her off Belle Isle, and further signals on the 11th showed that she was now moving to the north-west. It was concluded that she had laid her mines off Bordeaux during the interval.

In actual fact, she had originally been ordered to lay them off Bordeaux, but on the 6th a signal from Nauen ordered her to report on traffic observations in the Biscay area and presumably - since she laid her mines off St. Nazaire and Belle Isle on the 7th - not to operate to the south. By the 16th she had moved westward; a signal was intercepted after she had encountered a convoy and had sunk the steamer *Wellington*. Nothing more was heard from her, and the French assumed that she reached her base at the end of September. When the steamer *Arca* was sunk north-west of Ireland on October 2, the loss was ascribed to an unidentifiable UB-boat operating in the vicinity. Actually *U-118* sank *Arca* and returned to Brunsbüttel only on October 14.

In October signals were picked up from two more minelayers. *U-157*, north-west of Lisbon on October 16, had mined that port three days earlier. On the 18th she signalled again as she began her homeward voyage. On the 22nd the new *U-119* was in the Bay of Biscay west of La Rochelle, presumably acknowledging the recall order, which had been sent out to all U-boats. It was uncertain whether or not she had laid any mines, for none were found off Biscay ports. It later turned out that she had not laid any.

The German minelaying activities, begun so auspiciously in early 1917, had finally ended with almost total failure, though this point is not reflected in the highly inflated statistics provided at the end of the German official history.[1] A more adequate picture is given in a British Admiralty report which was transmitted to the French in August 1918. It contained a survey of the mine problem from February 1917 onwards.

At first the Germans had continuously laid mines along coastal traffic

---

1 According to a table in Spindler, V., p. 346, the 'stated sinkings' due to mines in 1918 amounted to 509,890 tons, while the 'proved sinkings' were only 117,125 tons. Even the latter figure is too high, however, for the total tonnage indicated by Spindler's own narrative amounts to 81,949. The figure of 762,520 tons sunk by mines in 1918 (p. 352) is absolutely false. Admiral Spindler was not himself responsible for these figures.

routes, carefully placing them so as not to jeopardize their own later operations and therefore often relying on fixed navigational points either on land or at sea. The British answer was to sweep all areas constantly. In consequence, minelayers could safely return to locations where they had laid mines ten to fourteen days earlier. At this point they were laying nearly one field a day. British sweeping finally brought the East Coast routes under control, but the Germans then laid mines in more distant zones. When sweeping was provided all around the British Isles mine damage was considerably reduced. This was the situation in the autumn of 1917.

At this point the Germans changed their tactics. They stopped grouping mines systematically and laid them in diverse areas, often making use of delayed-action mines. The British were able to reduce the losses of minesweepers only by making new studies of the effects of the tides on mines and sweeping alike. They also rearranged shipping traffic and increased the use of Otter gear to cut mine cables. Sinkings declined as more U-boats were destroyed. The change was due to defensive minefields, hunter flotillas, and the better organization of the coastal air command - along with closer liaison.

By this time - the summer of 1918 - the U-boats were running heavy risks in coastal waters. Recently they had changed their tactics again, now using the 'Hindenburg system' of concentrating the attack on single vulnerable points. Innovation in the past had been chiefly operational. In the future the mine itself would probably be altered, since so far the only novelties had been the delayed-action mine and improved mine-sinkers.

This sensible analysis ends on a sober note doubtless due to the imminent commissioning of a whole new class of UC-boats. By August 28, however, fifty of the first 79 of these boats had been lost. Presumably the new ones would have turned out to be as vulnerable as their predecessors.

B. Special Operations: Ireland and Finland

At the beginning of the war the German government realized that Great Britain had an Achilles heel in Ireland, long restive under British rule, and that it might be possible to support an Irish rebellion. In November 1915, and again the next month, the Admiralty Staff stated their objections to using U-boats for supplying arms and ammunition in Tralee Bay on the west coast, but by the end of February 1916 they had prepared a scheme for using trawlers. Meanwhile Count von Bernstorff, the German ambassador in Washington, had cabled Berlin via neutral lines that the revolution in Ireland would definitely begin on Easter Sunday, April 23. In March, on behalf of Irish revolutionary leaders in America, he asked for 25-50,000 rifles, some machine guns and field artillery, and the services of some German officers. It was suggested that Sir Roger Casement, an Irish leader then in Germany, should remain there. Finally, on March 23 the General Staff asked the Foreign Office to inform Bernstorff as follows:

> Instead of three trawlers, a small steamer of 1,400 tons cargo will come. Lighters will have to be held in readiness. Anticipated that from April 8th onwards at 2400 there will be sent from Nauen, as introduction to the press service, the word FINN as sign that expedition has started. The word BRAN will be given if hitch occurs; a date after BRAN signifies that arrival of steamer has been postponed to this day. Wave length 4,800 metres. Advise experiment beforehand with Nauen reception.

On April 9 the steamer *Libau*, disguised as the Norwegian *Aud*, sailed from Lübeck with a cargo of 20,000 captured Russian rifles, four million rounds of ammunition, 10 German machine guns and a million rounds, and 400 kilograms of explosives. Sir Roger Casement finally persuaded the Germans that he too had to go to Ireland, and on the 12th he sailed with two companions aboard *U-20*. When the U-boat's diving rudder suffered damage she had to return to Heligoland, where she transferred her passengers to *U-19* on the 15th. On the night of the 20th *Libau* reached Tralee Bay but failed to make contact either with the Irish land forces or with Casement, who went ashore from *U-19* early the next morning.

Forewarned by intercepting the communications between Washington and Berlin, the British had been waiting for the arrival of the arms and of Casement himself. 'Hall was able to follow every move of the plotters', James wrote. *Libau* was intercepted south of Tralee Bay and forced to proceed to Queenstown, where she blew herself up outside the harbour. Casement was arrested on April 22 and hanged on August 3.

Karl Spindler, captain of the *Libau*, much later found three signals in the German records, which marked the end of the expedition. Two came in on April 23 and, from Rotterdam and Christiania, announced the sinking of the Norwegian steamer *Aud* off Daunts Rock, Queenstown. The third exhibits considerable confusion. It was sent from Bruges and Nauen to *U-19*. 'Expedition betrayed, suspend operations immediately, if possible inform steamer.' This signal was to be made on April 24 - although it was already known that *Libau* had been sunk. 'On April 24', Spindler wrote, 'Berlin must have had conclusive evidence of treachery.' One would suppose that it was provided by the signals of April 23. There is no reason to imagine that the Germans were aware of the extent of British surveillance.[1]

Though the Easter uprising had ended in disaster, the Germans continued to foment trouble in Ireland. On December 31 the Nauen radio

[1] Full details in K. Spindler, *The Mystery of the Casement Ship* (Berlin, 1931).

informed Count Bernstorff, the ambassador in Washington, that large quantities of arms would be shipped to Galway and Tralee between February 21 and 25, 1917. Irish pilots were to be sent to Germany to assist in the operation. Bernstorff's line of communication, however, was abruptly broken at the beginning of February as the United States reacted to the unrestricted U-boat campaign against shipping, and the arms did not arrive.

In addition, on February 9 the British captured the prize crew of *U-43* and found a diary one of them was carrying. In it was the notation that February 6 was 'the last day of rendezvous with the boat in Tralee'. The submarine had come chose to the coast and had even entered Tralee Bay, but had failed to make contact.

Late in October plans were made for another uprising in Ireland, and the German minister in Berne cooperated enthusiastically. The Admiralty Staff in Berlin, however, were unwilling to participate, chiefly because they were given only three weeks to plan and act.[1]

Another scheme, this time in April 1918, worked out even less satisfactorily. The Germans were planning to send arms by U-boat during May, and on April 6 *U-19* sailed for the Bay of Galway, landing an Irish agent on Crab Island during the night of the 11th-12th. At 0240 on the 12th she signalled that she had accomplished her task. Directional interception placed her just west of Galway Bay, and it could easily be inferred that her task had been related to some activity there. In fact, the agent was soon arrested and the plan had to be abandoned.

Greater success attended the German efforts to support revolution in Finland, late in 1917. All six minelayers of the Kurlhand Flotilla were actively engaged during October, but in November one of them was lost. On November 12, *UC-57* sailed from Danzig in order to transport six men of a Finnish battalion, as well as arms and ammunition, to the vicinity of Helsingfors. Her mission was accomplished on the 17th, when her captain told Finnish officers that on the way out he had scraped mine cables. On the night of the 18th *UC-57* lay on the bottom before heading back to Danzig. The next day Danzig radio sent her a warning message: her voyage was being observed by the enemy. It is not certain that she received this signal, for she did not arrive at Danzig. The Danzig radio made repeated calls for her to report her position, on November 24, 25, 27 and 30, and even on December 7. She had probably encountered the Russian mines again.

On December 10, since naval operations against Russia in the Baltic were at an end, the Kurland Flotilla was disbanded and the five remaining minelayers were sent to join the High Seas Fleet and the Flanders Flotillas.

1 Correspondence in Spindler, op. cit., pp. 268-71.

C. The Mediterranean U-Boats

As far as the history of Intelligence is concerned, submarine warfare in the Mediterranean and eastward began with a striking German success. Since the spring of 1915 the Allies had been trying to force the passage of the Dardanelles and drive a wedge between Turkey and the Central Powers. Allied submarines were active in the eastern Mediterranean, and in May the German submarine *U-21* arrived on the scene, torpedoing two British battleships. In spite of heavy losses both French and British submarines were able to reach the Sea of Marmara and interfere with Turkish traffic.

Towards the end of October the French *Turquoise* spent a week in the Sea, on patrol in company with the British *H-1*, *E-12* and *E-20*. On the 30th, bound for her base, she ran aground near Akbasch, just north of the Dardanelles, and when she surfaced she found herself under the guns of a Turkish battery. Her captain showed the white flag, and ship was abandoned so precipitously that an alarm was still sounding when the Turks came aboard. No one had troubled to destroy *Turquoise's* confidential papers.

The consequences are reflected in the orders given *UB-14*.

Assignment: attack on enemy submarines in the Sea of Marmara. Reports on enemy: 1. An enemy submarine on November 3 and 4 off Mudania. According to information from *Turquoise*, presence of *E-12*, *E-20* and *H-1* in Sea of Marmara probable. 2. Rendezvous of enemy submarines between 0900 and 1000 and 1600 and 1700 in 2810/4045N. Operation: *UB-14* to sail at midnight November 4 and to be escorted out of the Bosporus by a gunboat. Transport of *Turquoise* from Palatia to Constantinople is to be expected on November 5.

Return: stand 2 sea miles east of the island of Proti November 7 at midnight; a gunboat will be waiting as escort. Light-signal B will be answered by a white star.

(signed) Souchon.

E-12 had actually returned to port on October 25, but of course she was not aware of the fate of *Turquoise*.

At 1600 on the 5th *UB-14* was waiting submerged at the rendezvous when her commander sighted an enemy conning tower. An hour and a quarter later he was in position, and his torpedo hit the target. He surfaced in order to pick up two officers and six men from *E-20*, returning to Constantinople that night. Two days later he went out again after a seaplane sighted another submarine in the rendezvous area, but this time he found nothing. After the Dardanelles expedition was abandoned, the U-boats had no further targets in the Sea of Marmara.

During 1916 the scene of action, and of Intelligence initiative, shifted to the west. The role of radio interception became more important. In the eastern Mediterranean, however, it had its difficulties, as H. C. Hoy pointed out.[1]

It was one of my duties to chart the movements of the German submarines on information supplied by 40 O.B. through their wireless intercepts. On their various journeys via the north of Scotland, when they were heading for the west coast of Ireland or the Bristol Channel, it was a comparatively easy matter to guess their destination and locate them. But when they were dodging about in the Ionian and Aegean Seas, they proved slippery customers indeed. They were literally here to-day and gone to-morrow. 40 O.B. might report that a U-boat was, for instance, off Andros, but though her wireless was working all the time neither we nor the Germans themselves could say where she might be to-morrow. The hundred and one possibilities of the Grecian Archipelago defeated us.

He tells of trying to track a U-boat 'known to be making for Corfu' and finally located off Rhodes. Only later it was found out that she had passed Cephalonia, Zante, Cerigo, Andros, Ikaria, and so on. A one eyed Greek agent had been supplying 'inaccurate and misleading reports' which brought Admiral Fisher to the boiling point. 'To hell with that one-eyed Greek!' he exclaimed.

Even when signals were intercepted and boats were identified the results were not very satisfactory. The French records for November 1916 list only two Mediterranean intercepts, one on the 3rd probably from *U-32* arriving in the Mediterranean after a cruise from Emden, the other on the 30th from a U-boat not identified at all but possibly *UC-20*, also bound for Cattaro. Two more are listed for December: these came from *U-52* and *U-47*, both heading for Cattaro after voyages from Germany. For January 1917, however, no Mediterranean intercepts are listed. Indeed, as late as July 1918 the Admiralty had made no systematic analysis of the call signs used in the Mediterranean.

In March 1917 two significant signals were intercepted from *U-64* - the first at 2200 on the 19th from a location 70 miles south, 75° west of San Pietro, Sardinia; the second at 2200 on the 21st from a similar location. The purpose of the first signal was clear enough. On the afternoon of the 19th the 18,400-ton French battleship *Danton* had been torpedoed and sunk southwest of Sardinia, with the loss of 296 men. The message sent that evening was obviously a report of the sinking, transmitted to the cruiser *Arkona* at Emden. According to Moraht it was made so that newspaper extras could

1 Hoy. pp. 74-75.

133

announce the sinking the next noon. The second signal identified the battleship more precisely. At the time of the sinking, she could be identified only as one of the *Danton* class; on the 21st, however, Moraht had begun his return and passed through the area again, picking up a seaman's chest from the wreckage and finding letters in it which showed that the ship was *Danton* herself. That night he transmitted this new information to *Arkona*.[1]

Other signals intercepted around this time showed only that a few U-boats, most of them unidentifiable, were arriving at Cattaro from Germany.

On June 11 another important signal was picked up, this time from *UC-52*. Engine trouble was compelling her to put in for repairs at Cadiz on her way from Germany to the Mediterranean. Another signal on June 29 at 0230 marked her departure. Naturally the British were not entirely dependent upon interception for information about her.[2]

> The progress of the repair was carefully watched by our agents at Cadiz, and when on the 27th they reported that she was ready to sail, our own submarine *E-38* went out and lay off the port to catch her. The U-boat slipped out two nights later when it was very dark and managed to get by *E-38* without being sighted. A sweep by four torpedo boats and four motor launches from Gibraltar also failed to locate her, and she reached the Adriatic safely, having carefully refrained from attacking any merchant ships.

Intelligence had provided the requisite information; the failure was operational.

Six signals intercepted during July were of unequal value. Three were ascribed to *U-47* - wrongly, since she was undergoing repairs from June 4 onwards. Actually they were made by *UC-25*, which announced her arrival south of Italy on the 1st and her successful laying of mines on the 4th. Two days later she was back in the Adriatic because of engine trouble. The other three signals could not be identified.

The French records mention only one signal picked up during August and September; this came from '*U-63*', north-west of Sicily on September 20. The ascription was evidently wrong, for *U-63* was in the Atlantic west of Gibraltar. Not until the end of October was a message of any significance intercepted.

On October 31, according to Newbolt, 'it was reported from the direction-finding stations at Alexandria and Port Said that two submarines were on the Palestinian coast'. This information was passed on to the British forces attacking Gaza, and 'the patrol vessels kept a specially sharp lookout'.[3]

1 R. Moraht, *Werwolf der Meere: U64 jagt den Feind* (Berlin, 1933), pp. 61-62.

2 Newbolt, *Naval Operations*, IV, p. 309.

3 Ibid., V, p. 79. The commander of the Pola Flotilla noted that 'a few days before *UC-34* was to be sighted there the enemy undertook a sharper lookout' (Spindler, IV, p. 484).

The lookout was a little premature, for on October 30 signals had been intercepted from an unidentified submarine (probably *UC-34*) in 3034/1830E. and from *UC-38* in 3736/2030E. Since neither location can be called 'on the Palestinian coast', it is evident that what Alexandria and Port Said actually picked up consisted of the orders transmitted to these two U-boats by the German radio station at Nauen.

Early in November both submarines arrived off Gaza and Ascalon. *UC-34* operated there without result during the week beginning November 4; *U-38* arrived on the 10th, making a signal at 0300 on the 11th and torpedoing a destroyer and a monitor that afternoon. By the 13th she had headed for home and sent an intercepted message from 3422/2655E., presumably reporting her achievements.

Seven signals were picked up during December, but they showed only that *UB-66* was arriving off Cattaro from Germany on the 6th (according to Spindler she reached Cattaro on the 10th) and that *U-65* was returning from a cruise on the 10th. Three signals north of the Otranto Straits on December 12 were ascribed to 'UB-c', but apparently nothing could be made of them. In all probability they came from the outward bound *UB-49*, reporting an attack made on her by an enemy submarine.

The most detailed information acquired about Mediterranean U-boats during 1917 seems to have concerned the new UB-boats which were being sent out from Germany. Between September 9 and October 6, while *UB-49* was interned at Cadiz, agents were able to learn that she had left Germany about August 25 and had sunk five ships of 11,859 tons en route, damaging another one of 5,646 tons. After she escaped from Cadiz and reached Cattaro nine days later, it could be calculated that her speed had been about 6.5 knots and that therefore her fuel supplies must have been running low.[1] Further information was obtained during October from a Greek captain who had been taken aboard *UB-50* in the Mediterranean on her way from Germany to Cattaro in September. He reported that each morning the U-boat went out to sea, returning towards the coast at night in order to intercept shipping. She had two torpedoes; he estimated that she had already fired seven. The cook had told him that *UB-50* had come out to the north of Scotland and usually cruised on the surface at 6 knots. (This statement must have cast some doubt on the calculations about the fuel of *UB-49*.)

At the end of the year prisoners were taken off *UC-38*, depth charged in the Aegean Sea on December 14. They discussed their cruise to the Syrian coast in November, for which they had received orders from Nauen on October 30. On their last cruise they had left Cattaro at 1600 on December 1

---

1 According to P. Ritter (ed. G. Bock), *Ubootsgeist: Abenteuer und Fahrten im Mittelmeer* (Leipzig, 1935), p. 99, she had lost 10,000 litres of oil when rammed by a British steamer on September 9. Spindler (IV, p. 351) does not mention this episode.

and had laid mines in the Gulf of Patras on December 3-5. Most of the mines were then swept up, though the French patrol boat *Tubereuse* had already been sunk by one of them on the 6th.[1]

An Intelligence summary circulated early in February 1918 was partly based on statements made by these prisoners. Certainly they did not make the statement that the Mediterranean was essentially safe for U-boats and that the Pola flotilla was a good place for rest. They did have something to say about minelaying procedures [2] and stated that U-boats in the Mediterranean sometimes refuelled at small bases on the Turkish and Syrian coasts.

Meanwhile the British kept close watch on the new U-boats which were being sent to the Mediterranean. By December 10 they were aware that UB-66 had arrived at Cattaro the day before. A signal intercepted at noon on January 10 showed that she had gone out again and was off Beirut. Thereafter, however, no clear trace of her could be observed. She probably sank the steamer *Windsor Hall* north-west of Alexandria a week later; then she disappeared.

Signals were also making it possible to follow the course of UB-68 out from Kiel into the Baltic on December 15 and west of southern Ireland on the morning of the 23rd. Other signals from the Adriatic on January 8, ascribed by the French to UB-62, must have indicated the arrival of UB-68 off Cattaro.

A signal on December 25 showed that UB-69 was being delayed by bad weather, and the next evening she had anchored off Borkum. On the 29th/30th it was plain that she had passed through the Straits of Dover, since she was in the Channel and moving westward. Apparently she was sunk off Bizerta on January 9 while attacking a convoy.

Two of the three boats sent south during December 1917 were thus immediately sunk, and there was a considerable delay while three more were completing their trials. Orders were finally issued, during February and March, for UB-70, UB-71 and UB-105 to sail for Cattaro, and as the British were aware UB-70 did sail in February but had to return because of an accident.

On April 4 UB-71 left Kiel with UB-105. The next evening, UB-105 was in the Little Belt (Danish waters) when first she was lightly rammed by UB-71 and then, half an hour later, stranded on the coast. Soon after midnight she radioed for help but heard no response. She was unable to get clear for twenty-five hours and then returned to Kiel for repairs and refuelling. The British listened to her calls with considerable interest. Before she got free an Allied agent photographed her (see Plate 10) and soon got his picture into

1 Spindler, IV, p. 485.
2 'Wherever the watch is not too strong, minelaying at night and on the surface. In patrolled areas, during the day at 15 metres and full speed.'

friendly hands. It was important for the study of the large UB-III class of submarine.

On April 13 Nauen informed *UB-71* that *UB-105* had sailed again on the 11th. Three days later the French picked up a signal from *UB-71* herself, 350 miles west of Ushant, and the British read her signal as indicating that she had encountered no difficulties thus far. On the 17th she and *UB-105* were both informed that *UB-70* had sailed from Kiel.

The signal from *UB-71* gave a clear indication as to when she might be expected to enter the Mediterranean. Newbolt describes the consequences. 'On April 17 Admiral Heathcoat Grant ordered such vessels as he could assemble for the purpose to occupy successive patrol lines near the Straits of Gibraltar, and four days later *UB-71* was sunk by motor launch No. 413 . . . whilst on her way to Pola to reinforce the Adriatic Flotilla.' Actually *UB-71* got through the Straits, only to encounter the patrols to the east. She was speeding eastward on the surface when *ML-413* switched on her bow lights to avoid a collision. The submarine abruptly changed course and dived, followed down by four depth charges. At daylight oil and wreckage were found on the surface.

This sinking left *UB-70* and *UB-105* still in transit. On the 29th Nauen informed all three boats that at Gibraltar the patrols were very strong; they should watch out for motor boats. That day *UB-70* was west of Gibraltar, where she sank the steamer *Valdivia*. *UB-105*, however, was the first to get through. On the morning of May 1 both the French and the British picked up a signal from her, giving her position and reporting having sunk 18,000 tons of shipping. She reached Cattaro on May 8.

On May 5 *UB-70* also reported, though her signal was not received at Pola. She had gone through the Straits on the Spanish side and was heading for Cattaro. Nothing more was heard from her. The wartime guess that she was depth charged on the 8th is mistaken, since the submarine attacked - and damaged - was *U-38*. *UB-70* simply disappeared.

On May 7 the German radio ordered *UB-71* to report her location, for she should have entered the Mediterranean several days earlier. Neither she nor *UB-70* made any report, and only *UB-105* reached her destination, arriving at Cattaro on the 8th.

May 8 was the day when another U-boat was sunk, this time in the Sicilian Sea. At 0900 the French interceptors picked up a signal from *UB-48* in 3607/1328E. Soon afterwards the sloop *Wallflower*, escorting a convoy from Alexandria to Marseilles, took action against a submarine. Her log contains a record of the brief encounter.

10.22 Sighted periscope ahead about 400 yards; proceeded full speed.
10.28 Let go depth charge which failed to explode. Turned to starboard.

10.33 Dropped two charges. Second explosion observed 30-50 yards from explosion of depth charges. Position: 3607N/1328E.

French Intelligence concluded that the submarine was *UB-48* and that she had been damaged by the depth charges.

What happened, however, was that the homeward-bound *UB-48* had made her signal to *U-32*, who informed her that she was following a large convoy heading to the north-west. The convoy, including a large transport, was being escorted by a British destroyer. *UB-48* could not participate, since she had fired all her torpedoes. As she left the scene she picked up an 'Allo' signal from the convoy, indicating that the presence of *U-32* had been observed. Presumably Cattaro radio picked up the signal of *UB-48*, for that afternoon *U-32* was ordered to repeat a garbled message about shipping traffic. Naturally she did not reply. On May 24 she was instructed to exercise great caution in steering for her base and in making signals.

Cattaro was concerned, it would appear, because interception seemed to have played a part in two episodes during May. On the 15th the French interceptors located *U-39* in 3705/0140E. Three days later she arranged to meet *UB-50*, somewhat to the west, and was promptly bombed by aircraft. The attack was repeated four hours later. Unable to dive because of damage, she reached Cartagena for internment that afternoon. (There she was photographed in dry-dock by an Allied agent.[1]). The other case was that of the homeward-bound *UB-52*, torpedoed on May 23 in the Adriatic to the east of Durazzo, Italy. During the previous week she had been making signals and it could only be concluded that they had been intercepted. One of them had been made on the evening of the 23rd after passing through the Otranto Straits; *UB-52* expected to reach Cattaro the next morning.

The interrogation of a survivor shows how useful interception could be. He refused to give the number of his boat, but the British first informed him that it lay between 50 and 60, then gave him a folded piece of paper. If he would state what the number was, he could open the paper and see that the British already knew it. He gave the number and then opened the paper. On it was the number 52.

In June another U-boat was followed from signals she made. On June 8 the German radio announced a meeting between *U-64* and *UC-53* for 0600 on June 13 in 3610/1730E., and on the 12th *U-64* announced her arrival there. At this point Allied forces did not attack either boat, but at midnight on June 16/17 *U-64* revealed her position near a convoy she was following. The convoy escorts, on the alert, took care of her that afternoon when she attacked the convoy.

Only two more U-boats were known to be sunk in the Adriatic or the Mediterranean. One was *UB-53*, out from Pola on August 1 and unaware

1 See Plate II.

that the Otranto Straits mine barrage had recently been extended to the east. After nearly fifteen hours under water, her commander believed that he was through the field. As *UB-53* surfaced her stern struck two mines and water began pouring in. Two hours later she sighted a destroyer and two trawlers. The crew abandoned ship. The other was *UB-68*. Off Malta on the afternoon of October 4 she torpedoed a steamer and then lost trim. She came to the surface, where gunfire from another steamer forced her to surrender. Her captain was Karl Dönitz, who was to become Grand Admiral in World War II. Naturally no information was released about the sinking, and on October 30 the British picked up a signal ordering her to report her position.

Meanwhile two more new UB-boats had reached the Mediterranean. These were *UB-128* and *UB-129*; signals from both were intercepted and read. The old *U-35* and *U-38* returned to Kiel without attracting notice. In September the Germans planned to send *UB-67* and the new *UB-130*, *UB-131* and *UB-132* out to the Mediterranean. They were to radio news of safe arrival when north of Algiers. The situation worsened rapidly, however, and these boats were retained in Germany for the final battle in the North Sea.

D. Special Operations: Spain and North Africa

In southern waters the German U-boats were often employed in special operations, and the Allies watched over these with equally special care. For instance, on June 6, 1916, *U-35* left Cattaro with orders to visit Cartagena, Spain, and deliver a letter from the Kaiser to the King of Spain, and on June 21 she accomplished this task. The frequent signals she made were picked up by stations at Bizerta, Cape Bone, and Bone, and the French sent out hunters to look for her - though she escaped from them. A little later Room 40 in London intercepted and read 'a bitter complaint from the Ambassador in Madrid that the U-boat which had reached Cartagena - though its visit had a most excellent effect on public opinion in Spain - had not brought the ciphers and propaganda material for which he had repeatedly asked.'

At the beginning of October *U-35* returned to Cartagena, this time to pick up three German officers who had been interned in Spain; one of them was Kapitän-Leutnant Wilhelm Canaris, later commander of a Mediterranean U-boat but more famous as chief of the Abwehr (counterespionage) from 1935 until it was dissolved in 1944. Once more the Allies were aware of the submarine's movements, and on October 8 planes tried to bomb her in the Adriatic. They failed, and the submarine shot down one of them.

Another cruise in February 1917 was equally closely watched. *U-35* made signals in the Ionian Sea on the 8th and near the Balearic Islands on the 17th. In the interval she had not been idle. As the French were aware, on the

14th she had disembarked two agents near Cartagena, and soon afterwards the Spanish had discovered buoys floating off Cape Tinoso. These, it was found, marked the location of cases of explosives, along with secret correspondence for German agents in Spain. According to James, 'this led to an angry protest by the Spanish Government, who believed the explosives were for use against their property'. Actually they were not aimed at Spain but at other neutrals. A letter to a German agent in America was intercepted during February and its text, quoted by Yardley, shows that similar plans were under way elsewhere.

> Advise immediately where U-boat or sailing boat material sacks can be sunk on American coast - perhaps between New York and Cape Hatteras. Position must be free of currents. ... Water depth not more than 20 metres. ... The marking of sinking buoys is successfully carried out in Spain.

Apparently real success was actually achieved neither in Spain nor in America.

Meanwhile the Political Section of the German General Staff was trying to create trouble for the Allies in North Africa. As early as November 1915 *U-35* had been sent to Bardija in Libya, transporting ten Turkish officers and a small cargo of munitions. That December her sister submarine *U-38* sailed for the same location with the ex-consul Dr. Edgar Pröbster, a Turkish major, two Arab chiefs, and a cargo including 315 rifles, 93,000 cartridges, and 1,000 pistols. She also towed *UC-12*, a converted minelayer with a similar cargo, part of the way. On December 14 she put her cargo ashore at Bardija. Twelve days later *U-34* arrived there with more equipment, followed by *U-38* on February 10. In April *U-21* was sent to the coastal waters west of Tripoli with a mission including Oberleutnant Freiherr von Todenwarth, who was to remain active in the area until the end of the war. Heavy surf, however, and uncooperative Arab leaders prevented any landing from taking place, and von Todenwarth did not reach Libya until July, when he was landed from *U-39*. In October this submarine returned in order to pick up von Todenwarth, two Turkish officers, and an Arab chief.

During October 1916 an attempt was also made to promote revolt against the French in western Morocco. On the 18th the converted minelayer *UC-20* left Heligoland with Dr. Pröbster, two officers, and a Moroccan Arab named Larbi ben Achmed el Chabuli. A month later she disembarked the personnel and also unloaded weapons, ammunition, money, and gifts for the Arabs.

From their agents among the Arabs the French had learned of the submarine's arrival, and soon after *UC-20* left the coast the French patrol *Océan* found a rubber raft, a mile off shore, with rifles, cartridges, grease, and other items. *UC-20* had expected the raft to drift ashore. The German agents watched the patrol sinking it.

The mission succeeded in making contact with Marche-Abo, brother of the agitator El Hiba (as the French soon learned) but could get no farther without supplies. They received a letter stating that the submarine would soon return, but nothing happened. Pröbster's group wandered from Assaka to the Oued Draa, and on December 18 reached Cape Juby to ask for internment from the Spanish. Five days later they were sent on to Las Palmas in the Canaries.

The French, thus forewarned, were prepared for the revolt which the sultan Hibat Allah led at the end of January 1917, and soon suppressed it. Under diplomatic pressure Larbi ben Achmed was turned over to the French, who shot him at Casablanca.

During 1917 *UC-20* was employed in the Libyan service, making six trips with supplies to the coast near Misrata. She brought war supplies and sometimes picked up cotton, rubber, and other items for the return voyage. On May 22 she brought von Todenwarth to Misrata again, and there she met *UC-73*, fresh out from Germany and also engaged in transport. During the rest of 1917 the latter submarine visited Misrata three more times. The submarines were disturbed only once. This was when *UC-20*, late in August, was attacked by an Italian torpedo boat and bombed by Italian planes - without result.

According to Dinklage, writing in 1939, the Turkish general Nourri Pasha, in command at Libya, never knew the day when a submarine would appear off the coast. For this reason he maintained Arab posts in the dunes between Misrata and Djebel el Melfa, and Allied spies apparently infiltrated them.

Dinklage's statement is wrong, for the Allies were constantly intercepting and reading the series of signals which Nauen transmitted 'für GOD' (GOD being the call letters of the receiver). The 1917 series included the following two signals.

2 October 1917. Für GOD No. 37.
UC-73 arrives about 5 October for Todenwarth. Please send some *Tinsoel* (?) and if ripe also dates for the Admiralty Staff and General Staff, together with the bill. Eichel.

Tinsoel may mean olive oil, often transported by U-boat, as were dates and even date-bread. It is odd to think of risking a U-boat in favour of luxuries for staff officers.

29 December 1917. Für GOD No. 51.

UC-20 arrives the morning of December 31.

The first day mentioned, October 5, proves to have been exact, though the second was four days too early.

During 1918 precisely the same situation obtained. Almost all the Für GOD signals were intercepted and read.

15 January 1918. Für GOD No. 6.
First:*UC-73*: her arrival time was accidentally not announced.
Second: the arrival of the next U-boat will be about mid-February.

Obviously Nourri Pasha had complained because of the fact that *UC-20* and *UC-73* had arrived off Misrata together on January 3, thus requiring a double complement of porters. The next to arrive was actually *UC-73*, which unloaded and loaded between February 18 and 26.

28 January 1918. Für GOD No. 7.
The next U-boat will bring a transmitting station. Nourri has suggested that a *Deutschland* [U-cruiser] be sent to Misrata with a large supply of artillery munitions. He asserts that he has many captured Italian guns in Tripoli, without ammunition. Please send a statement by the next boat as to how many and what kind of such guns are there and what kind of ammunition and how much is required.
18 February 1918. Für GOD No. 8.
UC-73 arrives about February 17.

UC-73 did arrive, as we said; but nothing was ever done about sending a cruiser.

A signal intercepted on March 9 had to do with another arm of the naval service. It explained that the Zeppelin *L-59* would be operating in the central and eastern Mediterranean and would be marked beneath by a black cross and on the 'arm' with Turkish flags. This signal was especially interesting because on March 10-11 the Zeppelin bombarded Naples, from the 20th to the 22nd made a cruise to the Nile Delta, and on April 7 headed for Malta. That night, however, the German submarine *UB-53* watched her burning in the sky over the Adriatic.

Later in March two signals for von Todenwarth showed that he was in regular communication with German radio, although none of the signals he made was ever intercepted. On March 23 the American Navy in Paris took part in the work of interception and sent Sims a message from Berlin to an 'unknown station probably Mediterranean Sea'. It obviously belongs to the Für GOD series, even though it is not recorded in the Army's collection. It read as follows: 'Calculate U-boat 73 [*UC-73*] arriving 24 March or 26 March.

Requesting some oil made of dates.' Because of the lack of communication between Army and Navy, not to mention between Americans and Italians, nothing was done about the signal. *UC-73* could lie off Misrata unhindered on the 25th.

About this time, however, the Germans evidently began to wonder how secret their communications were, for on April 10 and 13 GOD was informed that for security reasons the arrival of U-boats would no longer be announced.

Further signals made during the summer had to do chiefly with the transport of cargoes from Misrata and with political propaganda for circulation among the Arabs. No attempt to attack the submarines seems to have been made. On October 1, however, a more significant message was picked up. 'Mine-boat has sailed, more information orally through transport-boat.' Apparently the two boats in question were *UC-20* and *UC-73*, and early in October both were damaged by Italian patrols off Misrata.

The end was drawing near. On October 29 orders were sent von Todenwarth to return by the next boat. The next day another order instructed all German personnel to board *UC-73* when she arrived, and between the 31st and November 2 she picked up ten German passengers for transport to Germany. As she left the anchorage she was attacked by Italian motorboats but managed to reach the open sea.

The last signal of the series was made by POZ (Nauen) to MIRR (Tripoli) on November 6. The large minelayer *U-73*, being rebuilt at Pola, could not come to Misrata. (In fact she had already been scuttled.) All Germans were to board *UC-73*, presumed to be waiting off Misrata. The signal was a bit late, for the submarine was already on her way to Germany, where she arrived well after the Armistice.[1]

The whole Libyan operation was an exercise in futility, except in so far as it tied down Italian and other Allied forces. At the same time, we may wonder why so little was done with the intercepted Für GOD signals. *UC-20* was attacked in August 1917, *UC-20* and *UC-73* in October and November of the following year. Presumably it had been decided that the information constantly obtained from the signals was worth more than a U-boat or two. Conceivably this judgment was correct, but the information thus acquired had little practical value.

E. Cruisers Southward

By February 1917 it was fairly clear that the United States was going to enter the war on the Allied side, and the German Admiralty proceeded to rebuild the seven large submarines of the *Deutschland* class, originally

---

1 Quotations from these intercepts come from a collection of U.S. Army Intelligence documents in the Walter Hines Page Library at Randolph-Macon College in Virginia.

intended for mercantile use. The *Deutschland* herself, which had made two voyages to America during 1916, was actually ready for war operations on February 19. From the beginning, the British were well informed about these boats. They listened with interest as *U-156* headed outward through the Sound in the Baltic on October 17 and reported her location in the North Sea on the 20th and the 24th. On the 24th they also heard Nauen informing the cruisers that a Holland-American ship bound for America was carrying valuable objects including diamonds. Since only *U-151* was in the Atlantic, and she was off Dakar, the message did not call for any action.

More significant news soon came in from another source. Since April the British had been in possession of the German diplomatic code, which was used for signals between the Admiralty Staff in Berlin and the Naval Attaché in Madrid. Early in November the Admiralty Staff informed Madrid that two submarine cruisers could meet a sailing vessel off the Canaries and take on a total of eighty tons of wolfram ore. The date of the meeting could not be read, but it could not be too far in the future. Meanwhile British agents reported that the schooner *Erribero* at Bilbao was loading wolfram ore for an undisclosed destination. At the end of November another signal gave the date as December 25 and the location of the rendezvous as on the southwest side of Ferro Island (Canaries).

Madrid soon postponed the date to the new year, and in mid-December the Naval Staff set it for January 20 and after. On January 3 Madrid announced that the vessel had sailed and would be at the rendezvous on January 20. The reply from Berlin indicated that a slight hitch was developing, for it stated that *U-156* and *U-157* would arrive off Ferro between January 15 and February 1. Madrid replied that since the vessel had already sailed her orders could not be changed.

By radio *U-156* then arranged a rendezvous with *U-157* off Ferro for January 17. This signal too was intercepted, but it did not need to be read. *U-156* arrived at the rendezvous at 0700 on the morning of the date set, and at 1524 she sighted a periscope only about sixty yards away. As she headed for the open sea, the enemy submarine - the British *E-48* - fired three torpedoes at her. The first two passed ahead of her bow and exploded on the shore; the third hit her amidships but failed to explode. At 0400 the next morning she signalled to *U-157* that the rendezvous had been compromised and arranged for another location. The whole German scheme had ended in failure, and the schooner *Erribero* was captured.

Within a week Nauen warned the cruisers that a British submarine had been at the rendezvous and that Madrid thought she might have sunk both *U-156* and *U-157*. A few days later, however, the German radio transmitted more accurate information. Neither submarine had been sunk, although two of the crew of *U-156* had been washed overboard when she dived and were found on Ferro Island.

On February 20 *U-156* informed Nauen of her activities. She had sunk 23,000 tons of shipping, had bombarded Funchal in the Azores, and had been hit by a torpedo amidships. Obviously the last item referred to the attack made on her by *E-48*.

By this point two more cruisers had already sailed for the waters west of the African and Spanish coasts. These were *U-153* and *U-154*, whose activities could be followed from their frequent radio messages and attacks on shipping. By April 17 the American intelligence section, London, was informed that two British submarines were to operate against *U-154*. The next day an intercepted Nauen signal stated that *U-157* and *U-152* had returned to Kiel and that *U-151* had sailed. (*U-156* had reached home on March 10 and *U-155* was heading there.) The signal about *U-151* was to prove important in regard to operations off the American coast. At the moment the significant fact was that only *U-153* and *U-154* were on cruise in southern waters; they could be expected to make contact there.

Further information came in on April 26, when Nauen informed *U-153* that in the middle of May *U-62* would arrive off the Azores. During the week after, the only news from Nauen announced promotions in rank for the commanders of the two cruisers. On May 6, however, definite orders were transmitted. *U-153* was to operate to the north of Madeira and west of Gibraltar, while *U-154* was to patrol the waters either north or south of the Canaries. The next day the cruisers were informed that *U-62* would arrive off the Azores about May 10, and *U-153* was ordered to meet her.

The crucial signal was made at 0450 on May 9, when *U-153* instructed *U-62* to meet her in 3645/1200W. Just before midnight on the 10th *U-62* replied that she would reach the rendezvous at 1800 the next day, and *U-153* told her that she would arrive there from the south, with *U-154* at ten miles distance.

The stage was set; all that remained was for the actors to arrive. First on the scene was the British submarine *E-35*, out from Gibraltar, which sighted a 'low-lying object' in her periscope at 1600 on the 11th. Soon afterwards she identified the object as 'a large enemy submarine making slowly off northwards'. *E-35* pursued her unobserved, at 1818 firing a torpedo that missed. At 1825 she was only 500 yards away and fired two torpedoes at the German's fore and after gun turrets. Both hit, and when *E-35* surfaced she found a 'lake of oil' with wreckage in it. Three or four survivors were clinging to some woodwork. As the British submarine proceeded to pick them up, another enemy submarine appeared, two miles away, and *E-35* dived just in time to escape a torpedo.

U-62, late to the rendezvous, sighted a great cloud rising out of the sea on the horizon, and soon received a radio warning from *U-153*; the two boats met undisturbed on the 12th, a hundred miles to the south-west. That day Nauen urgently instructed *U-154* to report her position, but without avail.

On the 19th Nauen was still issuing instructions to both cruisers and informing them that on June 1 U-91 would proceed out to relieve U-62. On the 20th, however, the homeward-bound U-153 made a signal concerning her position, results, and estimated date of return. She also stated that on May 11 U-154 had been sunk by an enemy submarine.

British submarines continued to search for U-62 off the Azores, but without success, and her departure from the Azores and homeward journey could be traced from signals intercepted on May 29-31 and June 1. By June 6 she was located in the North Sea.

On June 18 the Admiralty informed Sims that U-91 had recently left port and that she was probably bound for the Azores. Knowledge of her sailing had been derived from signals made to escort vessels. Her destination was inferred from the Nauen signal of May 19. Thereafter her cruise could be accurately traced from such signals as those listed in the French records for June 24, west of the Biscay area, July 27, south-west of Ireland, and August 1, north-east of the Shetlands. The French reconstruction of her cruise rightly placed her west of Gibraltar from June 30 to July 10, east of the Azores July 11-21, and far west of Biscay July 24-27. It must be that some of her signals were read. The French report estimated her sinkings at 23,171 tons - a figure very close to the actual total of 23,712.

Since no further pairs of U-boats were sent to the Azores area, there was little opportunity for the British to crack communications. At the end of July the British learned from a prisoner taken off UB-124 that the cruiser U-157 had been seen at Kiel on July 9. By August 6, however, an intercepted signal proved that she was out in the Atlantic again. The French placed her far to the west of the Channel approaches. On August 20 Sims was informed that calls had been sent out for U-157 but no reply had been made. It would appear that a signal from U-22, off the Portuguese coast and in need of oil, water, and provisions, had not been read, although it was certainly intercepted. U-157 met her on August 26 near Madeira in order to transfer supplies. The British were impressed by her silence; indeed, on September 17 Sims was told that she had not spoken since the 6th (August).

On the 19th, however, she broke silence to inquire about German mines and U-boats off harbours in the Azores, and was told that there were none. It is hard to tell, therefore, why she was informed on October 10 that there were German mines off Punta Delgada and Horta. The message was irrelevant, in any event, since she was heading for Lisbon. On the 16th she made a signal to report that she had laid her mines there on the 13th. Two days later she repeated the information and stated that she was heading for home. Other signals on the 20th and the 21st showed that she was moving northward. She took no part in the final North Sea patrols because her fuel supplies were low.

The two cases in which British submarines surprised U-cruisers at meeting-places were based on the interception and decryption of signals. Since *U-156* was surprised in January 1918 and *U-155* was criticized by Cruiser Command for her excessive radio use during February, it remains a mystery why *U-153* and *U-62* were allowed to set a rendezvous by radio in May. The probability or even the possibility of Allied decryption should have proscribed the use of radio for this purpose. Only a misplaced confidence in British stupidity permitted the sending of the messages which directly led to the loss of *U-154*.

F. Cruisers to America

Three significant cruises made by U-boats during 1916 - one by *U-53*, two by the mercantile submarine *Deutschland* - had shown that if the United States entered the war it was likely that U-boats would operate off the American coast. During 1917 further visitations were almost constantly expected, and Admiral Sims in London spent a good deal of time insisting to Washington that U-boats could not sail westward without advance information being supplied by the Admiralty. Since the Admiralty apparently did not tell him how the information was obtained, it is not surprising that his arguments were not entirely convincing.

It was not until April 22, 1918, that a Nauen signal made it absolutely clear to the Admiralty that some submarine was on her way to American waters. This signal described the sailing of troop transports from Newport News and New York and indicated what their escorts and routes eastward were. The information was confirmed by another signal on April 27, and this time the recipient was definitely identified as *U-151* - known to have sailed about April 18 because of another signal. On April 29 Nauen made a signal indicating that *U-151* and *U-155* were probably fairly close together, in about 5230/1500W. According to an American Intelligence Section memorandum of this date, *U-151* was believed to be bound for South America.

Two days later the series of signals had been analysed. Sims was informed that according to 'reliable agents' *U-151* had sailed about April 19 to attack transports and cargo vessels, and that she was acquainted with the routes taken by both. She was taking the northern route across the Atlantic and proceeding at an average speed of 5 knots. On May 3 she reported her position in about 5100W., although there was some confusion in the decryption process; on May 6 Sims cabled Washington that the May 3 position was about 4900/2700W. (This was not correct.)

As she moved westward Nauen sent her further information. On May 14 she was told that all American harbours were guarded by patrols and that an excellent area for minelaying would be in Delaware Bay, south of Five Fathom Bank Lightship. The next day this information was in Sims' hands, and he immediately cabled Washington. Shipping was at once alerted, but secrecy was maintained in accordance with Sims' cable.

> There are circumstances which render it highly important that nothing whatever should be given out which would lead the enemy even to surmise that we have had any advance information concerning this submarine, even in the event of our sinking her, and that such measures as are taken by the department be taken as secretly as possible and without public disclosure of the specific reasons.

U-151 gave her own position and intentions away, precisely on May 15, when against orders she attempted to torpedo a British steamer in 3428/5609W, about a thousand miles east of Cape Hatteras. She herself soon heard the warning transmitted by the steamer, and six days later it was repeated to her by Nauen.

Between May 21 and June 3 *U-151* was very active off the American coast, cutting cables, laying mines and attacking shipping. Admiral Sims' cable from London on June 4 was a little out of date. 'Enemy submarine at present making course slowly towards Hatteras Lightship. British steamship reports sighting large enemy submarine in Latitude 36°' Further intercepts from Nauen were interesting but presented problems. On June 6 the cruiser was told that if the situation was favourable she should attack shipping off Halifax (she did not do so), and on the 11th she was instructed to cut the cable only if conditions permitted (she had already done so). A more significant signal stated on June 15 that the German ambassador Count Luxburg was returning from Buenos Aires on the Swedish steamer *Suezia*, which would put into Halifax.

Finally, on June 20 and 28 Nauen gave *U-151* details as to her return route and told her to get further information from *U-156* if she met her. A very strong British hunting patrol was waiting for her off the Shetlands, but her only encounters were with submarines on July 13 and 14. On the latter day Nauen warned her about the new minefield in which *U-86* had been damaged. On the 17th four torpedoes missed her in the Skagerrak, and she reached home safely.

According to Hoy, the Admiralty intercepted a signal on June 15 showing that *U-156* was sailing for American waters, and this news was immediately passed on to the Americans. There is no record of such an intercept in the American files, and it is more likely that the first indication of the voyage was picked up a week later, when Nauen informed her about the steamer route out of New York along the Long Island shore. On July 28 Nauen exchanged word with *U-156*, whose pistons were not working well; she intended to continue her voyage, however. The next day Sims cabled Washington. 'Second cruiser submarine at sea. At present off west coast of

Ireland. Her field of operations not yet known. Cannot reach longitude of Nantucket before July 15.'

Another cable on July 6 reflected further cruiser activity. 'Although there is no positive evidence, Admiralty thinks it possible that one and possibly two cruiser submarines perhaps of later type are at sea, whereabouts so far unknown. U-156 apparently in 4232/4350W. July 5 bound west.' During the post-war naval investigation Sims stated that the vagueness in cables like this was due to fear of compromising security. Actually he had been given specific information and had been asked to paraphrase it. For this reason we may assume that the British read a Nauen signal of July 4, certainly picked up by U-151: 'U-140 out through the Sound on July 2.' At first it could not be determined whether the new call letters belonged to U-140 or to her sister cruiser U-139. The location of U-156 was known because on the 5th she attacked the American Navy cargo boat Lake Bridge.

On July 13 both submarines were told by Nauen that there were several factory chimneys at Cape May, off which the light was not burning, while at Cape Henlopen there were oil reservoirs. Sims passed this news on to Washington on the 17th. On July 14 Nauen informed three U-boats that there were mines off the American coast (this was not correct) and that transports from New York passed through Nantucket Sound. Six days later Nauen indicated that another submarine had been late in sailing and that therefore the new cruiser was to operate between Nantucket and Cape Hatteras until the other boat arrived, about August 10. On the 24th, in consequence of a signal intercepted two days earlier, Hall informed Sims that U-156 would operate in the Gulf of Maine but in case of foggy weather would proceed to the Delaware.

This information was not as significant as the action which U-156 had already undertaken. Her orders had instructed her to begin her operation by laying mines to the east of Fire Island Light Vessel, within twenty miles of the coast, and she had done so between July 15 and 19. At 1105 on July 19 the armoured cruiser San Diego struck a mine ten miles southeast of Fire Island and sank within twenty minutes. Three more mines were found within the next twenty-four hours. U-156 headed north to attack shipping off Orleans, Mass., and Portland, Maine.

The identification of the new cruiser continued to vex the Admiralty, but on July 30 Hall was able to give Sims some information from prisoners taken off UB-124. 'It is considered very probable that U-140 started on her first cruise about the date mentioned [June 20], and has now arrived off the east coast of the United States, but there is no evidence of U-139 having sailed yet.' This conclusion obviously implied that a third submarine, mentioned in the Nauen intercepts of July 14 and 20, was now at sea, and further research must have led to the conclusion that she was a minelayer. In any event, Hall informed Sims on August 1 that he thought a new minelayer was on her way to the American coast and that she had attacked the steamer *Baron Napier* on July 26 in 4526/3256W. 'If so, I estimate that she can reach the longitude of Nantucket Lightship tomorrow, August 2.' Sims sent a cable at once. On August 7 he cabled again, obviously basing his recommendation on the Nauen signal of July 20. 'We feel so certain that minelaying submarine will operate in Vineyard Sound and Nantucket Sound August 10 that counter measures in mining are recommended.' His recommendations were not followed because of the risk to shipping, greater than that to a U-boat. *U-117* passed close to Martha's Vineyard, precisely on August 10. That day Hall gave Sims more information. When returning homeward, *U-140* would pass from Cape Hatteras to 50°W., then north-east towards the Orkneys; *U-156* would move from Halifax eastward along the 44th parallel, then north-east; and the new minelayer (*U-117*) would lay mines or perhaps simply attack shipping, between Cape Race and Halifax. (On September 2 he revised the route of *U-117*: from Cape Race to 54N. 27W.)

August 10 was also important because of the only encounter between an American destroyer and a U-boat in American waters. *U-140* was shelling the Brazilian steamer *Uberaba* when the destroyer *Stringham*, answering her call for help, arrived on the scene and dropped fifteen depth charges over the spot where the U-boat had dived. About forty-five tons of water were shipped through leaks, and three days later *U-140* realized she could not operate off the coast because of her oil track. On the 21st she headed for Germany.

Between this date and September 6 we have records of only two signals made by boats off the American coast. On the 17th *U-117* called *U-140* but received no reply. On the 23rd a mysterious, incomplete signal was picked up from *U-156* to U-boat Command, made in plain German: 'Why do you not give'? What her operator had in mind will never be known.

Meanwhile from Nauen detailed word about future operations off the American coast was intercepted early on August 8. It was passed on to Sims the same day. 'I learn from a reliable source', Hall wrote, 'that two converted mercantile type submarines [actually *U-152* and *U-155*] will probably leave Germany in the middle of August for the American coast. One of them will probably lay mines East of Atlantic City and Currituck; the other off St. John's, Newfoundland and Halifax. These two submarines are estimated to reach American waters about the second week in September'. A signal made by *U-155* on August 11 showed that she was leaving Kiel. Sims had already informed the Navy Department that her sailing was imminent, but that she would not arrive for some time.

Early in September the attention of the interceptors was concentrated on the homeward-bound cruisers. On the 6th *U-156* tried to make contact with Rugia, but she was not successful until early the next morning, when she reported having sunk 41,000 tons of shipping, including the American armoured cruiser *San Diego*, and having cut five cables. Her location was about 4530/3530W. Next to be heard from was *U-140*, who made a signal from 5130/3130W. At this point Rugia replied to *U-156*, instructing her to pass to the west of the new Northern Barrage, since mines were to be found in the eastern part and in Norwegian waters. On the morning of the 8th, since *U-117* had heard the signal from *U-140*, she first reported her own location to Rugia as 5337/2521W. and then began to arrange a rendezvous with *U-140*, since her fuel supply was running low. She wanted 20 cubic metres of oil, but *U-140* could spare only 10. On September 10 Sims was informed about these signals and was told that *U-117* was 'in difficulties'. A few days later *U-140* gave fuel to her off the Faeroes. Both submarines reported from the North Sea on September 18, and both headed through the Skagerrak without incident - except that on the 20th *U-117* finally ran out of oil and had to call for help.

On September 16 the interceptors had unexpectedly heard from the new cruiser *U-139*, east of the Shetlands. She had passed to the west of the new barrage at night and without incident. Two days later, north-west of Ireland, she signalled to *U-156* and asked her position. On the 20th *U-156* replied; she was five degrees to the west and wanted information about the barrage. Hall sent Sims a memorandum about the attempt of the two U-boats to communicate.

Perhaps it is a coincidence, but on the 20th the British and the Americans jointly laid new lines of mines in Area B of the Northern Barrage, just to the east of the Orkney Islands.

U-156 then gave the other cruiser submarine some counsel about the traffic routes along the American coast. She had found nothing in the Gulf of Halifax but much shipping between Halifax and New York. *U-139* proposed that the two submarines meet, and *U-156* offered the position 5804/1240W. After various delays the meeting took place that evening. Nothing more was heard from *U-156* until the morning of September 23, when her anxiety about the barrage and the route to Skagen led her to ask the outward-bound *U-161* for guidance. *U-161* tried to persuade her to make visual signals, but the cruiser refused because of 'shortness of time'. *U-161* then stated that she had not passed Skagen (since she had sailed from Heligoland through the North Sea) but that the route would be in accordance with mine-signal 37. She had answered only half of the cruiser's question, preferring not to reveal that she had gone through the Fair Isle passage. That evening *U-139* informed Rugia that she had met *U-156*, and the latter submarine was ordered to report her position and the date she expected to meet her escort.

On the morning of September 24, therefore, *U-156* gave her position in 475E. and stated that she intended to cross the barrage the next day, entering it in square 1660E., or 5956/0130E. The same afternoon she was instructed to take this route only by daylight and in calm weather, keeping a lookout for the glass balls that indicated the presence of mines.

Soon thereafter the destroyer *Marksman* and the submarine *L-8* left Kirkwall and headed for the U-boat's anticipated location. At 0740 on September 25 *L-8* 'sighted vessel nature undistinguishable' precisely in the correct position. She dived at once, but she lost sight of her target and could not pick it up on hydrophones. Surfacing an hour later, she spent the rest of the day patrolling the area, but without making contact. The next morning she met *Marksman* and after further fruitless patrol returned to Kirkwall. She had evidently been the last vessel to catch a glimpse of *U-156*.

The orders given *U-156* instructed her to report her estimated time of arrival at Skagen just as soon as she had crossed the barrage. No report was picked up, and at 1945 on the 26th the German command ordered her to make a signal, repeating the order the next day. On the 28th the Admiralty informed Sims that they had expected to hear from her and therefore supposed that she was 'in difficulties'. It is virtually certain that she encountered the minefield within a fairly short time after *L-8* sighted her. The Admiralty estimated that she was sunk in about 6000/0300E., but a location closer to 5945/0200E. is more likely.

U-139 was now outward-bound, perhaps heading for American waters, but she was not the only cruiser being tracked. On September 7 a *Deutschland*-class boat had attacked a ship in 4300/4550W. and therefore was certainly bound for America. Two days later the Admiralty so informed Sims. They added that as late as September 2 the other boat of the two expected to sail in August was still at Kiel. By September 16, however, a signal from Rugia to *U-152* and *U-139* suggested that *U-152*, the other *Deutschland*, had now sailed. Since both submarines were ordered to report their positions every night they could not have proceeded far to the west. Two days later it became clear that the first *Deutschland* had arrived off the coast, for a German mine was swept up and destroyed off Halifax. Evidently this had been laid by *U-155*.

On September 18 and 19 *U-152*, slowly heading south-west in the eastern Atlantic, reported on convoys she had missed, as well as on glass buoys she had sighted while crossing the Northern Barrage. On the 20th Hall gave Sims her location, and American patrols off the New Jersey coast were alerted. *U-155* had reached Halifax; it was therefore to be expected that *U-152* would head for Atlantic City and Currituck.

On hearing of the alert, Sims immediately sent a warning from London. Any information he transmitted was to be used in confidence. The Admiralty had been disturbed by the inadequate American security measures. 'Their experience in obtaining and handling highly secret enemy information has involved serious difficulties and dangers. Entirely apart from the danger of jeopardising the source of information there is also involved the safety of

19 18.	From *Kirkwall* to *Patrol* or at
..rs, Defects, &c.	Details of attacks, exercises, torpedoes run, navigation, employment of crew, and other remarks

4. 30 Stopped charging
7. 40 Sighted vessel nature undistinguishable 7. 45
Dived S/o 135° failed to pick up vessel on periscope
listened for her on Hydroplanes but failed to pick her up.
8. 40 Surface. proceeded 7.5 Knots.

9- 60. 252° proceeded to Rendez Vous.

)K.		Condition Air Groups									Noon position	Fresh water remaining	
ived	Remaining	1	2	3	4	5	6	7	8	9	Lat.		
	10430					2	2	00	ar			7¼ Tons,	
		1⁰	11	12	13	14	15.	16	17		Long.		

EXCERPT FROM THE LOG OF THE BRITISH SUBMARINE *L-8* FOR
SEPTEMBER 25, 1918. The object sighted was *U-156*, viewed for the last time.
Reproduced by permission of The Public Record Office, London.

agents.' This statement was not, of course, entirely truthful. More important, however, it does reflect the tremendous value which Hall rightly placed on keeping secret the fact that the British were intercepting and reading every relevant signal.

Because of this continued secrecy it was possible to read a signal made on September 25 to both *U-155* and *U-152*, informing them about the convoy route from Cape Race to St. John's, Newfoundland. Only *U-155* was in any position to use the information, but she was already heading for southern waters. On October 10 Nauen instructed both U-boats to leave American waters and head for the Azores. Nothing was heard from either submarine until they appeared, far to the east, early in November.

As for *U-139*, she made signals nearly every day until October 4; these served only to show that she had proceeded toward the Azores. On the 4th, however, she gave more information, stating that she had begun her homeward journey on the 1st because all periscopes had been damaged when she struck a sinking steamer. Leaks in the conning tower kept her from diving deep, and her radio was not working well. A signal picked up by the French on the 6th showed that she had moved north and west, but on the 9th she was back to the south-east. She had continued her operation and was going to work on the surface off the Azores. By the 16th she had proceeded farther west in the Atlantic, but on the 21st, when the war on shipping ended, she was recalled with the other U-boats, moving slowly up the Irish coast and reaching the North Sea too late to take part in any battle there. Many of her signals were picked up by the French and the British but not received at home.

In writing the story of the cruise of *U-139*, Admiral Spindler was unable to make use of her war diary, missing from the German files. To judge from details provided by Laurens in his *Histoire de la guerre sousmarine allemande*, it fell into French hands at the end of the war.

V

THE END OF THE WAR

A. Final Curtain

BY EARLY OCTOBER 1918 the North Sea, once almost a German ocean, was practically a British lake. The Flanders Flotillas, shattered by depth charge, and mine had withdrawn to German safety. The British army was about to enter Bruges. Off the East Coast only a few submarines of the worn-out I Flotilla continued to operate. Nevertheless, the German Navy was not yet vanquished. U-boats continued to cross the Northern Barrage on their way to and from the Atlantic waters. The High Seas Fleet, in spite of rumours of mutiny, remained menacing.

Britons brought up on Erskine Childers' *Riddle of the Sands* could only imagine what surprises might lurk to the eastward, behind the German minefields in the Bight of Heligoland. They could also hope that the Admiralty were as well prepared as ever.

Naval Intelligence was fully cognizant of current U-boat operations, even though most of the submarines could not be identified any longer. The call letters had been drastically changed on September 21, and it was taking a long time to work out identifications. It was more important, as Admiral James points out, to know what they were doing than to identify each boat. The future was of course less definite than the present. Intelligence expected a German reaction to the pressure being imposed by the Allies on land and at sea. Mindful of the minefields which the Germans were still building up off the Scottish coast, they could only assume that some sort of action in the North Sea would result. This was the situation on October 21, when Nauen instructed all the U-boats to end attacks on shipping. The storm abruptly died down. From what quarter would it revive?

The Admiralty needed to know where the U-boats on cruise were operating, and this knowledge was available on October 21-22, with or without identifications. Five submarine cruisers were at sea. Three were far west of the Azores and one west of the Bay of Biscay. It could be assumed that they could not reach the North Sea for some time, although one of them, probably *U-151*, had just entered it. Four U-boats were in the Bay of Biscay or west of it; four more were south of Ireland; two were in the Irish Sea. It was unlikely that these boats would take part in any action soon. On the other hand, one to the west of Ireland could be expected back, along with two just north of the Northern Barrage and three which had not yet crossed it. The strength immediately available for any German plan thus consisted of seven U-boats. Certainly these submarines would be reinforced from Germany at the opportune time, but some indication of the German plan could be gained by close observation of the boats at sea.

A glance at the next page will show how information was taken from the intercepted communications. By the morning of October 24 Sims could be told that there were three U-boats in a sixty-mile square east of the Firth of Forth. Two more joined them that day, and on the morning of the 26th they were occupying clearly defined locations somewhat to the east. Another boat had arrived on the scene. On the 27th one more submarine arrived, making signals that day and the next. It was on the 28th that the long-awaited order came from Germany, giving the locations which six of the U-boats were to take up 'against warships' on the 29th. That morning Sims was informed that six or eight U-boats were now present in the sixty-mile square, and in the evening *U-43*, arriving from Biscay, reported that she was heading for her assigned position but would have to proceed homeward by the evening of the 30th because she lacked lubricating oil.

It was clear that the action had begun. A signal from *U-67* on the 26th had already suggested that other U-boats were on the move. Early on the morning of the 28th the British submarine *G-2*, on watch south-west of Norway, overheard German oscillator signals and was able to torpedo the outward-bound *U-78*. The Admiralty estimated that she had been bound for Kinnaird Head, Scotland. Actually she had been ordered to lay mines off the Dutch coast, but this now made no difference. That night *UB-116* made an attempt to enter Scapa Flow but was blown up by shore-controlled mines. Divers found the wreck the next day.

On the 28th a German signal was also received asking for the locations of *UB-123* (sunk October 18 or 19!), *U-46* (an error for *U-43*), *U-60*, *U-119*, *UB-94* and *U-122*. They had hoped that all these boats would take part in the North Sea operation, but answers intercepted during the next two days showed that only *U-43* could do so.

In spite of exact British information about the U-boat lines - on the morning of the 29th Sims was told that 'the latest orders' placed three submarines off northern Scotland and four more south of the Firth of Forth, all occupying north-south lines - it was impossible to send out hunters against them. Their arrival would have shown the Germans that their signals were being read, and the possible gain would not have amounted to much in view of the other submarines still prowling unobserved in the North Sea. The Grand Fleet and the other bases had been alerted. British submarines and aircraft were on watch. It was up to the Germans to make a move.

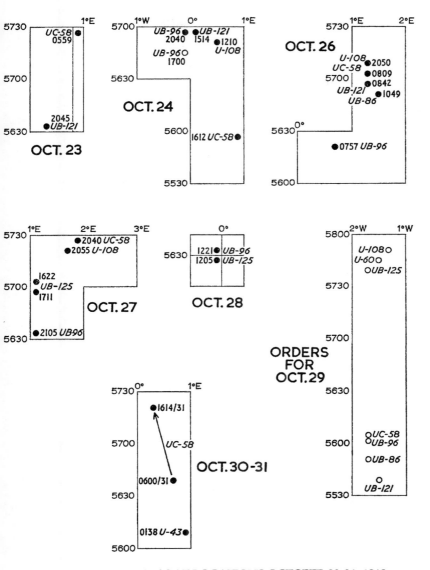

U-BOAT LOCATIONS OCTOBER 23-31, 1918

Admiral von Hipper had issued his orders to the High Seas Fleet on October 24, though he was dismayed when a junior officer reported, the next day, that there was a general rumour about a great naval battle during the coming week. Was there a traitor in the German command? The plan in question had been developed over a long time, beginning with the laying of minefields off the Firth of Forth earlier in the year.

The operations order itself was published at Paris in 1931. It read as follows. [1]

A. Information about the enemy
It is to be supposed that the enemy combat forces are in the ports of the east coast of Scotland, with detachments in the Tyne, the Humber, and the Channel.
B. Intentions
To engage the enemy under conditions favourable to us. For that purpose, night approach of the concentrated High Seas forces toward the Hoofden. Attack on combat forces or merchant shipping on the Flanders coast and in the Thames estuary, to lead the enemy to advance with detachments of his fleet towards the line Hoofden/German Bight. Our intention is to engage these detachments on the evening of Day 2 of the operation, or to have them attacked by torpedo boats during the night of Day 2 or 3.
C. Execution
1.Departure from the German Bight by day, out of sight of the Dutch coast;
2.Route through the Hoofden so that the attack on the Flanders coast and the Thames estuary takes place at dawn on Day 2;
3.Attack:
(a) against the Flanders coast by the commander of the II Destroyer Flotilla with *Graudenz, Karlsruhe, Nürnberg,* and the II Flotilla;
(b) against the Thames estuary by the II Scouting Group with *Koenigsberg, Köln, Dresden, Pillau,* and the II Half-Flotilla.
Covering of (a) by the fleet, (b) by the commander-in-chief of the Scouting Group (I Scouting Group);
4.Return so as to reach the combat area favourable to us, near Terschelling, one or two hours before nightfall on Day 2;
5.Protection of the return (Day 2) by part of the VIII Flotilla;
6.Minelaying by the leader of the IV Scouting Group, with the IV Scouting Group (supported with minelaying by *Arkona* and *Möwe*) and the VIII Flotilla, on the approach routes of the enemy, in accordance with Plan No. I;

1 The U-boats' assigned locations are given in Gladisch, VII.

7.Disposition of submarines on the enemy routes in accordance with Plan No. III;

8.Attack by torpedo boats during the night of Day 2-3, in case an encounter has already taken place, from near the Terschelling Light Vessel towards the Firth of Forth, in accordance with the orders of the commander of the torpedo boats. On the meeting of the torpedo boats with the fleet on the morning of Day 3 see the following order;

9.Entrance into the German Bight by the departure route or by Routes 420, 500 or 750, depending on the situation;

10. Air reconnaissance: if possible.

A singularly important part in this operation was to be played by the groups of U-boats, which were to attack units of the Grand Fleet as they hastened south from Scapa Flow and Rosyth. In addition, *UB-116* received orders, dated October 23, to proceed in to Scapa Flow on the night of October 28-29 or 29-30 and attack the Grand Fleet there. She sailed on the 25th.

The precise date of the plan is open to some question. When *UB-96* sailed on October 12 her commander was given a sealed order with instructions from the Chief of U-boats; he opened it when the war on shipping ended. Obviously the U-boats had advance warning of the coming battle, since their locations, in six or seven lines in the North Sea, had been assigned so early.

Der Tag never came, however. On the night of October 29 orders were given the High Seas Fleet to raise steam and head out through the North Sea, but at this point mutiny broke out. The Fleet did not sail. The U-boats were hurriedly informed that the action would be postponed, but as the mutiny spread this postponement was cancelled, along with the operation itself. The signal to this effect was read with jubilation on October 30. It was followed by an order to *U-78*, already sunk, to lay her mines and return. On November 2 the other U-boats were told to move homeward through the Baltic.

We cannot tell what would have happened if the German Fleet had sailed. There are too many intangibles. Both British and German losses would probably have been severe. The sortie could hardly have influenced the ending of the war, and if the Fleet had shelled London the peace terms would certainly have been even less favourable to Germany. The Germans had already lost the war. The U-boats had been defeated and the German armies had been rolled back. Even Ludendorff had stated on October 25: '*Es ist nichts mehr zu hoffnen, Deutschland ist verloren!*'

All that remained to be done was to prevent the return of the U-boats from the Mediterranean, a move which the Admiralty told Sims was imminent. Newbolt has described the Allied countermeasures. Across the

Straits of Gibraltar there were 'five lines of watching vessels, supported at their eastern end by three kite balloon ships and two submarines, which kept periscope watch'. On November 6 and 7 five trawlers and drifters, as well as eleven American submarine chasers, reinforced the patrols. On the 7th two of the U-boats were sighted between Gibraltar and Bizerta; the next day, farther to the west, *E-54* and the destroyer *Lyra* made ineffective attacks. On the night of the 8th- 9th a group of U-boats got through the Straits. *UB-49* and *UB-51* underwent depth charge attack but were able to escape. At 0715 on the 9th, off Cape Trafalgar, *UB-50* torpedoed and sank the old battleship *Britannia* and got away unscathed from the two destroyers escorting her. As Newbolt points out,

> she was destroyed by a German submarine within one of those zones which had been specially defended, and which, of all places in the high seas, should have been more dangerous to German U-boats than to Allied warships.

Though Germany had lost the war, the ablest U-boat commanders had lost none of their ability to sink or damage allied vessels.

The Allies derived some comfort from the notion that very early on the 9th two motor launches and the sloop *Privet* had depth charged *U-34* out of existence in the Straits. Their target was actually *UB-49* or *UB-51*. The old *U-34* had actually sailed from Pola on October 16 and from Spalato two days later, heading for Cape Matapan and an operation with other submarines. Nothing more was heard from her, and on the 23rd she did not answer radio calls from her base. It is possible that she was destroyed on October 20 or 21. After a hydrophone search on the morning of the 20th in the Straits of Otranto the destroyer *Lizard* dropped twenty depth charges on a U-boat, and the next night the trawler *John Bowler*, also using hydrophones, dropped nine charges in 3914/1933E. *U-34*, then, was sunk, but not while passing through the Straits of Gibraltar.

B. The Summing up

The war came to an end, but the rigorous secrecy of wartime continued to enshroud the work of the Admiralty's Intelligence Division. People in the know could easily read between the lines in *Brassey's Naval Annual* for 1919. 'Probably no greater compliment was ever paid to a department of the Admiralty than that of the German officers, who declared that every movement of their Fleet became rapidly known to the Intelligence Division. It was, indeed, the persistent and ubiquitous knowledge gained by the British Navy and centred in the Intelligence Division that was chiefly instrumental in paralysing the initiative of the German Fleet and thus bringing about its surrender. ... The most striking feature in the expansion of the Intelligence Division was the introduction of civil ability, with the object of gaining the help of experts of all kinds. Men of science and letters, eminent scholars, lawyers and linguists, and travellers acquainted with all countries, were brought into the Service. This was, perhaps, the boldest and most successful thing done by Admiral Hall.'

The experts departed from Whitehall and resumed their careers as financiers, dress designers, professors, and bishops. Several professors received knighthoods. Ronald Knox translated the New Testament. All kept the secret faithfully, and in 1920-21 when the United States Senate investigated the American conduct of the naval war Admiral Sims refrained from giving away any unnecessary information about British procedures.

Indeed, a semi-official history of naval intelligence described British activities in remarkably incorrect fashion. 'A careful checking up of the facts after the armistice was signed with Intelligence obtained during the war showed an uncanny accuracy, and it is an admitted fact that their agents in Germany conveyed to the Admiralty accurate information on every movement of enemy vessels. The source of this information and method of conveying same was never revealed, but it is a matter of simple deduction that the Admiralty had and maintained a splendidly organized spy system in the heart of the Central Empire.' The point to which simple deduction could lead is indicated in the memoirs of Sir Bertram Hayes, commander of the transport *Olympic* during 1918.[1]

Our Naval Intelligence Service must have had trustworthy sources of information during the war, as they seemed to know where every submarine was located. I have heard it said by more or less responsible people, that it was Admiral von Tirpitz himself who was giving us the information, and I have also heard speculations as to how much he was paid for doing so. Whether he was the source or not, the fact remains that the information was accurate.

With Hayes's last sentence we heartily agree.

A young American named Leighton, who worked with Admiral Sims's staff in London and in 1920 described his work, almost - but not quite - gave the secret away. He insisted that direction-finding was the key to success.

It was the custom of submarines to communicate with their headquarters in Germany almost nightly by wireless. The messages were always in a highly secret code, and might, or might not, be eventually deciphered by the Admiralty. The chief interest in them was

---

1. *Hull Down: Reminiscences of Wind-jammers, Troops and Travellers* (London, 1925), p. 239. For another false lead see D. McLachlan, *Room 39* (London, 1968), p. 230.

the opportunity they afforded to locate the submarine which sent the message. ... The Admiralty took the greatest care that this method of locating submarines should not be discovered by the enemy, for the authorities regarded it as the greatest secret in their possession; and there is no evidence to show that the Germans ever did discover it.

Leighton died in 1936, and we do not know whether or not he really thought that direction-finding was the greatest secret. In the French records there is much mention of radiogoniometry. At the same time, many of the U-boats are identified, and one would assume that if this much of a signal was read it was possible to read more. Comparison of some French comments with German signals, indeed, shows that some signals were read.

The Admiralty certainly kept secret the fact that nearly every German signal was read, even though students of naval history might well have wondered about the 'persistent and ubiquitous knowledge' mentioned in Brassey. What had been the function of the linguists in the Intelligence Division? Gradually, however, some of the concealed information was released. On October 23, 1926, the *Saturday Evening Post* published 'with official permission' an article entitled 'A War Secret'. This described the activities of divers who visited the wrecks of U-boats and brought up codes and charts from them. A certain 'Diver Miller' investigated 'no fewer than sixty sunken German submarines'. Since the details of the episodes were artfully garbled, it was impossible to identify any of the U-boats, and as far as one can now tell the total of sixty was considerably exaggerated. Books published in the early Thirties by Ferraby, Bywater, and Hoy maintained the practice of combining fact with fiction, and great emphasis was laid on the use of radiogoniometry. It is clear that questions sometimes arose, at least in Germany. Hashagen of *U-62* told how he had been in communication with two submarine cruisers, arranging a meeting with them 'by a few short signals'. One of them 'was fired at, exactly at the rendezvous, by a British submarine, and lost with all hands'. He was evidently suggesting (as he had suggested at the time) that the British could read German signals.

Bywater's book *Their Secret Purposes* (1932) disclaimed any substantial reliability. 'The purpose of this volume is to entertain rather than to instruct, and no historical importance is claimed for the disclosures it makes.' Indeed, in 1938 he said the same thing to me. 'Everything in this book is true as stated.' Nevertheless there was a good deal of information in the book. Winston Churchill had already told how the Russians acquired the basic German signal book from the cruiser *Magdeburg* and had sent it to London, thus providing the key to the U-boat signals. Bywater went on to say that 'every form of cipher submitted to the experts was read sooner or later, though sometimes the discovery of the key was a long process'. He also mentioned the importance of the psychological factor and quoted Sir Alfred

Ewing, Director of Naval Education (and in charge of Room 40 for a time) on the subject.

> The assumed stupidity of the British was a most valuable asset, and it was not apparently until the war was over that the Germans became aware how completely their confidential channels of communication had been compromised.

During the period before 1939, however, the Admiralty reviewed five sample chapters of Admiral Hall's memoirs and felt it necessary to inform him that 'publication should be withheld for the time being'. It was not until 1956 that a substantial account of Hall's work appeared; it was published by Admiral Sir William James, in charge of decryption during 1917 and 1918. In recent years some full accounts of decryption in World War II have cast light backward on the First. We may mention especially the studies by Ladislas Farago, *The Tenth Fleet* (1962), by David Kahn, *The Codebreakers* (1967), and by Donald McLachlan, *Room 39* (1968).

Naval Intelligence in 1914-1918 remains important today, not in the sense that it provides practical lessons for the present or the future, but in the sense that it shows how the crucial challenge of a new weapon was met and countered. We have tried to show how the U-boat was defeated not only by the men who manned convoys and Q-ships or those who laid mines and hunted submarines, but also by those who did the work of Naval Intelligence. Theirs was a new task, carried out in new ways. As Admiral James wrote in 1967,

> The day of the agent ended with the sailing era. Agents watching, say, the French fleet in Brest and seeing that the ships were crossing their yards and preparing for sea could slip across the Channel and report to Admiralty. But in the steam age there were no indications that the ships were shortly proceeding to sea and if an agent watching the harbour saw that it was empty one morning he could not pass the information to England in time to be of any use.

The work of agents would have been even more difficult in dealing with the elusive submarines whose essential strength lay in secrecy and surprise.

For this reason the work of interception and decryption was all-important, especially when it was coordinated and acted upon. For the anti-submarine war of 1914-18 it was perhaps the most significant contributor to British and Allied victory.

ADDITIONAL NOTES

A. Mysterious Losses

IN SPITE OF ALL the efforts made during the last fifty years to clear up the sinkings of those U-boats which were 'sunk without trace', a good many problems still remain. We hope that some of them have now been brought closer to solution, but a glance at the tables on pages in Chapter III will show how many question marks and 'unknowns' are still necessary. In this note we simply add a few comments on cases for which we have found a little further evidence.

U-69

On July 12, 1917, the destroyer *Patriot* sighted a U-boat in 6025/0132E. and dropped depth charges. Four hours later a violent underwater explosion brought a vast expanse of oil to the surface. Presumably it marked the end of a U-boat. In this case, two signals probably served to identify the submarine. First, at 0340 on July 11 *U-69* had signalled her position about 115 sea miles west-south-west of Lindesnes. Second, at 1425 on the 12th the IV U-boat Flotilla requested an escort for another submarine and stated that *U-69* was heading northward. The target of *Patriot* can have been only *U-69*, from which nothing more was heard.

UB-63

On January 14, 1918, the Admiralty were aware that *UB-63* was outward-bound under escort on the *Weg Mitte*. Two days later a directional intercept located her in the North Sea to the east of Peterhead, and the next day the same submarine was presumably sighted as she moved south along the Scottish coast toward the Firth of Tay. For this reason it was supposed that she was the U-boat depth charged there on the evening of the 28th; a sweeper found a new obstruction on the bottom. It appears, however, that no U-boat was there at the time, and *UB-63* had orders to head for the Irish Sea through the Straits of Dover. Conceivably she was sunk there on either January 30 or February 2. In the first encounter the British patrol *P-68* dropped depth charges on a U-boat but believed it escaped. In the second, the American destroyer *Allen*, escorting a convoy, dropped depth charges when a periscope was sighted close by. In either case, *UB-63* may have been sunk, but no proof can be provided. She made no signals while on cruise and did not return to port. Perhaps she was lost in the Dover Barrage on January

31 while homeward-bound (explosion in 5102/0116E.; no wreck), but there is no sufficient reason for thinking so.

UB-119

Another mystery can perhaps be brought somewhat nearer to a solution. On April 27 the new *UB-119* sailed from Heligoland through the Kiel Canal and out through the Baltic. At 0430 on the 30th she radioed her position as '038 beta IV', about 95 miles west-south-west of Lindesnes, Norway. Thereafter the German command heard nothing from her. Her orders were (1) to attack shipping in the North Sea and (2) at her commander's discretion to proceed onward to the north coast of Ireland, the North Channel, and the northern part of the Irish Sea. That she did so is clear from the location of two signals intercepted on May 8, the first from 5821/0718W., close to Flannan Island in the Hebrides, the second from 5716/0802W., west of South Uist. It looks as if she continued on into the Irish Sea, and if so she was probably the submarine attacked on May 19 in 5242/0503W, west of Cardigan Bay, by the American destroyers *Patterson* and *Allen*. No other U-boat in the Irish Sea reported a similar depth charge bombardment on that date. Oil and air bubbles came to the surface, along with what looked like 'a canvas muzzle bag, painted white'. These suggest that the U-boat was sunk. If so, she was *UB-119*.

UB-65

The loss of *UB-65* presents one of the most baffling mysteries of the U-boat war. On July 2 she sailed from Heligoland out through the North Sea, bound for the Bristol Channel, but she never returned. The only event that can explain her disappearance took place south of Fastnet, Ireland, on the afternoon of July 10. The American submarine *AL-2* was patrolling on the surface when she sighted something like a buoy three miles away. She had proceeded towards the location for only five minutes when she was suddenly shaken by a violent explosion. A geyser of water shot up, eighty yards away, and when it fell back *AL-2* could see six feet of an enemy periscope about a hundred feet beyond it. Lieutenant Foster of *AL-2* made a crash dive and tried to ram the U-boat; propellers running at high speed could be heard close by. A few minutes later, two submarines were heard on the C-tube. One was near by and running fast, while the other was proceeding more slowly. Within twenty minutes the faster submarine went silent, presumably dropping to the bottom in 300 feet. The other began emitting oscillator calls and continued for another twenty minutes, making the signal 'dash-dash-dash-dot' (=OE).

After Foster returned to Bantry Bay he was informed that two U-boats had communicated by radio about an hour before the encounter with *AL-2*, and that about midnight on July 10 the survivor made a signal presumably reporting the sinking.

It is practically certain that *UB-65* was sunk at this time. Probably the torpedo she fired at *AL-2* exploded closer to herself than to her target, and she ran at high speed in an effort to reach the surface. This effort failed.

The problem has to do with the other submarine which *AL-2* heard. First we should look at the signals which *UB-65* made or was thought to have made. The records of II Flotilla, to which she belonged, list two signals from her. On July 4 she was in the North Sea and reported that an enemy submarine had unsuccessfully fired two torpedoes at her. This was actually the British *G-.6.* whose three torpedoes had missed. In addition, it was thought that on July 17 she reported again, announcing her position in 1879E. and adding 'Nothing special'. This signal should not have been ascribed to *UB-65*, however, since the message was of the type sent by U-boats outward-bound. It must have been sent by *UB-89*, also belonging to II Flotilla. Oddly enough, the British interceptors also ascribed to *UB-65* several signals she did not make. On July 15 at 0700 a submarine south-west of Norway requested an escort for another U-boat. This was really *UB-62*, making the request on behalf of *U-102*, whose radio was out of order. Two more signals supposedly from *UB-65* on July 22 also came from *UB-62*.

As for the signal about midnight on July 10, the French records state that *U-92* made one at that time. Another, two hours later, definitely could not be read, and this was probably the signal supposed to contain a report of the loss of *UB-65*. German records show that the latter signal told how *U-92* was repairing extensive damage but could continue on cruise. Conceivably Foster's informants thought that the damage was due to the explosion on July 10; if they did, they were wrong.

No U-boat log contains a report of the incident, and only *U-60* was near the area on July 10. Her log for the day mentions only routine matters. The only other boat that could possibly have been involved was *UB-108*, out from Flanders on July 2 for the western Channel approaches. We have already seen, however, that she was almost certainly sunk on July 4.

We conclude that in spite of all appearances no other U-boat was on the scene when *UB-65* went down.

UB-104 and *UB-113*

After September 1 Flanders submarines out to Atlantic waters took the northern route. The cruises of four of them can be followed from their logs, but two did not return. (1) *UB-104* sailed from Zeebrugge for the western Channel approaches on September 6 and was apparently sighted from Fair Isle on the 9th at 1100. Two days later she was heard from in 5520/1020W. at 1806 when she exchanged recognition signals with *U-57*. These points suggest that her speed was between 6 and 7 knots and that she arrived in the western Channel about September 15, then sank three ships in Lyme Bay on the 16th and the 17th. Two more ships were attacked there on the 20th and the 21st; only *UB-104* can have been responsible for these attacks. It is at least possible that she remained in the area until 1725 on September 23, when the steamer *Aldershot* was torpedoed and sunk. After this encounter she probably returned to the north and was lost in the Northern Barrage. (2) Spindler, however, tentatively ascribes the sinking of *Aldershot* to *UB-113*, from whom nothing was heard after she sailed from Zeebrugge at 2135 on September 14, heading north about for the western Channel approaches. *UB-111*, out on the same day, did not pass through the Northern Barrage until the 20th, and perhaps *UB-113* was similarly delayed. She *may* have caused the heavy explosions which *U-55* noted near Fair Isle on the 20th and the 21st. According to Gröner she hit a mine off Boulogne on October 9, but neither French nor British records contain any evidence for this event. If *UB-113* was delayed in passing through the barrage, she did not sink *Aldershot*. If she went through on the 17th or 18th she could have done so.

B. Intelligence and the V U-Boat Flotilla

During the early months of 1917 a group of six UB-boats operated off the British East Coast under the command of II Flotilla (Heligoland). In May two of them were transferred to Kurland, thence to Flanders in July, and the others were transferred to IV Flotilla (Emden), to which three new UB-boats were added in August and September.

On September 10, 1917, however, all the UB-boats of IV Flotilla were transferred to the newly created V Flotilla, stationed at Bremer- haven under the command of Korvetten-Kapitän Jürst, formerly commander of *U-43*. Jürst's flotilla thus consisted of seven UB-boats from the IV Flotilla [1] and, in addition, the new *UB-64*, to the front on September 9. During the rest of the year 1917 nine new UB-boats were put under his command.[2]

These submarines continued to operate chiefly off the East Coast, although the newer ones were soon being sent to the North Channel approaches or as far as the Bristol Channel. The first of them to be lost was *UB-41*, which apparently struck a mine off Scarborough on October 4. At least three prisoners informed the British about her disappearance. One from *U-58* (sunk November 17) said that she was known to be lost and that she had belonged to the V Flotilla, stationed at Bremerhaven. Another from *U-48* (sunk November 24) said that for three months he had not seen a friend who was attached to *UB-41*. And a survivor from *UB-81* (sunk December 2) stated that the loss of this U-boat had been confirmed.

1 *UB-21, UB-22, UB-34, UB-61, UB-41, UB-62, UB-63.*
2 *UB-65, UB-67, UB-72, UB-73, UB-74, UB-77, UB-78, UB-82, UB-83. UB-74* was sent to Flanders in January, *UB-78* in February.

During November and December two more units of this flotilla fell victim to mines, *UB-61* off the Dutch coast and *UB-75* off the East Coast. The British do not seem to have obtained information about these losses for some time, although they were observing signals made by V Flotilla submarines and from a radio message sent in the northern North Sea on December 28 they rightly concluded that *UB-65* was completing a cruise begun earlier in the month.

The V Flotilla suffered another loss in January, when *UB-22* struck a mine in the Bight. During the same month *UB-63* disappeared. On January 16 and 17 she was heard and sighted off the Scottish coast as she headed southward, but there was no further news of her.

The French records show that the Allies were aware of several cruises undertaken during February by V Flotilla submarines (*UB-67*, *UB-73*, *UB-77*). They also believed that *UB-78* began a cruise in February and ended it in March, but this submarine's signal actually meant that she was arriving off Zeebrugge on February 18 to join the Flanders Flotillas. *UB-67* had made a signal in the northern North Sea on February 12 as she returned from the North Channel after sinking *Aurania* (13,936 tons), and *UB-77* had sent a whole series of messages.

31 January	0500	mid-North Sea
1 February	1500	north of Scotland
5 February	0800	north of Ireland
15 February	0300	west of the Hebrides
18 February	1530	south-west of Norway

By intercepting and reading the last signal the Admiralty were able to inform Sims on February 19 that *UB-77* had sunk the *Tuscania* (14,348 tons) on the 5th. Presumably this message was also the one that made it possible to determine the end of the cruise of *UB-73*, which returned to port with *UB-77* on the 21st.

Around this time, it would appear, something began to go wrong with several U-boats of the Flotilla. According to a German account, three of these submarines were definitely damaged by sabotage; these were *UB-62*, *UB-67*, and *UB-83*.[1] It is certain that after *UB-67* returned from her cruise, on February 16, she was in such poor shape that she undertook no further cruises until the very end of the war, while *UB-62* was not at sea between March 27 and July 11. (By the latter date she had been transferred to the II Flotilla.) In the latter half of February two new submarines added to the V Flotilla undertook cruises in the North Sea; these were *UB-86* and *UB-85*, and they were followed by *UB-87* in March. Some of the commanders were rather nervous; on March 1, north of Denmark, *UB-85* began to shell *UB-86*,

1 L. Freiwald, *U-Boots-Maschinist Fritz Kasten* (Munich, 1933), p. 277.

fortunately without hitting her.

Early in April the French picked up signals from two boats of the Flotilla in the North Sea. One of them, from an unidentified UB-boat on April 1, actually signalled the return of *UB-72*. The other was made by *UB-73* on April 7- outward-bound, as could be seen on April 25 when another signal from her was intercepted from the same general area.

Toward the end of March, however, a great deal more information about the Flotilla came into the hands of the Allies when three deserters left Bremerhaven and escaped to Holland, bringing with them not only verbal reports but also some of the official documents related to various submarines. In the Navy Department files there is a letter from the Admiralty dated April 9, and it reads as follows: '*UB-21, UB-77* and *UB-83* belong to the 5th Submarine Flotilla based on Bremerhaven. *UB-21* is commanded by Oberleutnant Scheffler. This information is of about February 18 and from a very reliable source.' The information was actually much more recent in date, but the documents which had come with it extended only to February. They included the log of *UB-21* for the period January 30-February 19, along with observations from her commander's war diary and the comments of Jürst (commanding the V Flotilla), and the log of *UB-77* for the period January 28-February 21. The latter log was especially valuable because it gave full details about the cruise during which *UB-77* sank the *Tuscania*. This U-boat had left Borkum on January 29 and headed north, meeting *U-86* on the 31st, and then proceeded north of Scotland to the North Channel area, arriving on February 5 and encountering *U-97*. About 1800 that day she sighted a large convoy escorted by destroyers and began her attack. At nightfall she fired two torpedoes at a large steamer and dived to 30 metres; a minute later there was a heavy explosion. *UB-77* waited for fifteen minutes before surfacing and then sighted a ship listing to starboard and sinking by the stern. At the same time she intercepted an SOS from the *Tuscania*. She dived again and worked her way under the destroyers to fire a third torpedo at 1945. During the rest of the night she remained in the area but could observe nothing because of the ceaseless movement of patrol vessels. She stayed in the North Channel until the 14th, when her fuel ran low, but bad weather interfered with her activities and she was unable to attack any other ships. On the 17th she passed Fair Isle and the next day she met the homeward-bound *U-97*. On the 20th, passing along the Danish coast, she arrived in the Bight.

Since the British did not obtain the logs of these submarines for later cruises (*UB-21*, March 15-April 1; *UB-77*, March 22-April 14) but did know that *UB-77* was on cruise during March and April, they evidently obtained what they did get late in March. During the last week of that month *UB-21*, *UB-77* and *UB-83* were at sea.

During April a deserter, possibly a different one, communicated with Allied intelligence at The Hague and stated that the V Flotilla included 15 U-boats on April 1; eleven more (*U-120-U-130*) were to be added on April 30. This statement was largely false, for only three of these boats had even been commissioned. He also wrongly said that *UB-62* had sunk the *Tuscania* and that she usually remained at sea for four or five weeks, though she was able to undertake cruises twice that long. He rightly stated that V Flotilla losses had included *UB-41* in September, *UB-61* in October, *UB-75* in December, *UB-63* in January, and - almost right - *UB-22* in February. Conceivably his mixture of fiction and fact was intended to find out what the Allies themselves knew about the flotilla.

In any event, several more losses were to take place almost at once. Details in the logbook of *UB-77*, including a carefully checked operations chart, showed where U-boats sent to the North Channel were likely to be working, and the Admiralty prepared a warm welcome for the next arrivals from Bremerhaven. On April 7 *UB-82* sailed for the North Channel. A German author says that a British agent gave advance notice of her sailing by placing a classified advertisement in a Continental newspaper.[1] If so, his effort was unnecessary. *UB-82* announced her location west of Lindesnes (Norway) on the evening of the 9th and north of the North Minch on the afternoon of the 11th. She was sighted in the North Channel approaches on April 12, 13 and 15. On the 17th drifters of the patrol sighted a periscope at the entrance to the Firth of Clyde and immediately dropped depth charges. Among the wreckage blown to the surface were two seamen's caps with ribbons from the IV and V Flotillas. Obviously *UB-82* had perished.

Meanwhile, though the Admiralty were not yet aware of the situation, the V Flotilla was being disbanded. Its collapse was doubtless speeded up when difficulties arose over the report of *UB-77*, back from the Irish Sea on April 14. Her commander claimed that he had sunk the liner *Celtic* (20,904 tons) on March 31 though he had been unable to attack another ship of the same class off the Isle of Man the next day. On the 15th, however, a German agent was able to transmit the news that the *Celtic*, though damaged, had been able to reach Peel on the Isle of Man on April 1 or 2. U-boat Command drew the obvious conclusion that she had not been sunk. On April 17 *UB-77* was transferred to I Flotilla. During the following week five more U-boats were transferred to II and III Flotillas, and as other boats returned from cruises they too were transferred. On May 19 the flotilla was deactivated. In an effort to salvage some propaganda value out of the report of *UB-77*, on April 19 the Nauen radio described her cruise and claimed that on the morning of March 31 she had sunk an 18,500-ton steamer, which left wreckage on the surface. She had actually sunk no ships.

Meanwhile on April 16 the last two sailings of V Flotilla boats had

1 L. Freiwald, *U-Boots-Maschinist Fritz Kasten* (Munich, 1933), pp. 279-80.

taken place. *UB-34* left for the East Coast, *UB-85* for the North Channel. The latter boat, out on her first extended cruise, made her presence in the North Sea known by three signals on the 18th and 19th. On the morning of the 20th she was sighted from Fair Isle and later bombed by a seaplane. A week later she unsuccessfully attacked shipping in the North Channel, and at 0330 on the 30th she was on the surface when she sighted a patrol and proceeded to dive. The temporary watch officer was the last to leave the deck. He did not close the conning-tower hatch properly, and water began pouring in as the boat reached 12 metres. The water soon reached 1.2 metres in the control room. When the order to surface was given, the engineer under-officer blew only the tanks forward; the boat lost trim and hung down by the stern. By the time the tanks aft were blown, so much water had entered that only the conning tower emerged on the surface. The men who came on deck to man the guns stood in water up to their knees. Inside the U-boat chlorine gas was bubbling up, and a short-circuit knocked out the ballast pump motors and one main motor. When the drifter *Coreopsis* opened fire and holed the forward ballast tank *UB-85* surrendered, sinking soon afterwards.

The prisoners described their cruise, stating that because of bad weather they had made only 6 knots in the North Sea - presumably this had been mentioned in *UB-85*'s signals - until 0900 on the 20th, when an airplane had forced them to dive off Fair Isle (this time does not agree with British records). They soon surfaced again and proceeded awash until 2100, then blew tanks and went ahead at full speed. Attacks on shipping had been unsuccessful.

They also provided rather full descriptions of the navigation apparatus for use with a leader cable, said to run out from Borkum, and of their hydrophones and oscillators. The radio, they said, was to be used only to report damage or to announce estimated arrival time when homeward-bound. A warrant officer surrendered his diary, which covered the activities of *UB-62* from January 1-20, on cruise off the Shetlands, and of *UB-85* from February 19-April 29.

The commander explained the obviously low morale of his crew as due not only to their lack of experience but also to influenza, from which many of them were suffering.

The interrogators also learned that V Flotilla was about to be disbanded, primarily because of 'lack of success' due to inexperienced officers and crews on board new submarines. Some of the prisoners were aware that three deserters had recently escaped into Holland and had probably taken secret documents with them.

More details about V Flotilla were provided when *UB-72* was sunk on May 12. Survivors stated that the crew had been assembled on April 20 to be told that the flotilla had been disbanded; their boat was being transferred to

II Flotilla at Wilhelmshaven. Three more boats, and probably two others, were to join II Flotilla, while five more, and probably another, would join III.

Repercussions from the collapse of the V Flotilla were apparently felt for some time afterwards. During the summer of 1918 the Allies received several reports about mutinies among U-boat crews but they rightly discounted most of them. Intelligence thought that one story might be true: during August several crews of U-boats belonging to the IV Flotilla refused to join up again after learning of losses due to mines. This information might be correct, since the IV Flotilla, it was thought, included several boats from 'the defunct 5th (Bremerhaven) Flotilla which is known to have been in a very poor state of discipline'. The analysis was wrong, for no V Flotilla U-boats were transferred to IV Flotilla.[1] It remains striking, however, that between July 30 and September 10 only six U-boats of the IV Flotilla undertook cruises.

In September a rather confusing report came in from a deserter.

It is generally believed in Germany that the large number of mines recently laid in the approaches to Cuxhaven is due to the fact that some members of the 5th Minesweeping Flotilla sold charts of the safe channels to the Allies, with the result that our submarines laid mines in them which caused several losses. The suspicions of the authorities are generally believed to have been aroused by the sudden affluence of one of the petty officers concerned.

Since no U-boats had been sunk in the Bight of Heligoland since January, the account is evidently somewhat garbled, and conceivably the V Flotilla in question was actually the V U-boat Flotilla. What remains clear is that the collapse of the V Flotilla continued to have an adverse effect on morale.

C. Strange Intelligence

In the middle of June what looked like very detailed information was supplied to the American Naval Attaché at Copenhagen by a German who claimed to have deserted from a U-boat at Kiel. He said that he served on the 'minelayer' U-70 until the spring of 1917, when he was ordered to the new U-125, a large boat which operated in the North Sea; in January 1918 he had become wireless operator on U-187. He had deserted because he did not want to embark on a six-months cruise to American waters. The Americans' suspicions were immediately aroused by his story, since U-70 was not a minelayer, U-125 had been commissioned only at the end of May 1918, and

1 It may have been based on the caps found in the wreckage of *UB-82*

U-187 was barely under construction. A little checking revealed that he was a German agent who had been expelled from Denmark six weeks previously but had been recalled by the head of the German spy network in that country.

He provided five lists of U-boats. The first contained the numbers of 46 submarines supposed to belong to the High Seas Fleet, but of these 30 were under construction (and were never completed), two were never even begun, one was in the Mediterranean (*U-73*), as the Allies were aware, and five had already been sunk (*U-61, U-75, U-103, U-106, U-154*). Only eight of the 46 bore any relation to reality. Presumably the list was provided in the hope of ascertaining what the Allies knew about the progress of U-boat construction. If the purpose was simply to mislead, the Germans were obviously underestimating enemy intelligence.

The last four lists were even more peculiar. One of them contained the numbers of fourteen minelaying UC-boats, of which three (all actually sunk during 1917) were said to operate from Zeebrugge, while the others were stationed at Wilhelmshaven. Of these eleven only four actually belonged to the I Flotilla (two had been sunk, one was under repair, and one was a *Schulboot*). One was in the Mediterranean, and six had been or were now stationed at Zeebrugge (four sunk, one under repair, one operative). We may perhaps assume that in offering this list the Germans were interested in what had become of UC-boats that had simply disappeared. Another list provided the numbers of fourteen UB-boats, some of which were said to be stationed at Zeebrugge. Actually none of them were presently stationed there. Nine had been sunk; two were used for training in the Baltic; one was in the Mediterranean; one had been transferred to Austria. A list of eight U-boats used for training was more reliable. Four of them really were used for training, but the list also included one submarine sunk as early as 1916 (*UB-7*), one transferred to Bulgaria, and two transferred to Austria. Finally, the agent listed twelve U-boats stationed at Pola or Constantinople. Of these only one (*U-21*) had ever been stationed there, and this submarine had returned to Germany in 1917. Nine had been sunk.

If we can assume that any rational purpose or purposes were in view when this mass of misinformation was compiled, it may be that the 'deserter' hoped that it would evoke some comment which would reveal something about Allied intelligence. One can hardly imagine that it was seriously intended to mislead, although prisoners taken off *U-103* in May had tried to give the impression that large numbers of new U-boats were in service.[1]

> There were eleven of them that came out together from Wilhelmshaven on May 2nd, protected by a destroyer escort until well at sea. They were all numbered in the hundreds, the highest being 196, so there must be a lot of new ones.

U-196 was also on the list provided in June, though it went up through *U-212*. Further assessment of this information must have led to its rejection.

1. E.K. Chatterton, *Danger Zone* (Boston, 1934), p.342.

REVISED LIST OF U-BOATS SUNK

This list is based on various sources, including the following:

1. The British document 'Submarine Losses Return' (C.B. 01292, O.X.O.), which underlies my article in U.S. Naval Institute Proceedings 64 (1938), pp. 66–77;
2. Revisions of this document provided by Captain A. C. Dewar, C.B.E., R.N.;
3. Admiral Arno Spindler, *Der Handelskrieg mit U-Booten*, and underlying documents;
4. E. Gröner, *Die deutschen Kriegsschiffe, 1815–1936* (Munich–Berlin 1937); second edition, Munich 1966.

I have tried to evaluate each instance, and it will be seen that in many details the list differs from earlier versions, both my own and those of others.

DATE	SUB.	CDR.	FLOT.	SAILED	OPERATION	LOCALITY SUNK	CAUSE
					1914		
Aug. 9	*U–15*	Pohl		Aug. 6	N. Sea	5835/0156E.	Rammed
Aug. 12	*U–13*	v. Schweinitz		Aug. 6	N. Sea	5833/0140E. ?	Unknown
Nov. 23	*U–18*	v. Hennig		Nov. 17	Pentland	5841/0255W.	Rammed
Dec. 9	*U–11*	v. Suchodoletz		Dec. 9	Channel	5129/0306E. ?	Mine
Dec. 18	*U–15*	Lemmer		Dec. 18	Belgian coast	5129/0311E.	Mine
					1915		
Jan.	*U–31*	Wachendorff	IV	Jan. 13	N. Sea S.	Unknown	Unknown
Jan. 21	*U–7*	König	I	Jan. 13	N. Sea S.	5343/0602E.	Torp. *U–22*
Mar. 4	*U–8*	Stoss	I	Mar. 4	Channel	5056/0115E.	Expl. sweep
Mar. 10	*U–12*	Kratzsch	I	Mar. 4	E. Coast	5607/0220W.	Rammed

Date	U-boat	Commander		Date	Location	Position	Cause
Mar. 18	U-29	Weddigen	IV	Mar. 4	Irish Sea	5816/0059E.	Rammed
Apr. 1+	U-37	Wilcke	II	Mar. 20	Channel	5104/0148E.?	Mine
May 23+	UB-3	S. Schmidt	M	May 23	to Smyrna	Unknown	Unknown
June 5	U-14	Hammerle	I	May 31	Forth	5713/0033E.	Gunfire
June 23	U-40	G. Fürbringer	II	June 18	Forth	5700/0150W.	Torp. C-24
July 2	UC-2	Mey	F	June 29	Lowestoft	5226/0148E.	Own mine
July 20	U-23	Schulthess	III	July 17	West Coast	5855/0014E.	Torp. C-27
July 24	U-36	Graeff	II	July 17	W. Hebrides	5907/0530W.	Q-Prince Charles
Aug. 16	UB-4	Gross	F	Aug. 13	Yarmouth	5246/0210E.	Gunfire
Aug. 19	U-27	Wegener	IV	Aug. 4	West Coast	5043/0722W.	Q-Baralong
Aug. 30+	U-26	v. Berckheim	B	Aug. 11	Baltic E.	Baltic	Russian mine?
Sept. 15	U-6	Lepsius	I	Sept. 9	N. Sea N.	5910/0509E.	Torp. E-16
Sept. 24	U-41	Hansen	II	Sept. 14	West Coast	4910/0723W.	Q-Baralong
Oct. 20+	UC-9	Schürmann	F	Oct. 20	Long Sand	Long Sand	Own mine?
Nov. 29	UC-13	Kirchner	Const.	Nov. 12	Black S.N.E.	4100/3008E.	Stranded

1916

Date	U-boat	Commander		Date	Location	Position	Cause
Mar. 16	UC-12	Fröhner	M	Mar. 12	Taranto	Taranto	Own mine
Mar. 22	U-68	Güntzel	IV	Mar. 16	W. Ireland	5154/1053W.	Q-Farnborough
Apr. 5	UB-26	Smiths	F	Mar. 30	Le Harve	4928/0002E.	Net
Apr. 25	UB-13	Metz	F	Apr. 23	E. Coast	5133/0245E.	Mine
Apr. 27	UC-5	Mohrbutter	F	Apr. 25	E. Coast	5203/0146E.	Stranded
May 27	U-74	E. Weisbach	I	May 13	Firth of Forth	5710/0120E.	Gunfire
May 27	UC-3	Kreysern	F	May 25	E. Coast	5135/0308E.	Mine
May 27+	U-10	Stuhr	Libau	May 27	Gulf of Finland	Unknown	Mine?
July 5	UC-7	Haag	F	July 3	E. Coast	5122/0307E.	Mine

DATE	SUB.	CDR.	FLOT.	SAILED	OPERATION	LOCALITY SUNK	CAUSE
July 7+	U-77	Günzel	I	July 5	Kinnaird Hd.	Unknown	Unknown
July 14	U-51	Rumpel	II	July 14	to W'haven	5355/0753E.	Torp. H-5
Aug. 4+	UB-44	Wäger	M	Aug. 4	to Constantinople	Unknown	Unknown
Aug. 21	UC-10	W. Albrecht	F	Aug. 17	E. Coast	5145/0320E.	Torp. E-54
Sept. 27+	UB-7	Lütjohann	Varna	Sept. 27	Black Sea	Unknown	Unknown
Nov. 3+	U-56	Lorenz	II	Oct. 13	North Cape	Unknown	Gunfire?
Nov. 4	U-20	Schwieger	III	Oct. 13	Bristol Ch.	5635/0810E.	Stranded
Nov. 6	UV-45	Palis	Varna	Nov. 6	Black Sea	Off Varna	Mine of Krab
Nov. 13+	UC-15	Heller	Varna	Nov. 13	Sulina Est.	Unknown	Unknown
Nov. 30	UB-19	Noodt	F	Nov. 22	Channel	4956/0245W.	Q-Penshurst
Dec. 6	UC-19	Nitzsche	F	Nov. 27	W. Channel	4941/0630W.	Depth charge
Dec. 7	UB-46	C. Bauer	Const.	Nov. 24	Sulina Est.	Bosporus	Mine
Dec. 13	UB-29	Platsch	F	Nov. 27	W. Channel	5109/0146E.	Depth charge
					1917		
Jan. 14	UB-37	Günther	F	Jan. 2	Channel	5007/0147W.	Q-Penshurst
Jan. 22	U-76	Bender	I	Jan. 9	North Cape	Hammerfest	Gunfire
Feb. 8	UC-46	Moecke	F	Jan. 25	Channel	5107/0139E.	Rammed
Feb. 8	UC-39	Ehrenraut	F	Feb. 7	E. Coast	5356/0006E.	Gunfire
Feb. 17	U-83	Hoppe	IV	Jan. 31	W. Channel	5134/1123W.	Q-Farnborough
Feb. 19	UC-18	Kiel	F	Feb. 16	Channel	4915/0234W.	Q-Lady Olive
Feb. 23	UC-32	Breyer	I	Feb. 17	Tyne	5455/0120W.	Own mine
Mar. 10	UC-43	Sebelin	I	Feb. 25	S. Ireland	6057/0111W.	Torp. G-13
Mar. 12	U-85	Petz	IV	Mar. 6	S. Ireland	4952/0320W.	Q-Privet
Mar. 13	UC-68	Degetau	F	Mar. 10	Channel	5017/0331W.	Own mine

Date	U-boat	Commander		Date	Location	Position	Cause
Apr. 21	UC-30	Stenzler	I	Mar. 30	S. Ireland	5519/0710E.	Mine
May 1	U-81	Weisbach	IV	Apr. 17	N. W. Ireland	5133/1338W.	Torp. *E-54*
May 8	UC-26	v. Schmettow	F	Apr. 30	Channel	5103/0140E.	Rammed
May 14	U-59	v. Fircks	II	May 14	W. Ireland	5533/0715E.	German mine
May 14/15	UB-39	Küstner	F	Apr. 23	Biscay	E. Dover	Mine
May 17/18	UC-36	Buch	F	May 16	Channel	Channel	Unknown
May 21	UB-36	v. Keyser-lingk	F	May 9	W. Channel	4842/0514W.	Rammed
May 24	UC-24	Willich	M	May 24	Medit.	Cattaro	Torp. Circe
June 7	UC-29	Rosenow	I	May 29	S. Ireland	5150/1150W.	Q-Pargust
June 12	UC-66	Pustkuchen	F	May 22	Bristol Ch.	4956/0510W.	Depth charge
July 7	U-99	Eltester	II	June 12	North Sea N.	5800/0300E.	Torp. *J-2*
July 12	U-69	Wilhelms	IV	July 9	S. W. Ireland	6025/0132E.	Depth charge
July 19	UC-1	Mildenstein	F	July 18	Calais	North Sea S.	Mine ?
July 26	UC-61	Gerth	F	July 25	Channel	5054/0139E.	Stranded
July 28	UB-20	Glimpf	F	July 28	North Sea S.	Off Ostend	Mine
July 29	UB-27	v. Stein	F	July 22	North Sea S.	5247/0224E.	Depth charge
Aug. 4	UC-44	Teben-johanns	I	July 31	S. Ireland	5207/0659W.	Own (?) mine
Aug. 12	U-44	Wagenführ	III	July 17	N. Channel	5851/0420E.	Rammed
Aug. 20	UC-72	Voigt	F	Aug. 12	French coast	4600/0848W.	Q-Acton
Aug. 21	UC-41	Foerste	I	Aug. 18	Tay	5602/0243W.	Own mine
Aug. 31	U-50	Berger	III	Aug. 30	W. Channel	5410/0445E.	Mine
Sept. 2	U-28	G. Schmidt	IV	Aug. 19	North Cape	7234/2756E.	Explosion
Sept. 3	U-66	Muhle	IV	Sept. 2	N. Channel	N. Sea S.	Mine
Sept. 5	U-88	Schwieger	III	Sept. 5	French coast	5410/0445E.	Mine
Sept. 10	UC-42	H. A. Müller	I	Sept. 1	S. Ireland	5145/0813W.	Mine

DATE	SUB.	CDR.	FLOT.	SAILED	OPERATION	LOCALITY SUNK	CAUSE
Sept. 11	U–49	Hartmann	IV	Aug. 30	N. W. Spain	4617/1442W.	Rammed
Sept. 12	U–45	Sittenfeld	III	Sept. 5	W. Ireland	5548/0730W.	Torp. D–7
Sept. 22	UB–32	v. Ditfurth	F	Sept. 10	W. Channel	5145/0205E.	Aircraft bomb
Sept. 26	UC–33	Arnold	I	Sept. 16	S. Ireland	5155/0614W.	Rammed
Sept. 27	UC–6	Reichenbach	F	Sept. 27	N. Sea S.	5130/0134E.	Mine-net
Sept. 29	UC–55	v. Lilienstern	I	Sept. 25	Shetlands	6008/0100W.	Accident
Sept.–Oct.	UC–21	v. Zerboni	F	Sept. 13	French coast	N. Sea S. ?	Mine ?
Oct. 3	UC–14	Feddersen	F	Oct. 1	N. Sea S.	Zeebrugge	Mine
Oct. 5	UB–41	Ploen	V	Sept. 30	E. Coast	5418/0021W.	Mine (German ?)
Oct. 7	U–106	Hufnagel	IV	Sept. 8	N. Channel	5400/0435E ?	Mine
Oct. 14 ?	UC–62	M. Schmitz	F	Oct. 11	W. Channel	Portland ?	Mine ?
Oct. 14 ?	UC–16	Reimarus	F	Oct. 2	W. Channel	N. Sea S.	Mine
Nov. 1	UC–63	Heydebreck	F	Oct. 18	Channel	5123/0200E.	Torp. E–52
Nov. 3	UC–65	Lafrenz	F	Oct. 22	W. Channel	5028/0017E.	Torp. C–15
Nov. 17	UC–51	Galster	F	Nov. 15	Plymouth	5008/0342W.	Mine
Nov. 17	U–58	G. Amberger	II	Nov. 12	S. Ireland	5137/0812W.	Depth charged
Nov. 18	UC–47	Wigankow	F	Nov. 17	E. Coast	5403/0022E.	Rammed
Nov. 18 +	UC–57	Wissmann	Kurl.	Nov. 12	to Danzig	Gulf of Finland	Mine
Nov. 24	U–48	Edeling	III	Nov. 22	W. Channel	5117/0131E.	Stranded
Nov. 29	UB–61	T. Schultz	V	Nov. 26	S. Ireland	5325/0458E.	Mine
Dec. 2	UB–81	Saltzwedel	F	Nov. 28	Channel	5027/0051W	Mine.
Dec. 6	UC–69	Thielmann	F	Dec. 4	Channel	Cape Barfleur	Accident
Dec. 9	UB–18	Niemeyer	F	Dec. 1	W. Channel	4917/0547W	Rammed
Dec. 10	UB–75	F. Walther	V	Nov. 29	E. Coast	Flamb. Hd.	Mine

Date	U-boat	Commander		Lost	Area	Position	Cause
Dec. 13	U-75	Schmolling	I	Dec. 13	N. Sea S.	5359/0524E.	Mine
Dec. 14	UC-38	Wendlandt	M	Dec. 1	E. Medit.	3832/2034E.	Depth charge
Dec. 19	UB-56	H. Valentiner	F	Dec. 18	Channel	5057/0123E.	Mine
Dec. 25	U-87	v. Speth-Schülzburg	III	Dec. 8	W. Channel	5256/0507W.	Rammed
				1918			
Jan. 7	U-95	Prinz	IV	Dec. 28	W. Channel	4959/0512W.	Rammed by steamer
Jan. 8	UC-50	Seuffer	F	Jan. 7	Biscay	5050/0126E.	Mine
Jan. 9	UB-69	Klatt	M	Dec. 26	to Pola	3730/1038E.	Explosive sweep
Jan. 19	UB-22	Wacker	V	Jan. 19	E. Coast	5427/0635E.	Mine
Jan. 26	U-109	Ney	IV	Jan. 24	W. Channel	5053/0131E.	Mine
Jan. 26	U-84	Roehr	IV	Jan. 1	W. France	5153/0544W.	Rammed by patrol
Jan. 26	UB-35	Stöter	F	Jan. 17	Channel	5103/0146E.	Depth charge
Jan. —	UB-66	Wernicke	M	Dec. 29	E. Medit.	Unknown	Unknown
Jan. —	U-93	Gerlach	IV	Dec. 29	W. Channel	Unknown	Unknown
Jan. —	UB-63	Gebeschus	V	Jan. 14	Irish Sea	Irish Sea	D/c Jan. 30-Feb. 2
Feb. 8	UB-38	Bachmann	F	Jan. 29	Channel	5056/0125E.	Mine
Feb. 12	U-89	Bauck	III	Feb. 2	N. Channel	5538/0732W.	Rammed by escort
Mar. 10	UB-58	Löwe	F	Mar. 9	Channel	5058/0114E.	Mine
Mar. 11/15	UB-17	Branscheid	F	Mar. 11	N. Sea S.	Unknown	Unknown
Mar. 15	U-110	Kroll	IV	Feb. 27	N. Ireland	5549/0806W.	Depth charge
Mar. 19	UB-54	Hecht	F	Mar. 1	Channel	5100/0119E.	Mine

DATE	SUB.	CDR.	FLOT.	SAILED	OPERATION SUNK	LOCALITY	CAUSE
Mar. 26	U-61	Dieckmann	II	Mar. 3	Irish Sea	5148/0552W.	Depth charge
Mar.-Apr.	UC-79	Krameyer	F	Mar. 20	Biscay	Unknown	Unknown
Apr. 11	UB-33	Gregor	F	Apr. 6	Channel	5055/0117E.	Mine
Apr. 17	UB-82	Becker	V	Apr. 7	W. Channel	5513/0515W.	Depth charge
Apr. 21	UB-71	Schapler	M	Apr. 5	to Pola	3558/0518W.	Depth charge
Apr. 22	UB-55	Wenninger	F	Apr. 21	St. Nazaire	5101/0120E.	Mine
Apr. 25	U-104	Bernis	II	Apr. 10	W. Channel	5159/0626W.	Depth charge
Apr. 30	UB-85	Krech	V	Apr. 16	Irish Sea	5447/0527W.	Gunfire
May 2	UB-31	Braun	F	Apr. 16	Channel	5101/0116E.	Mine
May 5 +	UB-70	Remy	M	Apr. 15	to Pola	Unknown	Unknown
May 8	U-32	Albrecht	M	Apr. 14	W. Medit.	3607/1328E.	Depth charge
May 8 +	UC-78	Kukat	F	May 2	Channel E.	5055/0134E.	Mine
May 9	UB-78	Stosberg	F	Apr. 18	W. Channel	4950/0140W.	Rammed
May 10	UB-16	v. d. Lühe	F	May 6	N. Sea S.	5206/0201E.	Torp. E-34
May 11	U-154	Gercke	K	Feb. 16	Azores, etc.	3645/1200W.	Torp. E-35
May 12	U-103	Rücker	II	May 3	W. Channel	4916/0451W.	Rammed
May 12	UB-72	Träger	II	May 1	W. Channel	5008/0241W.	Torp. D-4
May 17	UC-35	Korsch	M	Apr. 28	W. Medit.	3948/0742E.	Gunfire
May 19	UB-119	Kolbe	III	Apr. 27	Irish Sea	5242/0503W.	Depth charge
May 23	UB-52	Launburg	M	Apr. 27	W. Medit.	4146/1835E.	Torp. H-4
May 26	UB-74	Steindorff	F	May 11	St. Nazaire	5032/0232W.	Depth charge
May 31	UC-75	Schmitz	F	May 22	E. Coast	5357/0009E.	Rammed
June 17	U-64	Moraht	M	June 11	Medit.	3807/1207E.	Gunfire
June 20	UC-64	Schwartz	F	June 18	Brest	5058/0123E.	Mine

181

Date	U-boat	Commander	Flotilla	Date	Location	Position	Cause
June 26	UC-11	Utke	F	June 24	Shipwash	5155/0141E.	German mine
July 4	UB-108	W. Amberger	F	July 2	W. Channel	5100/0119E.	Mine
July 10	UB-65	Schelle	II	July 2	Bristol Ch.	5107/0942W.	Explosion
July 12+	UC-77	Ries	F	July 11	Portland	Unknown	Unknown
July 19	UB-110	W. Fürbringer	F	July 4	E. Coast	5439/0055W.	Depth charge
July 20	UB-124	Wursdorff	III	July 6	N. Ireland	5543/0751W.	Depth charge
July 27?	UB-107	v. Prittwitz	F	July 26	E. Coast	?5424/0024W.	Depth charge ?
Aug. 3	UB-53	Sprenger	M	Aug. 1	E. Medit.	3958/1901E.	Mine
Aug. 8	UC-49	Kükenthal	F	Aug. 1	Plymouth	5020/0326W.	Depth charge
Aug. 13	UB-30	Stier	F	Aug. 6	E. Coast	5432/0035W.	Depth charge
Aug. 14	UB-57	Lohs	F	Aug. 3	Channel E.	5133/0305E.	Mine
Aug. 19+	UB-12	Schooler	F	Aug. 19	North Downs	Unknown	Unknown
Aug. 28	UC-70	Dobberstein	F	Aug. 21	E. Coast	5432/0040W.	Depth charge
Aug. 29	UB-109	Ramien	F	July 27	Azores	5104/0114E.	Mine
Sept. 8	U-92	Ehrlich	III	Sept. 4	Biscay	5900/0130W. ?	Mine
Sept. 9	UB-127	Scheffler	I	Sept. 4	N. Channel	5915/0130W.	Mine
Sept. 10	UB-83	Buntebardt	III	Sept. 7	St. George's	5828/0150W.	Depth charge
Sept. 16	UB-103	Hundius	F	Aug. 14	French coast	5052/0127E.	Depth charge
Sept. 25	U-156	Feldt	K	June 16	Amer. coast	5945/0200E. ?	Mine
Sept. 29	UB-115	Thomsen	F	Sept. 18	E. Coast	5514/0122W.	Depth charge
Sept. ?	U-102	Beitzen	II	Sept. 1	W. Channel	5920/0055E. ?	Mine
Sept. ?	UB-104	Bieber	F	Sept. 6	W. Channel	5930/0044E. ?	Mine
Sept. ?	UB-113	Pilzecker	F	Sept. 14	W. Channel	Unknown	Unknown

DATE	SUB.	CDR.	FLOT.	SAILED	OPERATION	LOCALITY SUNK	CAUSE
Oct. 4	*UB–68*	Dönitz	M	Sept. 25	W. Medit.	3556/1620E.	Gunfire
Oct. 16	*UB–90*	Mayer	II	Sept. 23	Bristol Ch.	5755/1027E.	Torp. *L–12*
Oct. 18	*UB–123*	Ramm	III	Sept. 26	Irish Sea	5945/0220E. ?	Mine
Oct. 21 ?	*U–34*	Klasing	M	Oct. 18	Medit.	3914/1933E. ?	Depth charge
Oct. 28	*U–78*	Vollbrecht	I	Oct. 25	N. Sea S.	5602/0508E.	Torp. *G–2*
Oct. 28	*UB–116*	Emsmann	III	Oct. 25	Scapa Flow	5850/0304W.	Mine

183

BIBLIOGRAPHY

Anonymous, 'A War Secret', *Saturday Evening Post*, October 23, 1926
Bywater, H. C., *Their Secret Purposes*. London 1932
Bywater, H. C., Ferraby, H. C., *Strange Intelligence*. London 1931
Chatelle, A., *Le base navale du Havre*. Paris 1949
Chatterton, E. K., *Danger Zone*. Boston 1934
Chatterton, E. K., *Gallant Sailormen*. London 1936
Corbett, Sir J. S., Newbolt, H., *Naval Operations*, I – V. London 1920 – 31
Crompton, Kapitän-leutnant, *Englands Verbrechen an U41*. Gütersloh 1940

Dinklage, L., *U-boot-fahrer und Kamelsreiter: Kriegsfahrten eines deutschen Unterseebootes*. Stuttgart 1939 [UC – 20]
Dönitz, K., *Memoirs: Ten Years and Twenty Days*. New York 1959
Dorling, T., *Swept Channels*. London 1935
Doughty, L., 'The Effect of Depth Charges on Submarines', *United States Naval Institute Proceedings*, 61 (1935), pp. 353 – 57

Ewing, A. W., *The Man of Room 40: The Life of Sir Alfred Ewing*. London c.1939

Farago, L., *The Tenth Fleet*. New York 1962
Freiwald, L., *U-Boots-Maschinist Fritz Kasten*. Munich 1933

Gladisch, W., *Der Krieg in der Nordsee*, I – VI. Berlin, 1922 – 37; VII. Frankfurt/Main 1965
Grant, R. M., *U-Boats Destroyed: The Effect of Anti-Submarine Warfare 1914 – 1918*. London 1964
Gröner, E., *Die deutschen Kriegschiffe 1815 – 1945*, I – II. Munich 1966
Harbord, J. G., *The American Army in France 1917 – 1919*. Boston 1936
Hashagen, E., *U-Boats Westward!* New York 1931
Hayes, Sir B., *Hull Down*. London 1925
Hoy, H. C., *40 O.B., or How the War was Won*. London 1932

James, Sir W., *The Eyes of the Fleet*. London 1956 (= *The Code Breakers of Room 40*. New York 1956)

Kahn, D., *The Codebreakers*. New York 1967
Keyes, Sir R., *Scapa Flow to the Dover Straits,*. (II) London 1935

Laurens, A., *Histoire de laguerre sous-marine allemande*. Paris, 1930
Leighton, J. L., *Simsadus: London*. New York 1920
Lorey, H., *Der Krieg in den türkischen Gewässern*, I – II. Berlin 1928

Ludendorif, E., *Meine Kriegserrinerungen 1914 — 19 18*. Berlin 1920

Marder, A., *From the Dreadnought to Scapa Flow*, III. London 1966

Martini, N. von, *Bilddokumente aus Oesterreich-Ungarns Seekrieg*, I — II.Graz 1939

McLachlan, D., *Room 39*. London 1968.

Navy Department, U.S., *The American Planning Section in London*. Washington 1923

Navy Department, U.S., *German Submarine Activities on the Atlantic Coast of the United States and Canada*. Washington 1920

Navy Department, U.S., *The Northern Barrage*, I — II. Washington 1920

Newbolt, H., *A Naval History of the War 1914 — 1918*. London, c. 1920

Newbolt, H., *Submarine and Anti-Submarine*. London c. 1918

Ritter, P., *Ubootsgeist: Abenteuer und Fahrten im Mittelmeer*. Leipzig 1935 [*UB — 49*]

Robinson, D. H., *The Zeppelin in Combat*. London 1962

Rose, H., *Auftauchen ! Kriegsfahrten von 'U53'*. Essen 1939

Roskill, S. W., 'The U-Boat Campaign of 1917 and Third Ypres', *Journal of the Royal United Service Institution*, 104 (1959), pp. 440 — 42

Rowan, R. W., *The Story of Secret Service*. Garden City, N.Y. 1937

Scheer, Admiral, *Germany's High Sea Fleet in the Great War*. London 1920

Schwarte, M., *Die Technik im Weltkrieg*. Berlin 1920

Sims, W. S., *The Victory at Sea*. New York 1920

Spindler, A., *Der Handelskrieg mit U-Booten*, I — IV. Berlin 1932 — 41; IV (reprint). Hamburg 1965; V. Frankfurt/Main 1966

Spindler, K., *The Mystery of the Casement Ship*. Berlin 1931

Thomazi, A., *La guerre navale dans la Mediterranee*. Paris, 1929

Tirpitz, Grand Admiral von, *Memoirs*, I — II. London c. 1920

Vidil, C., *Les mutineries de la marine allemande 1917 — 1918*. Paris 1931

Yardley, H. O., *The American Black Chamber*. New York 1931

INDEX OF PERSONS, VESSELS AND LOCATIONS